THE POETRY
OF SURREALISM

An Anthology

BOOKS BY MICHAEL BENEDIKT

Poetry

MOLE NOTES

SKY

THE BODY

Theatre Anthologies

THEATRE EXPERIMENT

With George Wellwarth

MODERN SPANISH THEATRE

POST-WAR GERMAN THEATRE

MODERN FRENCH THEATRE:
THE AVANT-GARDE, DADA AND SURREALISM

Translations

TWENTY-TWO POEMS OF ROBERT DESNOS

RING AROUND THE WORLD: SELECTED POEMS OF JEAN L'ANSELME

THE POETRY OF SURREALISM: AN ANTHOLOGY

THE POETRY
OF SURREALISM
An Anthology

*With Introduction, Critical Notes
and New Translations*

by Michael Benedikt

Little, Brown and Company — Boston–Toronto

FIRST EDITION

T 01/75

Acknowledgment of permission to reprint poems and
translations included in this anthology appears on
pages 373–375.

LIBRARY OF CONGRESS CATALOGING IN PUBLICATION DATA

Benedikt, Michael, comp.
  The poetry of surrealism.

  Includes bibliographical references.
  CONTENTS: 1. Poetry.
  1. French literature — 20th century — Translations
into English. 2. English literature — Translations
from French. 3. Surrealism — France. I. Title.
PQ1113.B4 1974   840′.9′108038   74–8014
ISBN 0–316–08897–8
ISBN 0–316–08808–6 (pbk.)

Designed by Barbara Bell Pitnof

*Published simultaneously in Canada
by Little, Brown & Company (Canada) Limited*

PRINTED IN THE UNITED STATES OF AMERICA

With thanks to

Michel Heine

for his insightful as well as technical help
on these translations;
and for his interpretations
of many difficult passages.

Introduction

IT SEEMS ASTONISHING that some fifty years following the founding and first flourishings of the Surrealist movement, and despite the publication of anthologies such as this in many countries, throughout the world, there should not until now have been a single anthology in English of its poets. For the most part, readers here have had to find the major Surrealist poets embedded in the few existing anthologies of miscellaneous twentieth-century French poetry. Often, they have been accompanied by strange bedfellows indeed, and usually represented by such abbreviated quantities of works as to blur both the overall quality of poets involved and the uniqueness of the movement from which they derive strength. In this more concentrated selection, focusing in most cases on major figures, we hope to represent something more of the extent of both this uniqueness and this excellence.

But why such delay?

The answer can probably be found in what has been, until relatively recently, the curiously insular nature of twentieth-century Anglo-American literary practice.

Resist as we may the idea of "isms" in politics, literature and art for almost two centuries now have transformed themselves in such terms. And the fact is clear that French Symbolism, the literary movement of international significance prior to French Surrealism, was just being discovered here and in Great Britain many years after its leading exponents flourished in France. Perhaps as a result of our natural orientation toward the idea of English literary primacy, we too often tend to forget that the celebrated and crucial "discoveries" of Laforgue by Eliot, Gautier by Pound, and Rimbaud by Hart Crane — not to mention the less particularized but no less influential discoveries of the French Symbolists by Stevens, Aiken and MacLeish — came between a half- and a quarter-century after the French writers ended their work and were regarded as established, even "classic," writers elsewhere. It was, of course, partly the aftermath of these already tardy revelations which produced the Symbolist-oriented, classicist, and esthetically conservative literary criticism that dominated American writing from the early 1920's through the 1950's.

Plainly, the pattern of delay has been repeated once again with regard to French Surrealism. The movement is considered to have been at its height during the first fifteen years following its founding in 1924, and to have ended with the beginnings of World War II. During this period the English-speaking poet was apt to be just beginning to come to terms with this earlier international literary cycle.

But, although word of Surrealism had reached these shores through translations in a few avant-garde periodicals, it was not until the mid-1950's and the early 1960's that several poets of substantial stature began to reflect awareness of the Surrealists. During the 1950's, for example, direct influence was registered among the major members of the San Francisco or "Beat" poets — Allen Ginsberg, Gregory Corso and Lawrence Ferlinghetti especially — the result in part of the contact with the internationalist perspectives of the poet-critic Kenneth Rexroth. More direct signs of influence appeared among the members of the original group of "New York School" poets, especially in the work of John Ashbery, Kenneth Koch, and the late Frank O'Hara, all of whom had spent some time in Paris. In the early 1960's Surrealism also became effectively operative in a range of by-and-large independent writers who had already accomplished widely recognized, distinguished work in a less experimental mode during the previous decade: W. S. Merwin, Louis Simpson, James Wright, Donald Hall, Robert Bly and David Ignatow (who had also experimented with Surrealism in the 1930's). Among poets of my own generation, the list of sympathetic or influenced writers would be much longer, if not too extended to tabulate. A brief but suggestive survey appears in the introduction to the revised edition of Anna Balakian's *Surrealism: The Road to the Absolute.*

True, many of this new and so far largest wave of indigenous-internationalist poets have also been influenced by European and Latin American writers whose work, it is generally agreed, would itself not have been quite the same without Surrealism — I am thinking of writers of the stature of Grass, Celan, Alberti, Garcia Lorca, Neruda, Vallejo, et cetera, not to mention French writers such as Michaux and Bonnefoy, Char and Queneau (though the two latter poets, participants in group Surrealism during their formative years, specifically requested to be omitted from Surrealist "annexation" here — the term is Queneau's). But this of course only renders still greater the honor of presenting this initial anthology of the first Surrealist poets.

II

Fortunately, in contrast to the paucity of Surrealist translations — in poetry particularly — the number of critical and historical works recounting Surrealist history and theory is large indeed. For example, the reader might find helpful such recently published chronicles, originally written in English or translated, as Maurice Nadeau's *A History of Surrealism*, with its introduction by Roger Shattuck; Mary Ann Caws's *The Poetry of Dada and Surrealism* and her *André Breton*; Anna Balakian's aforementioned *Surrealism* and her *André Breton: Magus of Surrealism*; Nicholas and Elena Calas's *The Challenge of Surrealism*; Herbert Gershman's *The Surrealist Movement in France*; J. H. Matthews's *Introduction to Surrealism, Surrealist Poetry in France* and *The Surrealist Novel*; Nahma Sandrow's *Surrealism: Theatre, Arts, Ideas*; Roger Cardinal and Robert Stuart Short's *Surrealism: Permanent Revolution*; and Fernand Alquié's *The Philosophy of Surrealism.*

In nearly all these works, one essential point seems to stand out with respect to Surrealism's relation to poetry — or, indeed, its relation to any creative medium. Surrealism's uniqueness can be traced to a paradox. While in retrospect we are apt to see Surrealism as one more movement which has generated outstanding works of art, the fact remains that in most of its major documents and manifestos, Surrealism was not particularly anxious either to associate its aims with nor draw its methods from art alone; often it insisted on doing just the opposite. It is quite characteristic that the movement's founding document, *Manifeste du Surréalisme* (*Manifesto of Surrealism*), issued by André Breton in 1924, begins not with literary polemics, but with broad generalizations on such general subjects of philosophical cast as "the world," "life," "fate," "destiny," and "freedom." Indeed, it makes sense to consider with particular care this document, issued by Surrealism's virtually unchallenged leader during its most definitive (and, in the opinion of some critics, most significant) years.*

Breton's point of departure, and perhaps Surrealism's most fundamental (not to mention grandiose) assumption, is that man is in a crisis. Man has lost touch with himself. He can no longer think of himself in terms of great sustaining generalities, which create his sense of reality. Perhaps the individual man who regards himself as sophisticated, and even a member of the intelligentsia, "knows what women he has had, what silly affairs he has been involved in; he is unimpressed by his own wealth or poverty. . . ." But it is precisely the welter of trivial personal details, primarily technical and essentially irrelevant, which has overwhelmed him and weakens him still, so that "though he may later pull himself together upon occasion, having felt that he is losing by slow degrees all reason for living . . . still . . . he will hardly succeed. This is because he henceforth belongs body and soul to an imperative practical necessity which demands his constant attention. None of his gestures will be expansive, none of his ideas generous or far-reaching." As a consequence, he is bound to accept the idea of a world which is fundamentally hostile to his more personal desires, a world which is now and will always remain unrelated to his own inward interests. Perhaps Breton's largest complaint in the Manifesto about things as they are appears in its final peroration: "This world is only relatively in tune with thought. . . . Existence is elsewhere."

* Although Breton's approach subsequently changed somewhat, this happened mainly as the absolute prescriptions of one time became the relative prescriptions of a later period, the theoretical core remaining intact. This initial document, in which it appears that the feelings of Breton's associates were also elaborated, remains not only historically seminal but also conceptually comprehensive.

Fortunately, two escapes exist from the insignificance of all that happens. One is recollections of childhood, the memory of which, Breton indicates, affords a temporary, sentimental, and ultimately illusory respite. The other is in the "imagination [which] alone offers some intimation of what can be; and this alone is enough to remove to some slight degree the terrible injunction." Still, imagination's ability to be enough and its actually *being* enough are two different things. Man's thought, of the possession of which he likes to assure himself, is not free. Man has become estranged from his own imagination. An implacably hostile if frequently unaware status quo has conspired to insist subtly, with all the force of its inert weight — which is to say with all the energy that so-called social imperatives can command — on adherence to systems of thought that bind the mind. Breton characterizes these systems as "the old antinomies hypocritically intended to prevent any unusual ferment on the part of man, were it only by giving him a vague idea of the means at his disposal, by challenging him to escape to some meaningful degree from the universal fetters."

In other words, in order to bring about change, it is not enough to alter convention; far more important is challenging the realities upheld by convention. A revised social imperative, based on the premises of the mind, needs to be established.

As a beginning, Breton proposes that, instead of accepting the idea of the necessary separation of man's inner and external reality, desires and the world, or dreams and hard facts, we consider the possibility of effecting a unity. One of the key definitions of Surrealism in the Manifesto revolves around this: "I believe in the future resolution of these two states, dream and reality, into a kind of absolute reality, a Surreality, if one may so speak." In the Second Manifesto, Breton names additional antinomies man has set up as if deliberately to thwart himself, and identifies their dissolution as the subject matter of Surrealism:

> Everything tends to make us believe that there exists a certain point of the mind at which life and death, the real and the imagined, past and future, the communicable and the incommunicable, cease to be perceived as contradictions. . . . search as one may, one will never

find any other motivating force in the activities of the Surrealists than the hope of finding and fixing this point.*

It is the aim of the Surrealist esthetic to cultivate a technique for locating and situating this "point of the mind," and to place it in an active relationship with an otherwise psychically destructive reality. Of course, the Surrealist is all too familiar with the fact that poetry (the poetry of the past) "bears within itself the perfect compensation for the miseries we endure," but Breton insists in the name of Surrealism that "it can also be an organizer, if ever . . . we contemplate taking it seriously!" For Breton, taking poetry "seriously" means, in the final analysis, refusing to predicate it on technique alone, or, at least, on any technique alien to the mind. Art is for the Surrealist poet "a question of going back to the sources of poetic imagination and, what is more, of remaining there." In short, just as all men must discover their proper reality, the poet, in what is really an implicitly collaborative effort with other men, must discover his. And, Breton insists with confidence that "the way to these regions is clearly marked . . . so that attaining the true goals is now merely a matter of the travelers' ability to endure."

* This particular tenet of Surrealist theory is often overlooked or misunderstood by even the most sympathetic of Surrealism's distant observers, who tend to see Surrealism as recommending an existence identical to the state of dreaming. In fact, as Breton indicates, Surrealism aims at the yoking of the "opposites" of dream and fact in the interest of the proliferation of their reciprocal relations, with the ultimate hope of fusing them. As if to render distorted or sentimental versions of the so-called Surrealist "dream" less likely, Surrealist declarations on this point have a particularly uncompromising quality. For example, Robert Desnos insists: "For me, it is less a question of having accepted as real certain facts formerly considered illusory than of placing dreams and reality on the same plane without caring whether it is all false or all true" (*Journal d'un apparition*, 1926); Benjamin Péret: "It is not a matter . . . of apologizing for poetry at the expense of rationalist thought, but of rebelling against the blatant contempt for poetry among the partisans of logic and reason despite the fact that both these were originally discovered also, as derivations from the unconscious . . . in brief, we must reduce once and for all the artificial opposition created by sectarian minds coming from both sides of the barrier they have erected together, between poetic thought, which used to be called pre-logical thought, and logical thought, between rational and irrational thought" (*Anthologie des mythes, légendes et contes populaires d'Amérique*, 1959).

xii

New Hanover County Public Library
Main Library
11/13/2013

Thank you for using self-checkout!

**********4170

34200006901397
'Sec-' (BC): Color :
Date Due: 12/04/2013 11:59:00 PM

34200004104556
'Sec-' (BC) Empire of light :
Date Due: 12/04/2013 11:59:00 PM

34200001825252
'Sec-' (BC): The poetry of surrealism:
Date Due: 12/04/2013 11:59:00 PM

34200004748147
PhotoSpeak :
Date Due: 12/04/2013 11:59:00 PM

Monday and Tuesday 9 A.M to 8 P.M.
Wednesday and Thursday 9 A.M. to 6 P.M.
Friday and Saturday 9 A.M. to 5 P.M.
Telephone Renewals: 910-798-6320
Website: www.nhclibrary.org
Checked Out / # Not Checked Out
4 / 0

The technique of traveling this road is proposed in the two definitions of Surrealism, dictionary and encyclopedia, which Breton offers "once and for all." The dictionary definition is:

> SURREALISM, noun. Psychic automatism in its pure state, by which one proposes to express — verbally, by means of the written word, or in any other way — the actual functioning of thought. Dictated by thought, in the absence of any control exercised by reason, exempt from aesthetic or moral preoccupation.

It is a definition extraordinary enough to continue to project threat even today; it is interesting to contemplate how the definition sounded in 1924! Of the three exemptions Breton claims, perhaps the least shocking is the claim to moral purity and impunity. In contrast to the established English poets, many of whom were still recovering from Victorian reverberations, French poets had been demanding such liberties for decades. Also reason, or at least reason of the eighteenth-century variety, had already been questioned by the nineteenth-century Romantics. (Later, Breton said he felt a particular kinship with the German Romantic philosophers, particularly Hegel.) It was the idea of proceeding without esthetic preoccupation or even, as it might be translated, "concern" that challenged most. For this idea attacked what had heretofore been one of art's most time-honored tenets: the idea of art as largely craftsmanship, that of art as artifice.

The shock was accentuated by Symbolist literary lessons. Had not French Symbolism's still-living representative, Paul Valéry, often spoken of the *donnée*, or "given inspiration," as the *least* significant aspect of the art work?* Had not Valéry's teacher and Symbolism's great mentor, Stephane Mallarmé, taken for his

---

* In view of Valéry's survival to 1945, it may seem a bit premature to "bury" his poetry in the Symbolist *fin-de-siècle*. Yet it is a fact that nearly all of Valéry's verse, except for several poems written around 1920 after a two-decade abandonment of verse, was composed during the 1890's. Soon after the compilation of *Charmes* (Charms, N.R.F., 1922), with its handful of new verses, Valéry discontinued writing poetry again, this time for good.

central subject the difficulty of poetry, the birth of the poem being seen metaphorically — and rather self-dramatizingly — as an act involving interminable labor pains as well as all the other responsibilities of child-rearing?

It was precisely this stress on *work* as the criterion for the determination of virtue which Breton was challenging. This above all was a myth contributing to the divorce of action and dream. (Breton did not quote Rimbaud's statement, "The hand pushing the pen is worth the hand pulling the plow," but he might have.) At bottom, the work myth is another false antinomy, another contribution to "this dog's life," adding to the separation of "man and his reality" (the phrase is by Paul Eluard, one of Breton's many close collaborators.) What interests the Surrealist, Breton states unequivocally, is "the astonishing ease of everything."

Perhaps even more threatening than the recommended departure from calculation in art and related areas was the suggested association with science. Breton's second, encyclopedia, definition underlines this:

> SURREALISM. n. Philosophy. Surrealism is based on the belief in the superior reality of certain forms of previously neglected associations, in the omnipotence of dream, in the disinterested play of thought. . . .

Breton had been a medical student before the First World War and had served as an intern in various military psychiatric wards. In this initial manifesto he openly acknowledges his debt to the techniques of exploration of the mind, particularly those of "free association" as proposed by Freud.* But Breton went

* In 1924 Breton actually visited with Freud, describing their meeting in one chapter of his autobiographical *Les Pas perdus* (*Lost Steps*, 1924). Not unpredictably, the scientist's response to the Surrealist program was somewhat puzzled. The October, 1924, issue (Number 5) of the Surrealist periodical, *La Révolution Surréaliste* (*The Surrealist Revolution*) presented the Breton-Freud correspondence, including a line summing up the great psychologist's reaction: "Perhaps I am not meant to understand Surrealism, for I am so removed from art." That Breton himself grew increasingly aware of a difference, rather than a similarity, of aims is suggested by a statement in the Second Manifesto remarking on the unfortunate necessity "to compensate for what is insufficient about the penetration of so-called 'artistic' states of mind by men who are for the most part not artists but doctors." Despite the fact that Breton was later to dedicate his essay, *Les*

beyond that, placing the disinterested play of thought at the very heart of literature. Breton was claiming that such deadly serious "play" had relevance to art not only as style but also as content. This "automatic writing," as he termed it, was valuable to the artist "not only as a method of expression on the literary and artistic level, but in addition as a first step toward a general revision of the modes of knowledge."

This claim to be bringing objective fact to light, as in scientific research, is at the core of the Surrealist proposal. Breton speaks with a seriousness which is characteristic of the best Surrealist spirit when he argues: "If the depths of our minds contain within them strange forces capable of augmenting those on the surface, or of waging a victorious battle against them, there is every reason for us to seize them; then, if need be, to submit them to the control of our reason." The key phrase here, as throughout Surrealism, is *"our* reason." The term, which appears in various versions and paraphrases throughout the work of Breton and his fellow Surrealist poets, suggests that the nature of true reason is negotiable, a relative reality only, rather than the absolute for which it is so often taken. Also, in the Second Manifesto, as if representing the imagination were ultimately a kind of political necessity, Breton proposes that through the enfranchisement of the unconscious, "the imagination is about to regain its rights." There is much in Surrealism lending itself to speculation that the ultimate goal of its works is establishing the unconscious — with its reason based on human desire rather than on the unreal code of social imperatives — on a plane from which it might prevail.

In 1924, the same year the first Manifesto was issued, the

Vases communicants (*The Communicating Vessels*, 1932) to Freud, and published an angry letter enlisting public protest against the doctor's rumored imprisonment by the Nazis, the schism was clear-cut, and is succinctly characterized by Anna Balakian, who notes that while Freud wished to "explore" the unconscious, the Surrealists proposed to "colonize" it. It is also to Balakian that we owe the detailed anatomization of Breton's debt to the French psychologist Pierre Janet, whose *L'Automatisme psychologique* (*Psychological Automatism*, 1889) had recommended as a means of penetrating the minds of subjects, "Let the pen wander automatically on the page, even as the doctor penetrates the mind." Balakian points out that Breton had doubtless become acquainted with one of the numerous subsequent editions in medical school, where it was used as a text while Freud (not translated into French until 1930) remained relatively unknown.

first Surrealist periodical appeared, edited by the poet Benjamin Péret and the critic Pierre Naville. Consistent with the desire to objectify was the format of the magazine, *La Révolution Sur-réaliste* (*The Surrealist Revolution*), which was designed to approximate the straightforward style of professional scientific journals. Also reflecting the struggle toward objectivity was the title chosen for the Surrealist center, the Central Bureau of Surrealist Research, established in 1925 with Antonin Artaud as its director. Throughout Surrealism's history, it is necessary in order to grasp it in its own terms, to translate the term not in its all too frequently misconstrued form, "non-realism," or worse yet, "fantasy," but rather according to its actual linguistic sense, as "super-realism."

The role of poetry in Surrealism's process of reevaluation has the most demanding implications for the writer. The Surrealist poet's work is a proof of vision and a personal testimony of faith in the attainability of Surrealism's goal of "the transformation of the world." But it is also much more. Every single poem by each poet is not only an esthetic gesture, but also an action. Each is not only a testimony, but a reality. To read a Surrealist poem is to survey a territorial tract — however modest in size — of liberated space.

IV

How much of this Surrealist theory was actually carried into practice? Certainly the Surrealist poem is poetry transformed. Still, though there were never nearly as many Surrealisms as there were Surrealists, the diversity of approach was considerable. And, despite the firm tone of the tenets we have transmitted, which we hope may suggest the armature from which the larger Surrealist structure may be deduced, Breton himself made room for such variations.* Though he remarked in the first

---

* The variations in approach to automatic writing were especially enormous. Even as he recommended a supraesthetic approach, Breton must have taken into account the fact that the individuals to whom he recommended automatism were, at least chronologically, artists before they were Surrealists. The approaches vary from that of Benjamin Péret, whose work suggests an automatic approach at all times, to that of Philippe Soupault, whose poems (despite his collaboration on early automatic texts

Manifesto that he was defining Surrealism "once and for all" —
and was to a remarkable degree correct about that — he also
emphasized that "we are not now attempting to establish a
definitive Surrealist pattern" and announced: "I believe in the
pure Surrealist joy of the man who, forewarned that all others
before him have failed, refuses to admit defeat. . . . The mate-
rial with which he must perforce encumber himself, his glass
tubes or my metallic feathers . . . is to me . . . a matter of
complete indifference. . . . As for his method, I am willing to
give it as much credit as I do mine."

At the very heart of the Manifesto lies an outright contradic-
tion. Intentional or not, it is a contradiction as productive to the
growth of Surrealism beyond its early years as any deliberate
allowance for variation.

Breton speaks of proceeding "without esthetic preoccupation."
But even without historical evidence and hindsight, it seems clear
that the Surrealist leader was always highly concerned about
esthetics. Throughout his writings, and not least in the scientifi-
cally-oriented first Manifesto, he uses the most esthetically
charged word in any language, "beauty." True, this beauty is a
new beauty — perhaps finally the ultimate *frisson nouveau* about
which French writers since Baudelaire and Rimbaud have so
often spoken; or even the "terrible beauty" which horrifies
artifice-upholding Yeats in his poem "Easter 1916"; but the
stated concern is for beauty, nevertheless, and is perhaps all
the more strong a concern for the insistence that such beauty
be new.

Compared to other definitions in the Manifesto, beauty's
definition has a passionate, even romantic ring. Almost as an
outcry, Breton insists: "Let us not mince words: the marvelous
is always beautiful, anything marvelous is beautiful; in fact

___

with Breton) have a crafted air. In general, it would seem that even though
they may have joined the movement after the experiments with automat-
ism were at their height, most Surrealists went through an intensely auto-
matic period. The works of the later poets included here, particularly
Prévert, are most obviously cases in point. It is as if automatism had been
used not only to produce the first drafts of poems, but the first versions of
poets; and that this submission of each poet to the "technique of inspira-
tion" was sometimes deliberately effected, perhaps with the expectation of
later extrication. J. H. Matthews compactly sums up the entire paradox of
the deliberate surrender of volition when he terms the Surrealists "con-
sciously unconscious artists."

only the marvelous is beautiful." Breton expands upon this assertion in the quasiautobiographical prose work *L'Amour fou* (*Mad Love,* 1938), characterizing all beauty as being, for him, necessarily "convulsive." "Convulsive beauty" is the result of the meeting, in one medium or another, of antinomies formerly considered incompatible. This meeting is meant to create a fusion, as in the stillness after a collision. This collision is most effectively registered using imagery. In *L'Amour fou* Breton singles out — with appropriate suddenness and as if on convulsive impulse — his own long-standing fascination with a photograph of a vehicle covered over with vines:

> There cannot, I insist, be beauty — convulsive beauty — except at the cost of the affirmation of the reciprocal relation which links the objects considered in its movement and in its repose. I regret not having been able to furnish, as a complement to the illustration of this text, the photograph of a powerful locomotive abandoned for years to the madness of the virgin forest. The fact aside that the desire to see such a thing has long been accompanied for me by a special exaltation, it seems to me that the surely magical aspect of this monument to victory and to disaster would better than any other have been of a nature to stabilize ideas.

Since society's ability to create antinomies is practically endless — as is testified to by the rareness of realized dreams — there is of course no limit to tractable categories. As one of the many pre-Surrealist foreshadowers of the Surrealist sense of beauty, Breton names the nineteenth-century prose poet Lautréamont,* who produced a new fusion by describing a certain sensation as being "beautiful as the chance meeting of an umbrella and a sewing machine on a dissection-table." In specifying this, with its wholly arbitrary listing of categories to be juxtaposed as

* It is interesting that a high place on Breton's list of Surrealist ancestors is given to two nineteenth-century writers with striking similarities: Rimbaud and Lautréamont, both prodigies who, with some dismay directed at the literary climate itself, gave up literature at very early ages: Rimbaud (1854–1891) at seventeen, Lautréamont (the pseudonym of Isidore Ducasse, 1846–1870) at twenty. Also, their writings most significant to the Surrealists are not in conventional verse, but in prose: Rimbaud's *Les Illuminations* (*The Illuminations*) and Lautréamont's *Les Chants de Maldoror* (*The Songs of Maldoror*).

a sort of prototype trope for the Surrealist sense of the beautiful, Breton is obviously recommending a celebration of the fusion of categories less for the sake of the categories to be combined, than for the sake of the beauty of the fusion itself.* The context is esthetic.

While this devotion to associations has the philosophical and esthetic bearing indicated, it clearly would have little meaning for Breton were not the nature and origins of the poetic image itself grounded in psychological truth, the Surrealist's ultimate reality. Among Breton's pathfinders is Pierre Reverdy, a pre-Surrealist contemporary who stressed this aspect of the image. In the first Manifesto, Breton quotes from notes on poetry published in 1918. Reverdy had written: "The image is a pure creation of the mind. It cannot be born from a comparison but from a juxtaposition of two more or less distant realities. The more the relationship between the two juxtaposed realities is both distant and true, the stronger the image will be — the greater its emotional power and poetic reality."

Also in contradistinction to the usual literary esthetics of comparison-making, which tends to regard such qualities as justness or decorousness as all-important, with calculation a major inspirational force here as elsewhere in human activity, Breton himself asserts:

> In my opinion, it is erroneous to claim that "the mind has grasped the relationship" of two realities in the presence of each other. First of all, it has seized

* A more modest exploration of the possibilities of juxtaposition occurred in an adoption of an old party game practiced as an amusement at some Surrealist meetings. At the top of a sheet of paper, the first "player" in this "game" would draw an object which he would conceal from the other participants, folding the page and leaving only a few lines hanging below the fold, which the next participant would use as a departure point for his own drawing. This would go on with as many players as wished to join. Some of the participants included, in addition to poets such as Breton, Louis Aragon, Benjamin Péret, and Jacques Prévert, such painters partial to the Surrealist approach as Yves Tanguy, Joan Miró, and Man Ray. In the initial Surrealist Manifesto, Breton mentions the possibility of receiving a primitive form of poetic inspiration this way, by cutting up newspaper articles and arranging them by chance into a poem (an approach which derives from certain Dada recommendations, which defined poetry itself as this and this alone). The game was called *cadavre exquis* or "exquisite corpse," after a phrase which emerged during a version of the game played with words: "the exquisite corpse drinks the new wine."

nothing consciously. It is, as it were, from the fortuitous juxtaposition of the two terms that a particular light has sprung, the light of the image, to which we are infinitely sensitive. The value of the image depends upon the beauty of the spark obtained; it is, consequently, a function of the difference of potential between the two conductors. When the difference exists only slightly, as in a comparison, the spark is lacking. . . . And just as the length of the spark increases to the extent that it occurs in rarified gases, the Surrealist atmosphere created by automatic writing . . . is especially conducive to the production of the most beautiful images. . . . Everything is valid when it comes to obtaining the desired suddenness from certain associations.

In the last phrase Breton identifies the element which, gathering up the implications of the Surrealist philosophy, dominates in the Surrealist poem itself.

v

With the image as touchstone, it is possible to consider — indeed, practically deduce — the nature of the Surrealist poem. Codifications can of course be catastrophically ineffective: in poetry especially there may be many exceptions. Maverick works may exist even within an otherwise consistent poet's output; there may be fresh explorations, or recidivist oversights. Nevertheless, Surrealism's esthetic seems consistent enough within the terms of its own self-proclaimed reason to encourage a few generalizations.

In *imagery*, for the philosophical and psychological reasons given above, the poem's images are apt to be extremely disparate, bringing together presences from wholly different realms to form the characteristic, juxtaposed Surrealist image — an image which differs from the conventional or "imagist" variety in that it is not only double in its comparisons, but three-termed or multiple as in Lautréamont's trope; and in that it risks distance of comparison among components. Not only individual lines but whole poems are structured so as to expose this extraordinary imagistic activity.

In *tone*, consistent with imagistic disparateness, the usual tonal distinctions do not apply and are often actively subverted. The noble and the absurd, the low and the high, the lyrical and the ironical, the mysterious and the humorous — all such tonal "antinomies" are denied and — at least it is to be hoped — fused. Moreover, such juxtapositions are attempted not only for the sake of familiar, perhaps "satirical," oppositions, but in such a way as to allow for a multiplicity of moods, representing a range of shadings such as is native to the mind beyond any superimposed idea of esthetic propriety.

In *diction*, since the mind tends to prefer the vernacular, rather than a more literary idiom, the ideal of "spoken thought" is present, the diction leaning toward the everyday. The accepted ideal of "dictional purity" — a "purity" apt to be manufactured according to traditional literary expectations and specifications, and therefore to the Surrealist hardly an indicator of fixed inner value at all and scarcely sacred — is discarded in the interest of dictional flexibility. The colloquial and the formal frequently intermingle, less because the Surrealist wishes to burlesque either than because the mind really works that way, and can comfortably contain both at the same moment.

In *rhythm and meter*, the poem reflects the fact that the mind often operates in sudden associative leaps, or in "convulsive" gestures, rather than in any metrically regular fashion. The most metrically irregular passages may appear juxtaposed with lines which "sing" as if on impulse. In the Surrealist's view, ordinary metrical yardsticks are discardable not only because they are literarily unnecessary, but because they are apt to be philosophically restrictive.

In *theme*, since the existing reality is fundamentally "out of tune" with thought, and since "the imagination is about to reassert its rights," a central theme is the imminence of change, and a longing for it that verges on revolt. Since the realization of even the most modest of such wishes is obviously so far in the future — as observation of the existing world confirms, perhaps above all in so-called "revolutionary" countries — the desire expressed is intense, suggesting the sexual. Insofar as longing and desire overlap, and insofar as the theme of "passion" in one or another of its various forms propels all its poetry, it might even be claimed that all Surrealist poems are love poems. Consistent with this, the most frequent targets of Surrealist satire are figures who wish to restrict desire, these satirical poems perhaps corresponding with those earlier poems of amorous frustration in which the lover angrily condemns forces separating lover and beloved.

In *subject matter*, since world and beloved tend to be identical, it is only logical that no part of either physical or global anatomy be regarded as indecorous. Indeed, the subject matter is not so much the objects involved as the poet's treatment of them, which is as "idées fixes," in the sense of erotic obsessions. With no more facetiousness than the Surrealist himself would court, one might say that the lover's stare and the poet's style are related, the lover's acts and the act of poetry corresponding. As a result, sexual realms which both society and its poets tend to join in forbidding cease to be forbidden, the usual considerations of "taste" in these matters being regarded as ideally personal, rather than derived from socially prescribed norms.

In *overall form*, instead of being dictated by ideas of form external to the mind, form is regarded as an extraneous concept, except as it responds to the demands of the individual poem. Perhaps even more urgently than in most conventionally structured writings, the point is consistency of attack within individual works. Often, particularly at the outset of poems, a certain "arbitrary" quality is fostered as if to allow this internalized formal integrity to stand out, reflecting the functioning of a "reason" which refuses to base itself on previously existing, worldly stereotypes. As with the values which we have just broken down very broadly into categories, this does not signify that form is ignored. Just as the Surrealist might insist that he is all the more concerned with beauty because his involvement is with an indigenous rather than an imposed esthetic ideal, his concern with all the qualities conducive to such beauty is all the more intense for his refusal to accept the ready-made definitions of others.

In *genre*, the poem is intended to have a life of its own with respect to which the whole notion of "genre" is virtually irrelevant. There is an obliteration of large as well as small boundaries which exist according to the traditions of art, but not necessarily according to the mind. According to inner requirements, the poem may discard verse altogether, moving toward visual or "concrete" formats, or the prose poem. As the poem moves toward prose, it may incorporate elements of drama or dialogue, fiction or narration, manifesto or monologue, maxim or proverb. These explorations of genres beyond verse are not ends in themselves, but — ideally speaking — are way stations along a route which anticipates passing through and breaking down still further boundaries, for example those between world and mind, and perhaps those two other monolithic antinomies: art and life.

VI

As testified to by the numerous essays, prefaces and monographs by Surrealism's members dealing with pre-Surrealist writers, individual Surrealists have been more than willing to acknowledge the impact of prior writers on their work. In the first Manifesto, Breton himself lists as forebears a whole roster of nineteenth-century (and other) authors in addition to Rimbaud and Lautréamont: Baudelaire, Bertrand, De Sade, Mallarmé, Jarry, etc. Nor is Breton shy about identifying directly contemporary inspirations, listing in addition to Reverdy, Guillaume Apollinaire, who one year before his death in 1918 and six before the founding of the movement, coined the term Surrealism — though without much exploring its meaning or significance.

By the time of the Second Manifesto, Breton had taken a somewhat different tack regarding influence. Yet in asserting "when it comes to revolt, none of us must have any need of ancestors," he seems to have done so not so much to deny influence as to proclaim his antecedents outdistanced. To us, the relationship of Apollinaire and Reverdy to Surrealism's poetry seems so essential that, without in any way implying membership in the movement, we have decided to represent their poetry here. It seems to us that translations of their poetry have still not been so voluminous as to render their presence uneconomical in terms of space.

Apollinaire and Reverdy aside, certainly the most important not to mention critically well-explored source of Surrealism was the Dada movement. Founded by Tristan Tzara and friends in

Zurich in 1916, it ended, according to the general consensus of opinion, after a brilliant flourishing on foreign soil, in Paris circa 1922–1923. Dada's very character as a movement suggests Surrealism as does its concern with chance and the psychologically spontaneous or "automatic," and its willingness to tear down formal structures both esthetically and philosophically. Yet, as Breton phrased it in his initial, pre-Manifesto collection of theoretical prose, *Les Pas perdus* (*Lost Steps*, 1924): "It shall not be said that Dada served any other purpose than to keep us in that state of absolute availability in which we find ourselves now and from which we shall now set forth with lucidity toward what claims us for its own." And that tremendous debts exist on both sides certainly cannot be doubted. Many of Surrealism's founding members were participants in Paris Dada; Breton himself was the principal architect of Tzara's move to Paris in 1919, as well as the leading interpreter of Dada to the Paris avant-garde until 1922 (see biographical note on Breton). And, Surrealism *is* to some degree the immediate result of an attempt to break definitively with the Dada outlook. For our own part, we accept the prevailing critical view of the distinction between the two movements: that while Dada's destructive aspect was essential and characteristic, nihilism's role in Surrealism is much less important — in fact is definitely subservient to its positive, if not actually optimistic, hopes. Though we have attempted to suggest the relationship to Dada here and in our biographical sketches of Tzara and Arp (two major Dada writers who were also for a time associated with Surrealism), properly to give an idea of the relationship of Dada to Surrealism might require another anthology, virtually the size of this one.*

* Possibly because of his lack of command of English, Breton mentions only two English-speaking authors in his list of forebears, Edward Young and Jonathan Swift, and does not at all refer to the English Romantic poets. This is especially surprising in view of the psychological concerns of two of the founding figures of English Romanticism, Coleridge and Wordsworth, whose work represents, as does Breton's, an extraordinary departure from the rationalist norms of the time. The *Lyrical Ballads* (published in 1798), the duo's early collaborative collection (such collaborative interest itself suggesting Surrealist concern for group activity), like Surrealism broke new ground in rejecting rationalism in the name of psychological concepts — here, the ideas about "association" and "involuntary memory" of the pioneering English psychologist David Hartley. Certainly the circumstances of the writing of one of Coleridge's best-known poems, "Kubla Khan" (1798), as recounted by the poet himself, suggest Surrealist

Which brings us to our principles of compilation generally.

Just as we have taken care in this introductory note to pay particular attention to Breton's first, basic, and perhaps most significantly far-reaching proposals, we intend in the following anthology to reflect activity in Surrealist poetry during its initial ten to fifteen years — its most energetic epoch, both theoretically and creatively, and a considerable life span for any movement in the arts. It is unfortunately necessary to follow this program in view of a disconcerting circumstance traced in detail by Surrealism's historians: the fact that at the very moment when Surrealism began to increase its influence, spreading internationally, the original movement became troubled with internal squabbles, the majority of its most remarkable members gradually departing until the start of World War II, which delivered something like a coup de grâce from without.

The reasons for these departures are difficult to pinpoint but seem related to the same causes: dislike of what was felt to be the excessively insistent demands of the movement for acts and

---

experiments with dream-dictated and trance-related compositions: "The author continued for about three hours in a profound sleep, at least of the external senses, during which time he has the most vivid confidence that he could not have composed less than from two to three hundred lines: if that indeed can be called composition in which all the images rose up before him as things, with a parallel production of the corresponden: expressions, without any sensation or consciousness of effort." Coleridge's philosophical approach, the result of a restlessness deriving from what he called "knowing, feeling, a man to be one, yet not understanding how to think of him but as two," his view of poetry as "whole soul'd activity," suggest that like Breton's, Coleridge's esthetic may have had a starting point in resistance to the imperatives of antinomies. The immediate product of this interest, registered both in and out of the *Lyrical Ballads*, is the humanized, informal diction of Coleridge's early "conversation poems," which in turn helped inspire Wordsworth's more celebrated attempts to write in "a language really used by men." This desire evolves in the later Wordsworth into attempts to situate the mind and its vernacular in poetry, if not outright efforts to approximate "spoken thought." Often confused with a quasinaturalistic desire to duplicate the diction of English countrymen — just as the subject matter of his landscape poetry is often confused with a preoccupation with local rather than psychic concerns — Wordsworth's subject is fundamentally the functioning of the poet's mind and memory. For all its references to local color, perhaps Wordsworth's best-known poem, the autobiographical "The Prelude" (completed 1805) is with good reason subtitled "The Growth of a Poet's Mind." The continuation of this psychologically sophisticated mode is also apparent in later Romantic poets, with their odes and other poems addressed, dedicated, or even entitled "To Psyche."

professions of allegiance; and a near-fear of Breton's incipient authoritarianism, a power even by the mid-1920's extending to censure and "excommunication" (as the critics of "Pope André" within the movement began to call it). Yet in retrospect, it seems only fair to point out that this exacting quality was one which produced a Surrealist movement in the first place, since it came into being thanks to a willingness to explore challenging ideas in a concerted group effort as drastic in its own requirements as the ideas it dealt with.

Today it seems clear that the conflicts which so upset the movement may not have been precisely as necessary as its parties had thought. As the classic example of the phase of the movement colored by these excommunications, we might consider the firings in the Second Manifesto of 1929. Though charges of wavering loyalty had been leveled against Philippe Soupault and Antonin Artaud as early as 1926–1927, in this later document Breton "definitively" expelled Soupault, Artaud, and Robert Desnos, all of whom had been among Surrealism's most active members. Yet despite the intensity of Breton's disdain, the fact of these firings seems to lose significance in view of several circumstances surrounding them. Clearly, they took place in terms having less to do with poetry than with matters external to it. For reasons somewhat puzzling in view of the Surrealist leader's intermittent pronouncements urging that Surrealism seek a larger audience, Breton had a curious and perhaps strangely shortsighted suspicion of the so-called popular or performing arts; all three writers had made successful forays into such frowned-upon areas as journalism, theatre, and film. More characteristic of Breton's generally explorative, open-minded temperament is the preface he thought fit to write for the 1946 edition of this same Second Manifesto, in which he remarks that he has come to recognize that with respect to such necessarily exacting demands as his own, it is only natural that "the worst offenders might well be those in whom one had placed greatest confidence"; and, openly regretting his exclusions, rescinds them. A corresponding willingness to be reconciled is seen in writings by the many members who left the movement of their own accord during the 1930's. Beyond mere nostalgia, most stated feelings of intense respect for their Surrealist background, which most acknowledged as formative years.

Since so many of the "breaks" with Surrealism were healed wholly or partially, and since most took place on the level of internal politics rather than poetics to begin with, we have not only included the excommunicated, a category which includes all but a few of the movement's major writers, but have also chosen to represent these and other Surrealists by using works dating from both before and after their "period" of formal Surrealist involvement. So that the reader may be better able to see for himself something of the far-reaching influence of the Surrealist spirit on its poets, we have included in the source list at the back of this book dates of composition of all poems.

As for the postwar years, and the efforts of Breton and a circle of new friends to revive the movement, we are fully in agreement with Roger Shattuck, when he remarks in the preface to the translation of Nadeau's history that "since 1939 it has been the shadow, not the stature of Surrealism, which has been lengthening." While the relative virtues of many later Surrealist poets is apparent, it is impossible not to feel simply on the basis of originality alone, that something was lost. Also, it is clear in most cases that the involvement with Surrealism of many of the later, self-proclaimed "adherents" is scarcely as essential to their development as association had been for earlier writers. As for the quality and significance of the movement as a whole, again we can only state our belief that even in the case of as unusual a literary movement as was Surrealism, it is the quality, not the professed allegiances, of the participants which is all-important, and worth representing. Certainly it is far more to the movement's credit to have created a great many major poets in its crucible rather than to have kept on casting increasingly attenuated shadows. That the movement eventually fell victim to the ravages of war seems to us hardly to detract from either Surrealism's lofty significance or its overall achievement; indeed, it seems only consistent with the movement's heroic posture that it might prefer an active death rather than the step-by-step decline in the historical nursing home into which some of its later proponents seem determined to enroll it.

True, Breton himself, while exiled in the United States, announced in a wartime lecture (*Situation du Surréalisme entre les deux guerres* [*Situation of Surrealism between the Wars*]): "I think I know . . . what the final hour of Surrealism would mean: it would be the birth of a new movement with an even greater power of liberation. . . . Because of that very dynamic force which we continue to place above all else, my best friends and I would consider it a point of honor to rally immediately around such a movement." Though Breton was probably as close to a genuine literary saint as our century can offer, one need not be a paradigm of sophistication to note that only a god himself — if not God himself — could adhere to the psychologically wrenching requirements inherent in such a statement.

Or perhaps the flaw is in the nostalgia evident in the comparison itself. Breton after all assumes the existence of a highly centralized movement to "rally around." Instead, the very force which placed the ideal of transformation in such a high position may well have already — even by the wartime years — transformed itself. Perhaps what Surrealism accomplished was to do more than merely persist, existing finally — as all literary movements must truly exist to survive — in terms of its impact on subsequent literature everywhere.

— MICHAEL BENEDIKT

Contents

xxx

xxxii

xxxiv

xxxvi

xxxix

THE POETRY
OF SURREALISM

An Anthology

GUILLAUME APOLLINAIRE

1880-1918

A POLLINAIRE, HAILED AS "THE LAST GREAT POET" by the young André Breton, was the first to use the term Surrealism and also the first major poet of the twentieth century consciously to apply Rimbaud's recommendation that the poet become "absolutely modern." His work is characterized by the use of the poetic image in the sudden, "marvelous" juxtapositions later favored by the Surrealists, reflecting the poet's interest in what he termed a "new spirit"; at the same time, his writings remain haunted by reminiscences of traditional poetic techniques and themes, as well as by outright nostalgia for the past. Characteristic of his awareness of his particular position in time is Apollinaire's observation in one poem that he stands in a no-man's-land between "Order and Adventure."

Apollinaire's very biography seems peculiarly the product of an internationalist era — one in which speedy travel (a specific and frequent theme in the poems) is possible. Born in Rome, the "illegitimate" son of an Italian and of a woman of allegedly aristocratic Polish birth (the poet's actual surname was Kostrowitsky), he was taken as a child to Monaco, where he received a French education. In 1899 the family settled in Paris; in 1901 he worked briefly as a tutor in Germany, where he met an English girl who was the first of a long series of great loves motivating much of the poet's writing, which is often erotic in bearing. It is also in the poems about Germany and his quest for the beloved there and in England, where he journeyed in 1904, that the note of larger longing which sounds throughout

the mature work is first heard. Gradually, the poet's erotic yearn-
ings evolve into still more ambitious expressions of desire for
the conquest of the world itself: a turning point occurs in the
relatively early poem in which the poet names his archetypal
beloved "Rosemonde" — "the rose of the world." It is with
Apollinaire that the late nineteenth-century Symbolist ideal of
the poet as a contented, more or less self-condemned dweller in
the "ivory tower" is definitively set aside.

After returning to France around 1905, Apollinaire worked
for a time as a journalist, but was soon drawn to the new paint-
ing then appearing in Paris. The first of his articles on the visual
arts, like his "Saltimbanque" or "traveling clown" poems of the
period, have as their subject some of Picasso's Pink Period work.
His first book of poems, *Le Bestiaire ou le cortège d'Orphée* (*The
Bestiary, or the Cortege of Orpheus*, 1910),[1] was illustrated by
Raoul Dufy, but was originally to have been accompanied by
Picasso's drawings. This interest culminated in 1913 with the
publication of *Les Peintres Cubistes: Méditations esthétiques*
(*The Cubist Painters: Esthetic Meditations*),[2] which both pre-
sented and helped to coordinate the still relatively unknown
school of artists and poets.

Just as Apollinaire's articles include prophetically apt estimates
of many of the major painters of the coming decade, his first
published prose work, a short story, *L'Enchanteur pourrissant*
(*The Decomposing Enchanter*, 1909),[3] with its picture of an
unfortunately dormant magician, is often seen as a prophecy
of Surrealism. Surrealism's taste for secular magic also seems
prefigured by the motto Apollinaire took, *J'émerveille* — "I mar-
vel." A more specific prophecy was his pioneering use of the
term Surrealism itself several years later, in the introduction to
his play *Les Mamelles de Tirésias* (*The Breasts of Tiresias*, 1917).[4]
Although reference to "Surrealism" also appears in a letter of
the period, in neither instance did Apollinaire much develop his
neologism's definition, though in the note prefacing the play's
published version, inklings of Surrealism are certainly present:

> To characterize my drama I have used a neologism
> which, as I rarely use them, I hope will be excused: I
> have invented the adjective Surrealist, which does not at
> all mean symbolic, as Mr. Victor Basch has assumed in

4

his article on the theatre, but defines fairly well a tendency in art which, if it is not the newest thing under the sun, at least has never been formulated as a credo, an artistic and literary faith.

The cheap idealism of the playwrights who followed Victor Hugo sought for verisimilitude in conventional local color, which as "photographic" naturalism produced comedies of manners . . . in order to attempt, if not a renovation of the theatre, at least an original effort, I thought it necessary to come back to nature itself, but without copying it photographically.

When man wanted to imitate walking he created the wheel, which does not resemble a leg. In the same way he has created Surrealism unconsciously.

Apollinaire's multifarious activities during the prewar period also included editing a catalogue of the "Enfer" (or section of forbidden books) at the Bibliothèque Nationale, writing prefaces for a collected edition of the Marquis de Sade,[5] the introduction to a new edition of Baudelaire;[6] and (in a less metaphysical vein of love poetry than the one in which he identified the body of the beloved with the body of the world) working as a part-time pornographer. His *Oeuvres érotiques complètes* (*Collected Erotic Works*, 1934; published posthumously)[7] comprise three volumes.

In 1913 *Alcools* (*Alcohols*),[8] Apollinaire's first full-length collection of poems, was published — its first line, "You're weary of this ancient world at last," setting the tone for his later poetic work, and perhaps for Surrealism itself. In *Alcools* alone, the technical approach ranges from the relatively traditional imagery and regular structures and meters of the poet's earlier models, to extremely "free" verse. The mixed texture and quick pace of modern experience is a constant preoccupation throughout, but is captured with particular daring in such poems as "Monday Christine Street" and "Earth-Ocean," which seem to consist entirely of half-heard, frequently interrupted, and, in general, strangely juxtaposed fragments of conversation, somewhat in the manner of the Cubist collages contemporary with them. Influenced by the operations of chance, the poems often present concatenations of outrageous, disparate imagery virually as ends in themselves, in something close to the purest Surrealistic manner. It was also in this collection that Apollinaire streamlined his poems by abandoning punctuation, striking it from the galley proofs. Other poems from this period of discovery, together with early verses, appear in *Il y a* (*There Is*)[9] compiled and published posthumously in 1925.

The last poems, published in Apollinaire's second important collection, *Calligrammes* (*Calligrams*, 1918),[10] are those in which the poet speaks with fullest awareness of his unusual position between (as he calls it in one of his last poems, "The Gorgeous Redhead") "Order and Adventure." *Calligrams* also offers the poet's own versions of the seldom-attempted visual poem, many of them written on the battlefield, where Apollinaire was an artillery officer. One of the sources of "Concrete Poetry," Apollinaire's visual poems also foreshadow the Surrealist "poem-object," and the Surrealist interest in the bridging of genres generally.

Toward the end of his life the poet began a concentrated exploration of the medium of theatre — an exploration complicated by military service between 1916 and 1918. His death occurred on Armistice Day, 1918, the result of influenza contracted in the aftermath of an operation to remove a shell fragment from his skull. One of Apollinaire's last works, the play *Couleur du temps* (*The Color of Our Time*, 1918),[11] carries his lifelong concern with the conflict between old and new into new realms, and seems to prophesy that this struggle would continue — since, as the play suggests, it is this very struggle which defines life.

OTHER PRINCIPAL WORKS

L'Hérésiarque et cie. (tales: Stock, 1910; reissued 1922, 1945; tr. by Remy I. Hall as *The Heresiarch and Co.*, Doubleday/ Anchor, 1966); *Le Poète assassiné* (novel; Bibliothèque des Curieux, 1916; reissued N.R.F., 1945; tr. as *The Poet Assassinated* by Ron Padgett, Grossman, 1970); *Le Flâneur des deux rives* (memoirs: Ed. de la Sirène, 1918; reissued N.R.F., 1928); *La Femme assise* (novel: N.R.F., 1920); *Anecdotiques* (journalism: Stock, 1926); *L'Esprit nouveau et les poètes* (essay originally published in 1918 in *Le Mercure de France*: Haumont, 1946; tr.

6

by Roger Shattuck, together with poetry and other prose in *Apollinaire: Selected Writings:* New Directions, 1950); *Lettres à sa marraine* (letters: Haumont, 1948; reissued N.R.F., 1951); also many volumes of love and other poems posthumously assembled from personal letters and other manuscripts between 1947 and 1952, all collected (together with the plays) in the standard collected edition issued in the "Bibliothèque de la Pléiade" series of N.R.F. (1956). Selected poetry: *Apollinaire: Selected Poems,* tr. Oliver Bernard (Penguin Books, 1965). Selected writings: in addition to the Shattuck volume, *Apollinaire,* "Poètes d'aujourd'hui" No. 8 (Seghers).

HOTEL

My room is shaped like a cage
The sun slips its arm in through the window
I always said there was nothing like smoking to create a few
    fine mirages
So I light up my cigarette with a sunbeam
I don't want to work anymore now I want to smoke

— M. B.

1909

The woman had a dress
Of Turkish cloth
And her tunic with a border of gold
Was made of two panels
Attached to each other at the shoulder

Her eyes were dancing like those of angels
She was laughing and laughing
She had a face with the colors of France
Blue eyes white teeth very red lips
She had a face with the colors of France

Her dress was cut low in a circle below her neck
And her hair dressed like Mme. Récamier
With fine naked arms

Shall we never hear midnight sound

The woman in a dress of Turkish cloth
And a tunic with a border of gold
Cut low in a circle
Took her curls for a walk
Her band of gold
Accompanied by her little shoes with buckles

She was so beautiful
That you would never have dared love her

I loved atrocious women in the abysmal quarters of the city
Where some new beings were born every day
Their blood was iron, their brains fire
I loved I loved the people clever with machines
Luxury and beauty are nothing but scum
This woman was so beautiful
That she frightened me

— ROBERT BLY

AUTUMN

A bowlegged peasant and his ox receding
Through the mist slowly through the mist of autumn
Which hides the shabby and sordid villages

And out there as he goes the peasant is singing
A song of love and infidelity
About a ring and a heart which someone is breaking

Oh the autumn the autumn has been the death of summer
In the mist there are two gray shapes receding

— W. S. MERWIN

SAFFRON

This meadow is sickly but pretty in the fall
Cows pasture there
Filling themselves with poison
Saffron color of tree-rings and of lilacs
Flowers there your eyes are like those flowers
Near-violet like their rings and like this autumn
And my life for your eyes slowly fills itself with poison

The school-children run up with a racket
Playing on the harmonica but very neatly jacketed
They gather saffron flowers which are like their mothers
Daughters of their daughters and colored like your eyelid
Which flutters as flowers are fluttered by the mad wind

The shepherd softly sings
While slow and lowing the cows abandon
Forever this meadow blooming evilly in autumn

— M. B.

ZONE

You're weary of this ancient world at last

O Eiffel Shepherdess the flock of the bridges bleats this morning

You're tired of living in Greek and Roman styles

Antiquity has touched the automobiles
Only religion is still new religion
Still simple as the hangars of Port-Aviation

In Europe the Church alone is never ancient
The most advanced European is Pope Pius X*
And you beneath the windows whom shame prevents
From entering a church and there confessing
You read prospectuses posters catalogues which sing
Poetry for today as for prose there are newspapers
A thousand titles incidents of crime
Portraits of great men at twenty-five centimes

I saw a pretty street today whose name I forget
Sparkling and clear it announced the sun like a trumpet
Managers workers and pretty typists trek
Along it four times daily six days a week
At morning three times there the siren groans
A noisy bell barks there toward noon
Signs and writings on the walls
Posters placards parrot-calls
I like the graces of that busy street
Between Rue Aumont-Thiéville and l'Avenue des Ternes you'll
   find it

Now there's the young street and you're still a little tot
Your mother swaddles you only in blue and white
You're very pious and with your oldest friend René Dalize
The pomps of the Church are the things you mostly prize

* In May, 1911, Pope Pius X gave the Papal Benediction to a French pilot,
Beaumont, first winner of the Paris-Rome air race. The gesture received
wide publicity, and Apollinaire was clearly much impressed by it. [Trans-
lator's note.]

It's nine o'clock the gas a low blue flame you slip from the
  dormitory
And all night in the college chapel pray
While the eternal adorable depth of amethyst
Shapes forever the flaming glory of Christ
The beautiful lily that we all grow there
The inextinguishable torch with the red hair
The pale and scarlet son of mother's grief
The tree of which each prayer is a leaf
Twin-trunk of honor and eternity
It is the star with six rays
God dying on Friday and revived on Sunday
Christ surpasses pilots in his flight
He holds the record of the world for height

Christ apple of the eye
Fruit of twenty centuries he can fly
And changed to a bird this age like Jesus rises
The devils look up at him from the abysses
They say he imitates Simon Magus of Judea
They cry since he is stellar call him stealer
The angels stunt around the pretty stunter
Icarus Enoch Elijah Apollonius of Thyane
Float around the first airplane
Sometimes they part giving way to those on the Eucharist
Raising the Host eternally priest after priest
At last the airplane perches with open wings
A million swallows arrive the sky sings
Come flapping crows owls and hawks
Ibis of Africa flamingos storks
The roc in verse and fable read
Gripping Adam's skull first human head
The screaming eagle dives from the horizon
And from America comes the little hummingbird
From China come the pihis long and supple
They have one wing only and fly in a couple
Then too the dove in purest pride
The lyrebird the peacock argus-eyed
The phoenix that is born from his own pyre
A moment covers all with ash of fire

12

The three sirens from the perilous straits
Arrive singing their sweet notes
And all eagle phoenix and pihis of China
Fly with the airliner

Now you are walking in Paris in the crowd alone
On every side herds of buses groan
Love's anguish has you by the throat
As if you never should be loved again
You'd be a monk if this were the old reign
You find yourself with shame upon your knees
You mock yourself with laughter bright as Hades
The sparks of laughter gild your deepest life
It is a picture hanging in a somber museum
To look at it severely you sometimes come

Today you walk in Paris the women are bloodstained
It was and I would wish to forget it was then beauty waned

Surrounded with leaping flames Notre Dame at Chartres looked
    down on me
The blood of your Sacré-Coeur at Montmartre drowned me
I'm sick of hearing the windy pieties
The love from which I suffer is a shameful disease
The image possessing you makes life a sleepless woe
This fugitive image is with you wherever you go

Now you're on the Mediterranean shore
Under the citrus trees that all year flower
With friends in a boat you bask
This one is Nissard there's a Mentonesque and two Turbiasques
We see with terror the deep devil-fish
and among the algae fish-faces of Christ

You are near Prague in a hostel-garden
You feel quite happy there's a rose on the table
Instead of writing your little tale in prose
You examine the canker that sleeps in the heart of the rose

Dismayed you see yourself outlined in St. Vith's agates
That day you were so sad you stood at death's very gates
You look like Lazarus in love with light
The hands of the clock in the Jewish quarter turn

Backward and you also recoil in your life
Climbing to the Hradchin* you hear at night
Czech songs in the taverns

Here you are at Marseilles among the melons

Here you are at Coblenz Hôtel du Géant

At Rome beneath a Japanese medlar-tree

In Amsterdam with a girl you think is pretty
She's ugly and engaged to a student from Leyden
Rooms for rent Cubicula locanda
Three days I remember there and three more at Gouda

You are at Paris you have been arrested
And dragged to judgment like a criminal

You've carried out some sad and happy travels
Before perceiving the illusion and the age
At twenty and at thirty felt love's rage
I have lived like a fool and much time wasted
You can't look at your hands I could sob out
For you for my beloved your fearful rout

You regard with tearful eyes the wretched emigrants
They believe in God they pray the women nurse their infants
They fill with their smell the station of Saint-Lazare
Like the magi they have faith in their star
They hope to make some money in the Argentine
And come back to their country with a fortune
One family carries a red quilt like a heart
That eiderdown and our dreams are a world apart
Some of these emigrants will rent a hole here
On Rue des Rosiers or Rue des Ecouffes
I've often seen them at evening out for the air
Like checker-pieces moving in starts and fits
They're mostly Jews their bewigged women sit
Like mummies in the back rooms of the stores

You stand before the counter of a crapulous bar
You take a two-sou coffee with the beggars

* A hilly district of Prague [Translator's note].

14

You are the night in a great restaurant

These women are not wicked but they have their cares
All even the ugliest has made men shed tears

She is the daughter of a Jersey cop

I hadn't seen her hands so hard and chapped
I have great pity for her belly's contours

Debasing my mouth the poor girl has a horrible laugh

You are alone morning comes up
The milkmen tinkle bottles on the stoops

Night goes away like a beautiful Métive
Ferdine the false or Léa the attentive

And you drink this alcohol that burns like life
Your life that you are drinking like a brandy

Toward Auteuil bedward you go on foot
To fetish-gods of Oceania Guinea
Christs of another form and other culture
The lower Christs of hopes that are obscure

Adieu Adieu

Sun throat cut

— LOUIS SIMPSON

SALTIMBANQUES

For Louis Dumur

Across the field the traveling clowns
Go past beside the gardens
Before the doors of mist-enshrouded inns
Through churchless towns

Some children run out ahead of them
While others fall back dreaming
Each fruit-tree gladly resigns
Its burden when from far off they make their signs

The weights they bear are round or square
With tambourines and hoops gilt silver
Wise beasts the bear the monkey
Beg small coins along the way

— M. B.

16

PHANTOM OF THE CLOUDS

Since it was the eve of July 14
About four in the afternoon
I went out into the street to see the saltimbanques

These people who do tricks outdoors
Are beginning to be rare in Paris
In my youth one saw many more than today
They have almost all gone to the provinces

I took the boulevard Saint-Germain
And in a little square located between Saint-Germain-des-Prés
    and Danton's statue
I found some saltimbanques
The crowd that awaited them was silent and resigned to waiting
I found a spot in the general circle from which everything could
    be seen

Formidable weights
Belgian cities held up at arm's length by a Russian worker
    from Longwy
Black hollow dumbbells with a frozen river for shaft
Fingers rolling a cigarette as bitter and delicious as life

Numerous dirty rugs on the ground
Rugs with permanent pleats
Rugs which are nearly completely the color of dust
And on which a few yellow or green spots persist
Like a tune that will not leave you

See that thin wild-looking one
The ashes of his ancestors are emerging in his graying beard
He carries all his heredity in his face this way
Yet seems to be dreaming of the future
While mechanically turning a hand-organ
Whose sweet voice makes magnificent lamentation
With gurgling muffled groans and several clinkers

The saltimbanques didn't move an inch
The oldest had tights of a purplish rosy color which appears in

17

the cheeks of certain young girls who are lively yet very near
death

That rosiness nestles most in the lines around their mouths
Or next to their nostrils
It's a color full of treachery

That man over there could he be carrying on his back
The rotting coloring of his lungs

Arms arms everywhere were standing guard

The second saltimbanque
Was clothed only in his shadow
I looked at him a long time
His face entirely escapes me
He was a human without a head

Another looked like a bit of a bandit
Perhaps an ordinary street thief except absolutely debauched
With his floppy pants and suspenders
What he probably looked a lot like was a pimp dressing up for
business

The music stopped for a bit of a chat with the audience
Which bit by bit tossed the sum of 2 francs 50 on the rug
Instead of the three francs which the old one had set as the price
of a performance

But when it was clear that nobody would give anything more
They decided to begin
From under the organ a little saltimbanque came dressed
in tubercular red
With fur at his wrists and ankles
He cried out
And bowed bending out his forearms prettily
Hands open wide

With one leg tucked back to genuflect
He bowed to all four points of the compass
And when he stepped atop the ball
His slight body began so delicate a music that none of the
spectators could resist it

A tiny spirit without the least human burden
Everybody thought
And this music of shapes and forms
Drowned out that of the mechanical organ
Ground out by the man with his face covered with his own
    ancestors

The little saltimbanque turned a cartwheel
With so much harmonious grace
That the organ completely stopped playing
And the organ-grinder hid his face in his hands
With those fingers of his like descendants of his own destiny
Small foetuses which emerged from his beard
Renewed Indian cries
Angelic music from the trees
Sudden disappearance of the child

The saltimbanques lifted the great dumbbells at arm's length
They juggled with the weights

While each spectator searched in himself for the miraculous child
Century O century of clouds

— M. B.

THE MUSICIAN OF SAINT-MERRY

At last I have the right to say hello to all these beings I do not
   know
One by one they pass before me and reassemble further on
And still all that I can see of them is completely strange to me
But their hopes are no less strong than mine

I do not sing of this world nor of the other stars
I sing of all the possibilities of myself beyond this world and all
   the stars as well
I sing of all the joys of wandering and the delight of dying that
   way

On the 21st of the month of May in 1913
Death's ferryman together with St. Merry's many quick-tongued
   buzzing wives
Sent their splendor drifting abroad like a hundred million flies
When a man without eyes without a nose and lacking ears
Leaving the Sébasto district turned down Aubry-le-Boucher lane
The young man was darkly suntanned yet with strawberry circles
   on his cheeks
That man Oh! Ariadne
He was playing the flute but the music was conducting his steps
He stopped on a streetcorner along Saint-Martin
Playing the same song I'm singing now and which I just made up
   myself
The women he passed stopped as he went by
And came from all directions
When suddenly every bell in St. Merry began to ring
The musician paused and took a quick sip from the fountain
Which is at the corner of Simon-Le-Franc
Which is to say that it was when Saint-Merry finally shut up
That the stranger with the flute started up
And going back the same way he came reached the rue de la
   Verrerie
Which he walked down followed by his flock of females
Who kept coming out of the houses

20

Who kept coming out of the little side streets with wild and
  flashing eyes
Holding their hands out to the melodious seducer
He walked by very casually playing his song
It was terrifying the way he just walked along

Overheard elsewhere
Tell me at exactly what time does the next train leave for Paris

At that very moment
The pigeons of the Moluccas let their nutmeg droppings fly
Meanwhile
Catholic mission at Bôma what have you done with your sculptor

While elsewhere
She crosses one of the bridges linking Bonn with Beuel and
  disappears en route across Pützchen

Simultaneously
A girl in love with the local mayor

In some other section
Perfume-manufacturers whose creations virtually rival those cf
  poets

In sum O all you sarcastic mockers you haven't been able to
  make too much of men
You've barely been able to squeeze out your living from their
  misery
But we who die of our mutual separation
Hold our arms out and over those rails runs a long long train of
  merchandise

Sitting right beside me you were crying in the dark depths of the
  old-fashioned carriage

And now
You plainly look like me to me you look upsettingly just like me

We resemble each other like nineteenth-century architecture
All those tall chimneys looking almost just like towers

Now we are going higher much higher we no longer touch the
  ground

And while the world went on being so various and so alive
The women in the procession which was as long as a whole long
    day without bread
Followed the ecstatic musician down the Verrerie

Processions O processions
It was the same way when the king left for Vincennes
When the negotiators arrived in Paris
When thin commissioner Suger hastened in the direction of the
    Seine
When all the noise died down around Saint-Merry

Processions O processions
So great were their numbers that soon the women overflowed
Into the neighboring streets
All running as fast as they could
To catch up to and to follow the musician
Ah! my Ariadne and you Pâquette and you Amine
And you Mia and you Simone and you Mavise
And you Colette and you gorgeous Geneviève
All swept on by so shaken and so vain
With their light steps moving to the rhythm
Of the paradisial music filling
Their anxious ears

The stranger stopped for just a moment in front of an old house
    for sale
A deserted house
With broken windowpanes
It was a sixteenth-century structure
With a yard still used as a parking lot for the carriages they have
    for hire there
That is where the musician went in
His music as it died down became sensuous and slow
The women all entered the deserted empty house
Went in as one
Not one no not a single one turned around to look behind
They left without regret
For all that they were abandoning for good
They left without regret for either the light of day or their
    memories or their lives

22

And soon no one was left around the rue de la Verrerie
Except myself and one of the priests of Saint-Merry

We entered the old ruin

But found no one there
Now here it is evening
And all across Saint-Merry
You can hear the Angelus ring
Processions O processions

And when the king returned from Vincennes
He had with him a great flock of hatters
He had with him dealers in and sellers of bananas
As well as troops from the Republican Guard
O night
Flocks of sensuous feminine eyes
O night
You my grief and my own vain expectation
I hear the sound of a distant flute fading away

— M. B.

ROSEMONDE

For a long time at the foot of the stoop
Of the house where the woman went in
Whom I had followed for a good
Two hours at Amsterdam
My fingers kept throwing kisses

But the canal was completely empty
The dock too so nobody could see
How my kisses found once again
Her to whom my life had been given
One day for more than two hours

I named her Rosemonde
Hoping it would help me remember
Her mouth flowering in Holland
Then very slowly I began to proceed
To seek out the Rose of the World

— M. B.

MONDAY CHRISTINE STREET

The concierge's old lady and the concierge will be looking the
    other way
If you're a real man you'll come with me tonight
All we need now is somebody to watch the front door
While the other guy takes care of things upstairs

Three gas lamps burning
The boss's wife has T.B.
When you're through we'll have time for a fast game of
    backgammon
An orchestra conductor with a bad sore throat
If you ever get to Tunis you'll have to have some kief

That seems to make sense sort of

Enormous piles of plates a few flowers and a calendar
Smash crash splash
I'm into my landlady for just less than 300 francs
And I'd rather slice off my yes that's right I'd rather do just that
    rather than hand it over to her

I'm leaving on the 8:27
Six mirrors in there all just staring at one another
In my opinion we're only at the beginning of this mess
My dear Sir
You stink you dirty crapper
That lady's nose reminds me irresistibly of a tapeworm
Louise forget her furs
Well I haven't a fur to my name but I'm never in the least bit
    cold
The Dane perusing the train schedule puffs restlessly at his
    cigarette
The black cat crosses the bar-room floor

Those pancakes were certainly a big treat
Caught the clap
Her dress was filthy as her fingernails
No no it's absolutely out of the question

Here you are Sir
The malachite ring
Sawdust all over the floor
So it's true then what they say
The redheaded waitress took off with that clerk from the
  bookshop

A journalistic contact I used to know but not very well

Listen Jacques what I'm about to tell you is vitally important

Shipping company specializing in both passengers and freight

So he said to me Monsieur would you like me to see what I can
  do for you about getting hold of some paintings and etchings
All I have is one single solitary maid

And after lunch it's the Café du Luxembourg

As soon as we get there he introduces me to this big fat creep
Who tells me
Listen it's positively charming
At Smyrna at Naples or Tunisia
But for heaven's sakes where is it then already
The last time I stopped off in China
That must have been eight or nine years ago though
Honor often has a lot to do with the definitions of the day or
  with what the clock has to say
The major fifth*

— M. B.

* The final phrase, "la quinte major" is also slang for syphilis, a reference
of course not foreign to this poem [Editor's note].

26

EARTH-OCEAN
For Giorgio de Chirico

I built a house in the middle of the ocean
Its windows are the rivers flowing out of my eyes
Octopi swarm on all sides and cling to all the walls
Listen you can hear the rhythm of their triple heartbeats and
    the sharp sudden tapping of their beaks against the window
    pane

                  Damp dwelling
                  Fervent dwelling
                  Sudden season
                  Singing season

        Aircraft lay eggs
        Better watch out they're about to drop anchor

You'd better watch out for the ink they squirt
It was a good thing you abandoned the sky
The honeysuckle of heaven creeps ever higher
The earthly octopi pant
And so we foundation-layers grow closer and closer to becoming
    our own undertakers
Pale octopi of the chalklike waves O octopi with your beaks so
  · pale
All around this house there is this sea which you know so well
And which is never still

                                  — M. B.

THE LITTLE CAR

On the 31st day of the month of August 1914
I left Deauville a few moments before midnight
In a little car owned by Rouveyre

His chauffeur completed the trio

We said our farewell then to an entire epoch
Angry giants were looming over Europe at that time
Eagles were leaving their nesting places to wait for the sun
Voracious fish were rising from the deeps
Whole populations were madly rushing toward earthshaking
    encounters
The dead were trembling anxiously in their dark dwellings

Dogs were baying in the distance near the frontiers
As I traveled on I transported the opposing armies in my heart
I felt them assembling inside me then sending out their winding
    columns across the countryside
Also the forests the happy little villages of Belgium
Francorchamps with L'Eau Rouge with its peahens
Region of inevitable invasion
And the railway arteries where those who were going to die
Waved back one last time at a life alive with color
Ocean depths where monsters were stirring
In the empty shells of wrecks
Unimaginable heights where mankind locks in combat
Men battle men
Higher than any eagle flies
Only to fall quicker than any shooting star
I felt in myself new creatures with energies as yet unknown
Giving form to and then governing a universe refreshed
A merchant of inconceivable opulence and fantastic stature
Was setting out an extraordinary display of goods
And gigantic shepherds were driving ahead
Great silent flocks browsing on words as they went
They were what all those dogs along the road had been
    barking at

28

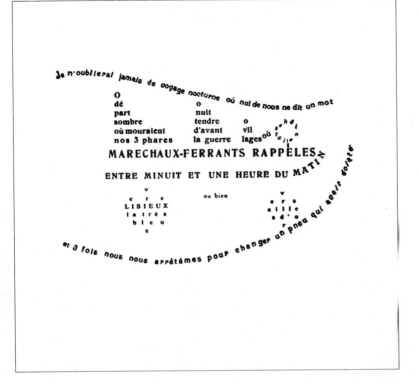

This poem section in calligram form by Apollinaire, which we reproduce here in the original typography, is translated in "The Little Car."

I'll never forget that long night's journey when no one said a word

O

dark   O

departure   tender   O

when all three   evening   vil

headlights failed   before the war   lages

w h e r e   w e r e   h u r r y i n g

B L A C K S M I T H S   R E C A L L E D

BETWEEN MIDNIGHT AND ONE O'CLOCK
IN THE MORNING

n   or maybe   v

e   a   r   e   r   s

L i s i e u x   a i l l e s

s o   v e r y   a l l   i n

b l u e   g o l d

and three times we had to stop to change a tire

And when having spent all afternoon passing through
Fontainebleau
We finally arrived in Paris
At the very moment when general mobilization notices were
    going up
It suddenly dawned on my comrade and me
That the little car had brought us into an age that was utterly
New
That although both of us were already fully grown men
We nonetheless had just been born

— M. B.

THE CARNATION

May this carnation announce to you the law of odors unpromul-
gated as yet but which some day will rule in our minds mcre
precisely and more subtly than the sounds which guide us
now I prefer your nose to all your organs O dear one it's the
throne of future knowledge

—M. B.

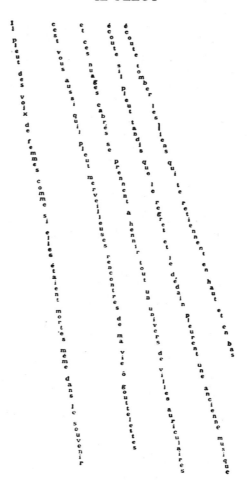

IT'S RAINING

It's raining women's voices as if they had died away even in
my memory
And it's raining you as well marvelous encounters of my life so
many droplets
Those clouds rearing there are beginning to neigh an entire
universe of cities of the ear
Listen when it rains while regretfulness and disdain keep
weeping out their ancient music
Listen to the binding ties falling away which still hold you
from above from below

— M. B.

LINKS

Cords made out of calls

Bells pealing across Europe
Centuries dangling down below

Rails connecting nations
We are only two or three men
Freed of all ties
Hold out your hands to us

Heavy downpour combing the clouds
Cords
Ties intertwined
Towers of Babel transformed into bridges
Giant Papal Spider
And all lovers are bound by just a single strand

Other ties more tenuous
Light rays of light
Cords and Concordances

I write to exalt you alone
O senses O my much cherished senses
Enemies of memory
Enemies of desire

Enemies of regret
Enemies of tears
Enemies of everything I still continue to love

— M. B.

HEART
My heart like a flame upside down

—M. B.

THERE IS

There is this ship which has taken my beloved back again

There are six Zeppelin sausages in the sky and with night coming
on it makes a man think of the maggots from which the stars
might some day be reborn

There is this enemy submarine slipping up beneath my love

There are one thousand young pine-trees splintered by the
bursting of the same shells falling around me now

There is this infantryman walking by completely blinded from
poison gas

There is the obvious fact that all that is happening here was
hatched a long time ago in the winding intestinal trenches of
Nietzsche Goethe and the metaphysicians of the town of
Cologne

There is the obvious fact that I'm dying over a letter which has
thus far been delayed

There are in my wallet various photos of my beloved

There are prisoners marching past with anxious faces

There is this artillery battery with its faithful servants hurrying
among the guns

There is the postmaster arriving at a trot on the road beneath
the single tree in silhouette

There is according to rumor a spy who infiltrates somewhere near
here invisible as the horizon as the horizon-blue French
uniform he has assumed for offensive purposes and in which
he is now most effectively camouflaged

There is erect as any lily the bosom of my beloved

There is this captain anxiously awaiting the latest radio despatch
to reach us via transatlantic cable

There are at midnight these details of soldiers sawing planks for
coffins

There are women somewhere in Mexico pleading with wild cries
for more Indian corn and maize

There is this Gulf Stream which is so warm and beneficial

There is this cemetery covered with crosses only five kilometers
away

There are all these crosses everywhere this way that way

There are paradisial persimmons growing on cactus-trees in
   Algeria
There are the long lithe hands of my love
There is this inkwell which I've made from a 150 mm shell I
   saved from shooting
There is my cavalry saddle left out in the rain
There are all these rivers blasted off their courses which will
   never go back to their banks
There is the god of Love who leads me on so sweetly
There is this German prisoner carrying his machine gun across
   his shoulders
There are men on earth who've never fought in the war
There are Hindus here who look with astonishment on the
   occidental style of campaign
They meditate gravely upon those who've left this place
   wondering whether they'll ever see them again
Knowing as they do what great progress we've made during this
   particular war in the art of invisibility

— M. B.

WHILE MARCHING AROUND
TO ATTRACT SHELLS

You who lead the column marching in step behind you
Through the clear night
Balls full, brain crammed with fresh images
Sergeant in charge of rice bread salt the one who throws the net
    into the canal beside the linden-trees
The exquisite essence of my Beauty is borne to me in the sudden
    odor of lilacs shedding early in the abandoned gardens we
    pass by

Some dusty Medics return to the trenches white as the arms of
    my love herself

I dream of having you night and day
I inhale you whole with the lilac smell

O doorways of your body
There are nine and once I opened them all
O doorways of your body
There are nine and for me now they have all been closed

At the first door
Perfect logic perished
It was do you remember that first day at Nice
Your left eye like some great snake slid
Into my heart
And may the doorway of the look of your left eye open once
    more

At the second doorway
All my strength just faded
It was do you remember in an inn at Cagnes
Your right eye fluttered like my heart
Your eyelids fluttered like flowers flutter in wind
And may the doorway of the look of your right eye open once
    more

At the third doorway
You can hear my aorta's throbbing
And all my veins which are swollen for the love of you alone
And may the doorway of your left ear open once more

At the fourth doorway
I am met and escorted by all the sounds of coming spring
And the straining ear hears from the beautiful woods
The song of love and nests rising
So sadly for soldiers at war
And may the doorway of your right ear open once more

At the fifth doorway
I deliver my very breath of life to you
It was do you remember in the train returning from Grasse
And in the shadows nearby quietly
Your mouth spoke to me
Those words of damnation so perverse and so tender
That I must ask myself O my wounded being
How I managed not to die of merely hearing them
O words so sweet so intense that when I think of them I think
    I can almost touch them
And may the doorway of your mouth open once more

At the sixth doorway
O pregnant with putrefaction O abortive war
Here are still springtimes with flowers
Here are cathedrals with their incense
Here are your armpits with their heavenly smell
And your perfumed letters that I keep nearby
Hour after hour after hour
And may the doorway of your left nostril open once more

At the seventh doorway
O perfumes of the past borne in by the breeze
Salty winds transmitting the taste of the sea to your lips
Marine odor odor of love under our windows the sea itself faded
    away
And the odor of orange-trees enveloped you with love
While you curled up in my arms
Quiet yes and quite screwed
And may the doorway of your right nostril open once more

At the eighth doorway
Two chubby-cheeked angels watch over two trembling roses
   supporting
The exquisite sky of your flexible form
And here I am armed with a whip made of moonbeams
A whole crowd of cupids crowned with hyacinths arrive
And may your derrière door open once more

At the ninth doorway
Love itself must come
Life of my life
I connect myself to you eternally
And through ideal unhasty loving
We will fulfill our passion purely or perversely
Perfectly according to our desire
Knowing all seeing all hearing all
I renounce myself in the deepest secret of your love
O shadowy doorway O doorway of living coral
Between two perfect pillars
And may that doorway again open which your hands understand
   how to open so well

— M. B.

THE GORGEOUS REDHEAD

Look at me now I stand before you here above all a man of
common sense
Knowing about as much of life and death as a living man can
know
Having experienced the joys and sorrows of love
Having been upon occasion able to assert his own ideas
Having a working knowledge of several tongues
Not entirely untraveled
Having seen battle in both the artillery and the infantry
Having suffered cranial contusion and been operated on under
chloroform
Having lost his best friend in the terrible struggle
I know about as much about the old and the new as any one man
can
And speaking now without any special prejudice toward the
outcome of this particular war
Strictly among ourselves and in our own interest my dear friends
I pronounce final judgment on this long argument between
tradition and invention
Order and Adventure

You whose mouths have been constructed in the image of God's
Mouths which stand for order itself
Indulge us a little be kindly when you compare us
With those who have been the previous paradigms of order
We who search everywhere for adventure

We are not your enemies
We only want to claim certain strange and unknown domains
Where Mystery flowers everywhere for whichever hands choose
to pick it
There are new flaming fires there are colors no one has ever seen
before
A thousand unimaginable phantasms
To which reality must be given

We want to explore true benevolence that vast land where all is
so silent and still

40

There is also time to reconsider time which can either be
   banished or else re-established
Pity those of us who go on forever fighting on some front line
Between no-man's-land and the future
Pity us our miscalculations pity us our sins

Soon it will be summer that season of such violence
And my childhood lies dead as the spring itself lies dead
O sun it's time to find some Burning Reason for being
                        And I wait
To follow forever the gentle yet glorious form
It may take so I may love it in her and in her alone
She materializes and attracts me the way a magnet might some
   needle
                 And looks for all the world to me
                 Like a gorgeous redhead

Her hair is "of gold" I suppose some might say
Like a lightning-flash which lasts
Or flames parading in a proud pavane
Among roses as slowly they fade and then are gone

So go ahead then laugh have a good laugh on me
Men from over all the earth but above all men from here and
   now
Because there are so many things I dare not tell you
So many things not a living soul will let me say
Have mercy

                                        — M. B.

FOREVER

For Madame Faure-Favier

Forever

We'll forge on further and further without ever advancing

Even from planet to planet
From nebula to nebula
The Don Juan of one thousand and three long-haired comets
Even without traveling off the earth
Seek new forces
And give phantoms due consideration

And thus that much of the universe forgets itself
Where are our great forgetters
Who will teach us to forget about such and such a part of the
world
Where is the Christopher Columbus to whom once again we will
owe the forgetting of an entire vast continent of creation

To lose

But to lose truly
To make room for discovery

To lose

Life itself to find triumph

— M. B.

Translations by Roger Shattuck

Use of these translations is permitted through the courtesy of New Directions, who at the date of this writing hold exclusive copyright on many Apollinaire poems. We therefore also offer versions by Roger Shattuck which appeared in the splendid, pioneering *Selected Writings*, first issued in 1948. — M. B.

SAFFRON

The meadow is poisonous but pretty in the fall
The cows graze there
Slowly poisoning themselves
The saffron ringed and lilac-colored
Blooms there your eyes are like that flower
Near-violet like their rings and like this autumn
And my life slowly poisons itself for your eyes

The school children come up noisily
Dressed in jackets and playing the harmonica
They pick the saffron flowers which are like mothers
Daughters of their daughters and are the color of your eyelids

Which move as flowers wave in a demented wind

The shepherd sings softly
While slow and lowing the cows leave
For ever this wide meadow evilly blooming in the autumn

ZONE

You are tired at last this old world

O shepherd Eiffel Tower the flock of bridges bleats at the
morning

You have had enough of life in this Greek and Roman antiquity

Even the automobiles here seem to be ancient
Religion alone has remained entirely fresh religion
Has remained simple like the hangars at the airfield

You alone in all Europe are not antique O Christian faith
The most modern European is you Pope Pius X
And you whom the windows look down at shame prevents you
From entering a church and confessing this morning
You read prospectuses catalogues and posters which shout aloud
Here is poetry this morning and for prose there are the
    newspapers
There are volumes for 25 centimes full of detective stories
Portraits of famous men and a thousand assorted titles

This morning I saw a pretty street whose name I have forgotten
Shining and clean it was the sun's bugle
Executives and workers and lovely secretaries
From Monday morning to Saturday evening pass here four times
    a day
In the morning the siren wails three times
A surly bell barks around noon
Inscriptions on signs and walls
Plaques and notices cried out like parrots
I love the charm of this industrial street
Located in Paris somewhere between the rue Aunont-Thiéville
    and the avenue des Ternes

Here is the young street and you are once again a little child
Your mother dresses you only in blue and white
You are very pious and with your oldest friend René Dalize
You like nothing so well as the ceremonies of church

It is nine o'clock the gas is down to the blue you come secretly
    out of the dormitory
You pray the whole night in the college chapel
While eternal and adorable an amethyst profundity
The flaming glory of Christ turns for ever
It is the beautiful lily we all cultivate
It is the red-headed torch which the wind cannot blow out
It is the pale and ruddy son of a sorrowful mother
It is the tree always thick with prayers
It is the double gallows of honor and of eternity
It is a six-pointed star
It is God who died on Friday and rose again on Sunday
It is Christ who soars in the sky better than any aviator
He breaks the world's altitude record

Christ the pupil of the eye
Twentieth pupil of the centuries he knows how
And turned into a bird this century rises in the air like Jesus
The devils in their abysses lift their heads to look at it
They say it is imitating Simon Magus in Judea
They shout that if it knows how to fly it should be called a flyer
Angels hover about the lovely aerialist
Icarus Enoch Elijah Apollonius of Tyana
Flutter around the original airplane
They separate occasionally to give passage to those whom the
    Holy Eucharist carries up
Those priests who rise eternally in lifting the host
The airplane lands at last without folding its wings
The sky fills up then with millions of swallows
In a flash crows falcons and owls arrive
Ibis flamingoes and marabous arrive from Africa
The great Roc celebrated by story tellers and poets
Glides down holding in its claws Adam's skull the first head
The eagle rushes out of the horizon giving a great cry
From America comes the tiny humming-bird
From China have come long supple pihis
Which only have one wing and fly tandem
Then the dove immaculate spirit
Escorted by the lyre bird and the ocellated peacock
The phoenix that pyre which recreates itself

Veils everything for an instant with its glowing coals
Sirens leaving their perilous straits
Arrive all three of them singing beautifully
And everything eagle phoenix and Chinese pihis
Fraternize with the flying machine

Now you walk through Paris all alone in the crowd
Herds of bellowing busses roll by near you
The agony of love tightens your throat
As if you could never be loved again
If you were living in olden days you would enter a monastery
You are ashamed when you catch yourself saying a prayer
You ridicule yourself and your laughter bursts out like hell fire
The sparks of your laughter gild the depths of your life
It is a picture hung in a somber museum
And sometimes you go to look at it closely

Today you walk through Paris the women are blood-stained
It was and I would prefer not to remember it was during beauty's
    decline

Surrounded by fervent flames Notre Dame looked at me in
    Chartres
The blood of your Sacred Heart flooded me in the Montmartre
I am ill from hearing happy words
The love from which I suffer is a shameful sickness
And the image which possesses you makes you survive in
    sleeplessness and anguish
It is always near you this passing image

Now you are on the shore of the Mediterranean
Under the lemon trees which blossom all year
With your friends you take a boat ride
One is a Nissard there is a Mentonasque and two Turbiasques
We look down in fear at the octopodes on the bottom
And amid the algae swim fish images of our Saviour
You are in the garden of an inn on the outskirts of Prague
You feel completely happy a rose is on the table
And instead of writing your story in prose you watch
The rosebug which is sleeping in the heart of the rose

Astonished you see yourself outlined in the agates of St. Vitus

You were sad enough to die the day you saw yourself in them
You looked like Lazarus bewildered by the light
The hands of the clock in the Jewish quarter turn backwards
And you go slowly backwards in your life
Climbing up to Hradchin and listening at night
In taverns to the singing of Czech songs

Here you are in Marseilles amid the watermelons

Here you are in Coblenz at the Hotel of the Giant

Here you are in Rome sitting under a Japanese medlar tree

Here you are in Amsterdam with a girl you find pretty and who
    is ugly
She is to marry a student from Leyden
There are rooms for rent in Latin Cubicula locanda
I remember I stayed three days there and as many at Gouda

You are in Paris at the *juge d'instruction*
Like a criminal you are placed under arrest
You have made sorrowful and happy trips
Before noticing that the world lies and grows old
You suffered from love at twenty and thirty
I have lived like a fool and wasted my time
You no longer dare look at your hands and at every moment I
    want to burst out sobbing
For you for her I love for everything that has frightened you

With tear-filled eyes you look at those poor emigrants
They believe in God they pray the women nurse their children
Their odor fills the waiting room of the gare Saint-Lazare
They have faith in their star like the Magi
They hope to make money in Argentina
And come back to their countries having made their fortunes
One family carries a red quilt as one carries one's heart
That quilt and our dream are both unreal
Some of these emigrants stay here and find lodging
In hovels in the rue des Rosiers or the rue des Écouffes
I have often seen them in the evening they take a stroll in the
    street
And rarely travel far like men on a checker board

There are mostly Jews their wives wear wigs
They sit bloodlessly in the backs of little shops

You are standing at the counter of a dirty bar
You have a nickel coffee with the rest of the riffraff

At night you are in a big restaurant

These women are not wicked however they have no worries
All of them even the ugliest has made her lover suffer
She is the daughter of a Jersey City policeman

Her hands which I have not seen are hard and chapped

I have an immense pity for the scars on her belly

I humble my mouth by offering it to a poor slut with a horrible
    laugh

You are alone the morning is almost here
The milkmen rattle their cans in the street

The night departs like a beautiful Métive
It is Ferdine the false or Leah the waiting one

And you drink this burning liquor like your life
Your life which you drink like an eau-de-vie

You walk toward Auteuil you want to walk home on foot
To sleep among your fetishes from Oceania and Guinea
They are all Christ in another form and of another faith

They are inferior Christs obscure hopes

Adieu adieu

The sun a severed neck

SALTIMBANQUES

To Louis Dumur

Across the plain the troop of clowns
Moves by along the garden walls
Before the doors of greying inns
Through churchless villages and towns

And children scamper out in front
While others follow dreamily
Each fruit tree submits readily
When from afar they give the sign

The weights they bear are round and square
And tambourines and gilded hoops
Wise animals the ape and bear
Beg for their keep along the way

PHANTOM OF THE CLOUDS

It was the day before July 14
About four in the afternoon
I went out to see the saltimbanques

Those men who do turns in the open
Are beginning to be rare in Paris
In my youth one saw many more than today
They have almost all gone to the provinces

I took the boulevard Saint-Germain
And on a litle square betweeen Saint-Germain-des-Prés and the
    statue of Danton
I found some saltimbanques
The crowd which surrounded them was silent and resigned to
    waiting
I found a place in the group where I could see everything

Formidable weights
Whole Belgian cities held up at arm's length by a Russian worker
    from Longwy
Black hollow dumb-bells with a frozen river for a shaft
Fingers rolling a cigarette as bitter and delicious as life

Several dirty rugs lie on the ground
Rugs with creases that will never come out
Rugs which are almost entirely the color of dust
And on which a few yellow and green spots still show
Like a tune which will not leave you

See that thin savage looking one
The ashes of his ancestors are coming out in his grey beard
He carries all his heredity in his face
And seems to dream of the future
While mechanically turning a Barbary hand-organ
Whose sweet voice wails marvellously
Gurgling false notes and muffled groans

The saltimbanques didn't move
The oldest wore tights of that purplish rose color which glows in

the cheeks of lively little girls who are near death
That rose nestles most in the lines around their mouths
Or next to their nostrils
It is a color full of treachery

Did that man carry thus around his waist
The vile color of his lungs

Arms arms everywhere mounted guard

The second saltimbanque
Was clothed only in his shadow
I looked long at him
His face escapes me entirely
He was a man without a head

Another one looked like an urchin
A good Apache but debauched
With his comic pants and garters
Wouldn't he have looked like a pimp getting dressed

The music stopped for a parley with the audience
Which tossed the sum of 2 francs 50 sou by sou on the rug
Instead of the three francs which the old one had set as the price
   of a performance

But when it was clear that no one would give anything more
They decided to begin
From behind the organ a small saltimbanque came out dressed in
   consumptive red
With fur at his wrists and ankles
He gave a few brief cries
And saluted with his forearms prettily held
His hands spread out

With one leg back ready to genuflect
He bowed to the four cardinal points
And when he balanced on a ball
His slim body became so delicate a music that none of the
   spectators could resist it
A tiny spirit without humanity
Everyone thought
And this music of shapes

Destroyed that of the mechanical organ
Which was ground by the man with his face covered with his
ancestors

The little saltimbanque turned a cart-wheel
With so much harmony
That the organ stopped playing
And the organist hid his face in his hands
With fingers like descendants of his destiny
Small foetuses which came out of his beard
New Indian cries
The angelic music of trees
The disappearance of the child

The saltimbanques lifted the great dumb-bells in their arms
And juggled with the weights

But each spectator looked in himself for the miraculous child
Century O century of clouds

THE MUSICIAN OF SAINT-MERRY

Finally I have the right to greet creatures whom I do not know
They pass in front of me and assemble further on
Whereas all that I see of them is unknown
And their hope is not less strong than mine

I do not sing of this world nor of the other stars
I sing all the possibilities of myself beyond this world and the
 stars
I sing the joy of wandering and the pleasure of dying thus

The 21st of the month of May 1913
Death's ferryman and St. Merry's ruddy buzzing wives
Millions of flies air out a splendor
When a man without eyes without a nose and without ears
Leaving the Sébasto turned into rue Aubry-le-Boucher
The young man was dark with a strawberry color on his cheeks
Man Ah! Ariane
He played the flute and the music guided his steps
He stopped at the corner of rue Saint-Martin
Playing the tune I am singing and which I made up
The women who passed stopped near him
Coming from all directions
When the bells of Saint-Merry began to ring
The musician stopped playing and took a drink from the fountain
Which is at the corner of rue Simon-le-Franc
Then Saint-Merry was silent
The stranger began his tune again on the flute
And retracing his steps walked as far as rue de la Verrerie
Which he turned into followed by his troop of women
Who came out of the houses
Who came out of the side streets with wild eyes
Their hands stretched out toward the melodious seducer
He strolled along indifferently playing his tune
It was terrible the way he went along

Then somewhere else
What time does a train leave for Paris

At that moment
The pigeons of the Moluccas voided nutmeg droppings
At the same time
Catholic mission of Bôma what have you done with the sculptor

Elsewhere
She crosses a bridge which links Bonn with Beuel and disappears
across Pützchen

At the same time
A girl in love with the mayor

In another quarter
Rivalled poetry with the refinements of perfumers

In all O mockers you have not gotten a great deal out of men
You have barely gotten a little fat out of their misery
But we who die from living far apart from one another
Hold out our arms and on those rails rolls a long train of
merchandise

Seated next to me you were crying in the depths of the fiacre
And now
You look like me you look distressingly like me

We resemble one another as in the architecture of the last century
Those high chimneys almost like towers

We are going higher now and touch the ground no longer

And while the world lived and changed
The cortège of women as long as a breadless day
Followed the happy musician in the rue de la Verrerie
Cortèges O cortèges
It is as when formerly the king left for Vincennes
When the ambassadors arrived in Paris
When thin Suger hurried toward the Seine
When the disturbance died out around Saint-Merry

Cortèges O cortèges
So great was their number the women overflowed
Into the neighboring streets
And hastened straightaway
To follow the musician

Ah! Ariane and you Paquette and you Amine
And you Mia and you Simone and you Mavise
And you Colette and you beautiful Genevieve
They passed trembling and vain
And their quick light steps obeyed the cadence
Of the pastoral music which guided
Their avid ears

The stranger stopped a moment in front of a house for sale
An abandoned house
With broken window panes
A sixteenth century house
The yard is used as a coach-house for carriages to rent
It is there that the musician went in
His music as it went away became more languorous
The women followed him into the empty house
And all went in in a confused band
All all of them went in without a backward look
Without missing what they were leaving
What they were abandoning
Without missing light life and memory
Soon there was no one left in the rue de la Verrerie
Only myself and a priest of Saint-Merry

We entered the old house

But we found no one there

Here it is evening
At Saint-Merry the Angelus rings
Cortèges O cortèges

When the king of old came back from Vincennes
A band of hatters came along
Banana merchants came
Soldiers of the republican guard came
O night
Flock of languorous glances of women
O night
You my grief and my vain expectation
The sound of a distant flute I hear as it fades away

OCEAN OF EARTH
To G. de Chirico

I built a house in the middle of the ocean
Its windows are rivers which flow out of my eyes
Octopus stir all around its walls
Listen to the triple beat of their hearts and their beaks which tap
    on the window panes
                  Humid house
                  Burning house
                  Rapid season
                  Season which sings
            Airplanes drop eggs
            Watch out for the anchor
Watch out for the ink which they squirt
It's a good thing you came from the sky
The honeysuckle of the sky climbs up
The earthly octopus throb
And then we are closer and closer to being our own gravediggers
Pale octopus of chalky waves O octopus with pale beaks
Around the house there is this ocean which you know
And which is never still

THE CARNATION

May this carnation tell you the law of odors which has not yet
    been announced and which one day will come to rule in our
    minds far more precisely and more subtly than the sounds
    which guide us
I prefer your nose to all your organs O my love. It is the throne
    of future knowledge

IT'S RAINING

It's raining women's voices as if they had died even in memory
And it's raining you as well marvellous encounters of my life O
   little drops
Those rearing clouds begin to neigh a whole universe of auricular
   cities
Listen if it rains while regret and disdain weep to an ancient
   music
Listen to the bonds fall off which hold you above and below

HEART

MY HEART like a flame turned upside down

THE PRETTY RED-HEAD

Behold me before all a man of good sense
Knowing life and of death what a living man can know
Having experienced the griefs and the joys of love
Having been able to assert his ideas on occasion
Knowing several languages
Having travelled a good bit
Having seen the war in the Artillery and Infantry
Wounded in the head trepanned under chloroform
Having lost his best friends in that frightful struggle
I know of the old and of the new as much as one man alone can
    know of them
And without being uneasy today about this war
Between us and for us my friends
I pronounce judgement on this long quarrel of tradition and
    innovation
                    Of Order and Adventure

You whose mouths are made in the image of God's
                    Mouths which are order itself
Be indulgent when you compare us
To those who have been the perfection of order
We who seek everywhere for adventure
We are not your enemies
We wish to appropriate vast and strange domains
Where flowering mystery offers itself to whoever wishes to
    pick it
There are new fires there and colors never yet seen
A thousand imponderable phantasms
To which reality must be given
We would explore goodness a vast country where everything is
    silent
There is also time which one can banish or call back
Pity us who fight always in the front lines
Of the limitless and of the future
Pity our errors pity our sins

Behold the return of summer season of violence

And my youth died like the spring
O Sun it is the time for flaming Judgement
                    And I wait
To follow for ever the sweet noble form
It assumes in order that I may love it alone
It comes and it attracts me as a magnet does the needle
                    It looks for all the world just like
                    My redhead darling my beloved

Her hair is really gold you'd say
A flash of lightning which endures
Or flames which dance a proud pavane
In roses as they slowly fade

But laugh laugh long at me
Men from anywhere above all men of this place
For there are so many things I dare not tell you
So many things you will not let me say
Have pity on me

ALWAYS

To Madame Faure-Favier

Always
We are going farther without ever advancing
And from planet to planet

From nebula to nebula
The Don Juan of a thousand and three comets
Without even rising from the earth
Look for new forces
And take phantoms seriously

And so many of the universe forget themselves
Who are the great forgetters
Who will know just how to make us forget such and such a part
   of the world
Where is Christopher Columbus to whom is owed the forgetting
   of a continent
                 To lose
But to lose genuinely
In order to make room for discovery
                     To lose
Life in order to find Victory

PIERRE REVERDY

1889-1960

Reverdy, with Apollinaire, was one of the most active and original writers of the World War I years, which Apollinaire saw as heralding a "new spirit." Hailed by André Breton in the first Surrealist Manifesto as "the greatest poet of the time," Reverdy's extraordinary poetic approach played a crucial role in creating the esthetic atmosphere from which Surrealism directly flourished.

Reverdy's initial collection, *Poèmes en prose* (*Poems in Prose*)[1] appeared in 1915; by 1917 he was collaborating with Apollinaire and the Cubist poet Max Jacob in editing the influential review *Nord-Sud* (*North-South*). Here were published many of the most far-reaching writings of the period, including the early verse of Breton, Soupault, and Aragon. It was around this time that Reverdy made the notes about the crucial role of imagery in poetry (beginning: "The poetic image is a pure creation of the mind . . .") which Breton quoted with such admiration in the 1924 Manifesto (also quoted and discussed in the introduction to this volume).

The early poems, in particular, are based firmly on daring mental associations, surprising imagistic leaps and sudden, untoward juxtapositions. Echoing with a strange presence, the haunted landscapes they purport to chart are, for all their outward references, those of the poet's mind in quest of its own nature. Often the work suggests catalogues of things seen; yet throughout is the sense that even the "simplest" ordering of material objects can convey the inadequacy of purely material definitions. This radical questioning of conventional definitions on both the philosophical and esthetic plane produces an atmosphere of spiritual crisis foreshadowing the Surrealist sense of the strangeness of being and the inadequacy of conventional, psychologically unsophisticated definitions of the self, both in literature and beyond. These visionary perspectives continue throughout the later work. Frequently, the earlier poems present landscapes populated by figures crushed beneath the sheer physical weight of the world (as in the "saltimbanques" or circus-clown poems, based loosely on certain Pink Period paintings of Picasso); soon they more openly begin to resemble interior monologues in which the poet's voice is heard questioning his own position in the material order. Although the later poems are all but prayers for a supernatural reply to his queries, and even for deliverance from this situation entirely, this quasireligious orientation is never presented using conventional religious personae. An uncompromisingly independent questioning of conventional explanations of being remains at their core.

Reverdy withdrew increasingly from the Paris literary world during the 1920's, finally settling in 1926 in an isolated region of the French countryside located, perhaps appropriately enough, near the Abbey of Solesmes.

Reverdy's voluminous writings consist primarily of poetry in both verse and prose, as well as three collections of notes on poetry, *Le Gant de crin* (*The Crêpe Glove*, 1927),[2] *Le Livre de mon bord* (*My Logbook*, 1948),[3] and *En vrac* (*Pell-Mell*, 1956);[4] and also include two early novels, *Le Voleur du Talan* (*The Thief of Talan*, 1917)[5] and *Le Peau de l'homme* (*The Skin of Man*, 1926);[6] a collection of tales, *Risques et périls* (*Risks and Perils*, 1930);[7] and the study *Pablo Picasso* (1924).[8]

OTHER PRINCIPAL WORKS

Principal collected volumes (poems): *Plupart du temps: Poèmes 1915–1922* (N.R.F., 1945 — includes *Poèmes en prose*, 1915; *Quelques Poèmes*, 1916; *La Lucarne ovale*, 1916; *Les Ardoises du toit*, 1918; *Les Jockeys camouflés*, 1918; *La Guitare endormie*, 1919; *Etoiles peintes*, 1921; *Coeur de chêne*, 1921, and *Cravates*

62

de chanvre, 1922); also *Main d'oeuvre* (Mercure de France, 1949 — includes *Grande nature,* 1925; *La Balle au bond,* 1928; *Sources du vent,* 1929; *Pierres blanches,* 1930; *Ferraille,* 1927; *Plein Verre,* 1940; *Le Chant des morts,* 1944–1948; *Cale sèche* [uncollected writings], 1913–1915; and *Bois vert,* 1940–1946). Selected poems: *Reverdy: Selected Poems,* tr. by Kenneth Rexroth (New Directions, 1969). Selected writings: *Reverdy,* "Poètes d'aujourd'hui," No. 25 (Seghers).

BELL-TOLL

Everything is extinguished
The wind goes singing by
  And the trees tremble
The animals are all dead
Nobody is left
    Look
The stars have stopped shining
  The earth stops turning
A head bends
  Its hair sweeps across the night
The last clock tower left upright
  Strikes midnight

— M. B.

DEPARTURE

The horizon lowers
    The days lengthen
    Voyage
  A heart hops in a cage
  A bird sings
    At the edge of death
Another door is about to open
    At the far end of the corridor
    Shines
    One star
A dark lady
  Lantern on a departing train

— M. B

SALTIMBANQUES

At the center of that parade, together with a dancing child, there is a man who lifts weights. His arms are tattooed in blue and are lifted to the skies, in testimony of their useless strength.

The child dances delicately, in tights several sizes too large for him; he is even lighter than the little balls on which he struggles to keep his balance. And when he holds out his money cup, nobody gives anything for fear of filling it with too heavy a weight. He is so thin.

— M. B.

SHOW FOR THE EYES

The heads leaning out beyond the line have all fallen now
People are at the windows shouting
Others are in the street
In the midst of all the noise and the laughter
Are animals never previously seen
The usual passersby
But with gold faces
The voices along the pathways
More pungent accents
Then toward noon the sun the trumpet fanfares
Happier men beginning to laugh aloud
Houses slowly opening their eyes
The doorsills greeting each other with wide smiles
And when the parade starts off among the dust
The child with eyes burnt by wonder
The blond boy the fearful angel
Shaken by the sight of all these people from altogether another
    world
Who don't look like everybody else
But whom you wish you could travel off with
Marvelous strangers who appear and disappear without ever
    dying
Evening lights its lamps
The show affixes its flares
The fiery dancer slips from her suitcase
The empty tights come to life once again
The wheel of fortune spins
The spotlight revolves
They leap back and forth through the scenery
While the low equivocal shadow of the circus
Grows dizzy with the sound of its own uproar
And while the child the dreamer of such magnificent dreams
Weeps because of his ugliness

— M. B.

FLOWER-MARKET QUAY

Delicate breast
   O
clouds
     In the waters where she drowned herself
     winter blasts no more
And
Far from the bank
He strolls off having slipped on his overcoat once more
The world looks in on her through her windowpane
She is dead so she smiles at all these people
         who have no idea what to make of this at all
Her little chest seems to stir
It's your own lips blowing at it
And her eyes are shut tight as they watch you
These gentlemen dressed in black
Their eyes are brightened by malice
"A little lady I've had certain dealings with on numerous
   occasions"
Misery passes with the wind
Sweeping up the streets
                She had lovely legs certainly
                She danced she laughed

And what will become of her now
Head turned away
She just asked to be left to sleep

                        — M. B

THE STRUGGLES OF WORDS

Torment wanders into the light beyond the roof. At midday, without sunlight. The walls are covered with snow, against a gray background. The eye stops and vainly seeks a better path.

They've rubbed away the designs that gave life to the crumbling walls. Some words raise themselves affirmatively. And the flood, too high, carries off the shore where the grass smooths the bank into well-combed hair. And while across the bluish rays turbulences whirl and slowly rise, silence falls heavily on the ground, without breaking.

— M. B.

CENTRAL HEATING

A tiny light
You see a tiny light coming down landing on your stomach and
    lighting you up
— A woman stretches out like an ascending flare —
Over there in the corner a shadow is busy reading
Her bare unencumbered feet are much much too pretty

Short-circuit in the heart-system
Engine breakdown
What electromagnet is still keeping me running
My eyes and my love are both taking the same wrong road

A mere nothing
A spark they strike only to let it go out again sometime later
I've had enough of the wind
I've had enough of the sky
Essentially everything visible is artificial
Even your mouth
Despite the fact that I warm up wherever your hand touches me
The door is wide open but I refuse to enter
I see your face but lack all faith in it
You're so pale
One night when we were unhappy we sat down together on a
    trunk
Men were laughing somewhere off in the distance
Nearly naked children walked by now and then
Water flowed by in perfect purity
Copper wire conducts the light
The sun and your heart are compacted of the same substance

— M. B.

HEARTBREAK

Oh everything is coming to an end
A slow music is being splashed drop by drop over the wall
One hand over somebody's mouth
The other without the side for touching or feeling
Naked Love jumps out the window
The beautiful portrait
A woman weeping in a torn chemise
Quite a good performance all this display of lofty passion
She sobs then departs for the heavens which are calling to her
The water and the tall trees
Despair of love utterly unaccompanied by violin
And yet always lying there in hiding is the snare
At the crossroads one summer evening an organ-grinder
Gave meaning to your melancholy
A delicate yearning
Of which nothing at all now remains
Every single friend is dead
And of their own accord their women have gone off to keep them
    company
You entered this game under an inauspicious sign
Well what have you decided to become an honest man or a thief
Nothing
I keep my skin concealed beneath my waistcoat
The wave of the future rolls on
I dissolve my smile in it
And across the distant rooftops look out at your logic
The world is so gay the world laughs out loud and so you do too
In one night I've lost both my age and my name

                                   — M. B.

TIME OF THE SEA

Far out, transported by the surgings of the moon on the crest of the waves, the air remained afire one moment longer. The sailors sing while unfolding evening with their sails. The East spreads its mysteries on the hard rock of the dock. Their eyes are full of imprecise images. And their memories in well-filled bags. The beacon, a low star that turns. And the distant visions draw nearer. Lands exchange climates. The customs officer sleeps, confined to his cabin. And his shadow moves off. Passing ships sink in the nocturnal dimness, flashing a last burst of light. The sun dissolves. Masts extend. The surges endlessly sift sacks of stars. And the sea spray dances with its own reflections.

— M. B.

THERE OR ELSEWHERE

The wings stay caught, trapped between the locked shutters. It's an enormous bird struggling to fly or the night straining at the hinges. The wind pushes more strongly than before. Impossible to remain standing in the midst of the walls, the moving floor, and the dancing glittering. Now the dust returns. A prayer is offered. Hands on the pavement. The brightness behind. And, to calm the spirit which departed at such great risk, a purer air descends once again. A glow comes from every surface, from the sharp-angled furniture. And the revived flowers, drifting around in their glasses, emerge from obscure corners.

— M. B.

AT THE END OF THE STREET OF STARS

The eyeglasses circumscribe themselves exactly around the new outline of the sky. Do the parts move together in order to look at one another? The moon and the sun hesitate, keeping their distance.

Meanwhile the hours fall more heavily and more lengthily than ever before.

Also, there are eyelids closing, clouds passing.

And a moment's repose and calm for those of us who've traveled so far. At a given signal, a finer hand, with lacquered red nails, lifts a curtain holding back the new day. And sleeping sun rays are visible. Water, standing on the grass. The numeral. And the street, where nobody goes by, enveloped in a long black cloak which, from time to time, shifts to one side.

— M. B.

FOREVER THERE

I have a need not to encounter myself anymore and to forget
  about everything
To speak with people I've never known
To shout without being heard
For absolutely no actual reason and in utter isolation
I know the whole world step by step down to the last
I want to tell my whole life's story without anyone there to
  overhear
Heads and eyes all turn away from me
Toward night
My head is a heavy full ball
Rolling across the earth making barely a sound

Vast distance
Nothing in front of me nothing behind me
In the emptiness into which I descend
A few gusts of air
Blowing around me
Cruel and cold
These come from doors only half-closed
On memories still not quite forgotten
The world is interrupted like some pendulum
And everybody is suspended for eternity
Like a spider an aviator slides down along a wire
Everybody dances around weightlessly
Between sky and earth
But a single light-ray escaped
From a lamp you forgot to put out
On the landing
No it's still not over
We're not finished yet with forgetting
And I still have the need to get to know myself just a little bit
  better

— M. B.

THE INVASION

This head
The eye distinct
The calm street of the port
    And the boats in from the sea
I take the direction of the wind on the avenue
That bears the coat-of-arms of the lanes
        Of the city

In summer
While others open their books
A treatise on medicine
Arithmetic
Geometry
Their glasses closed between eyes and life
The young student goes back up to his family
And the other in life
Having climbed over the iron gates
Without knowing where he is going
And the boat arrives bringing the sheep
The city has opened its side
The crowd enters
And now the bell's first note in a new key
Different kinds of children
And the fiery head of the sick companion
    All there is

— JOHN ASHBERY

CLEAR WINTER

The space of wrinkled gold where I passed the time
In the bed of December with descending flames
The hedges of the sky erect on the boundaries
And the frozen stars in the air which extinguishes them
   My head goes on to the north wind
      And the faded colors
         The water following the signal
All the bodies recovered in the field of showers
And the faces come back
Before the blue flames of the morning hearth
Around that chain where hands sound
Where eyes shine with the fire of tears
And which circles of hearts cover with a halo
The hard rays broken in the falling evening

— JOHN ASHBERY

LOVE AGAIN

I no longer want to go away toward those vast bowls of evening
To grip the icy hands of the nearest shadows
I can no longer put off this look of despair
Nor reach the great circles waiting for me out there
Yet it is toward those formless faces that I go
Toward those moving lines which still imprison me
Those lines my eyes trace in the vagueness
Those dim landscapes those mysterious days
Under cover of gray weather when love passes by
A love without an object burning night and day
Which wears out its lamp my chest so tired
Of fixing sighs which in turn die
Blue distances hot countries white sands
Shore where gold tosses where laziness takes root
Tepid wharf where the sailor falls asleep
Treacherous water which comes to flatter the hard rock
Under the greedy sun which is browsing on the foliage
Thought heavy with sleep blinking
Light memories with curls at the forehead
Nights of sleep without waking in a bed that is too deep
Efforts continually put off until tomorrow
Smile of the sky sliding in the hand
But above all homesickness for that solitude
O closed heart O heavy heart O deep heart
You will never get used to sorrow

— JOHN ASHBERY

ENDLESS JOURNEYS

All those seen from behind who were moving away singing
Who had been seen passing along the river
Where even the reeds repeated their prayers
Which the birds took up louder and farther on
They are the first to arrive and will not go away
They counted each step of the road
Which vanished as they went along
        They walked on the hard rock
At the edge of the fields they stopped
At the edge of the water they slaked their thirst
    Their feet raised a cloud of dust
And it was a coat embroidered by the sunlight
All who were going away
walking in that desert
And for whom the sky had now opened
Were still looking for the tip of land at the world's end
The wind that pushed them continued on its rounds
    And the door closed again
A black door
    Night

                — JOHN ASHBERY

ONE MORE EXPLANATION
FOR THE MYSTERY

All I can see, at the far side of the sky, is an enormous white dog chewing on the moon. And the dog is no cloud. If he doesn't belong to anybody, he'll go away. And we'll be able to see day again. But if this dog belongs to this man leaning against the mountain to watch us and laugh at us? The mysterious noises stop and darkness becomes denser. We are just about to take yet another trot about.

— M. B.

THE SPIRIT ESCAPES

So many books; A temple, whose thick walls are built of books. And inside, there where I had entered without quite knowing how, or without knowing where, I was suffocating; the ceilings were grey with dust. Not a sound. And all the great ideas moved no more; they slept, or were dead. It was so hot, so dark in this sad palace.

With my nails I scratched at the paneling and, bit by bit, I made a hole in the right-hand wall. It became a window and the sun practically blinded me but could not prevent me from looking out through it.

It was the street out there but now the palace had vanished. Already I was confronting a different dust and other walls surrounding the sidewalk.

— M. B.

THAT MEMORY

I saw you
I saw you in the distance in front of the wall
I saw the hole of your shadow on the wall
There was still some sand left
And your bare feet
Your footprints that went on and on
How would I have known you
The sky took up the whole background the whole space
At the bottom a little bit of land shining in the sun
And a little more space
And the sea
The star came out of the water
A ship passed flying low
  A bird
The line at the horizon from which the current was coming
The waves laughed as they died
Everything continues
No one knows where time will stop
   Or night
Everything is effaced by the wind
   We sing differently
   We speak with another accent
I recognize eyes which have stayed alive
And the clock that used to strike in the room
An hour late
The green morning that comes after a sleepless night
There is a laughing brook of clear water and other cries
In front of the door a silhouette which disappears
A face in the light
And in the midst of everything that lives and wakens
The same and single voice persisting
In my ear

       — JOHN ASHBERY

THE COLORS OF THE WINDOWS

The paved square
                some steps going by on the road
of the light passing by
                hastily
                and without your hearing it
At the four yellow corners
                fields in the sun
White stones in the night
                when you awake
Everything is flattened to two dimensions by the glare
                Even the light itself
And the furrow disappears in the distance
                The lit window
The highway signs
                the low retaining walls
                                dangerous roadways
All things lie down deeply in the evening during the revolving
                                towards fire
And this eyeball's pupil strains and then in the distance touches
  upon
                                the white body of mystery
The coach crosses the length and breadth of night
Nobody says a word
The windmill flaps its wings
And the noises of the air
Hide deep in the depths of the thicket
                And in some other ear

— M. B.

TRISTAN TZARA

1896-1963

TRISTAN TZARA WAS A CO-FOUNDER and the guiding spirit of Dada, the movement which, more than any other, led toward Surrealism.

Tzara was born in Bucharest. His first poems, written in Rumanian and posthumously collected and translated into French, combine an Apollinairean lyricism with an irony similar to but far less gentle than that of Jules Laforgue, the late nineteenth-century poet by whom the poems appear to have been influenced. Often, even in those relatively early days, their mood verges on pure Dadaist nihilism.[1]

In 1915 the poet left for Zurich to escape the draft; by the end of that year he had begun with a group of friends to conduct a series of literary soirées at various cafés and cabarets. Thanks largely to Tzara's leadership, these initial soirées became the characteristic Dadaist "manifestation," with its wildly nihilistic and anticultural overtones. It was in February, 1916, that Tzara found the word Dada by randomly slipping a paper-knife into a dictionary. Also in 1916 Tzara assumed the editorship of the magazine *Dada* and delivered from the stage of the Cabaret Voltaire the earliest Dada manifesto, *Manifeste de M. Antipyrine* (*Manifesto of Mr. Headache-Tablet*).[2] Two years later, at another Dada evening, he issued his second, and perhaps the best-known, of all Dada pronouncements: the *Manifeste Dada 1918* (*Dada Manifesto 1918*).[3]

As a direct result of what was described in the 1918 Manifesto as "Dadaist disgust" with the productions of official "logic" during World War I, Tzara's own poetry changed considerably during this time, developing what were at least originally intended to be "unartistic" qualities: an imagery in which men — even intelligent men — are pictured as machine-driven, while machines enjoy full lives of their own; chance or "illogical" associations of ideas; "artless" and even repetitious rhythmic or verbal patterns. The latter may also be the result of Tzara's study of "primitive" Maori poetry — this in the wake of Picasso's and Apollinaire's better known involvement with the sculpture of Africa and Oceania, respectively.

In 1919, at the urging of André Breton, who later wrote that among his circle of friends, Tzara had been "awaited like a messiah," the poet moved to Paris. Tzara's arrival stimulated a series of *succès de scandale,* modeled on events in Zurich. However, when in 1922 Breton proposed a retrospective "Congress" to examine and perhaps coordinate recent developments, Tzara bridled. And, at the 1923 performance of Tzara's play *Le Coeur à gaz* (*The Gas-Operated Heart*),[4] the future Surrealist group virtually sorted itself out in a riot of violent opposition to Dada. Although of course Tzara did not join the Surrealist group upon its founding after the publication of Breton's first Surrealist Manifesto in 1924, it is clear that without Tzara's example, not only Dada, but Surrealism as well, would have been a different, probably far less intransigent affair.

Although Tzara remained personally aloof from Surrealism's group activities, his poetry changed considerably during the 1920's. A more positive note was sounded, mechanical motifs giving way to visions of natural process, the life of nature becoming a metaphor for the human transformation of which the Surrealists also wrote with such hope. The work during this period is often as obstinately optimistic as the Dada work was determinedly nihilistic. In 1929, when Breton's Second Manifesto expressed a desire to effect a reconciliation (calling Tzara's writing "the only really situated poetry" with respect to Surrealism), Tzara finally joined the movement. His first act was to publish in *La Révolution Surréaliste* his finest sustained work, *L'Homme approximatif* (*The Approximate Man*),[5] a virtual epic examining the regenerative possibilities of language. His 1918 Dada Manifesto had described that movement as having "absolute and unquestionable faith in every god which is the immediate product of spontaneity." The earliest, Pre-Surrealist experiments with automatic writing, circa 1919, may be partly a result of this; and it is perhaps only appropriate that a reconciliation was demonstrated and effected in terms of this theme.

From 1930 to 1934 Tzara participated in most Surrealist activities, also contributing frequently to the successor-periodical to *La Révolution Surréaliste, Surréalisme au service de la Révolution (Surrealism at the Service of the Revolution)*. However, in 1934 a second though less violent break with Surrealism occurred, Tzara leaving the movement for work in the Communist party at the very moment when many of Surrealism's adherents were becoming disenchanted with Stalinism. Tzara's later poetry remained in a post-Dada mode, but adopted a more intimate tone, which is often pessimistic, even to the point of expressing a certain personal melancholy — the most startling contrast yet to the distancing, satirical stance of the earlier work.

During the Nazi occupation, Tzara was active in the Resistance, and after the war worked briefly for the French government. As do his final poems, his late lecture, *Le Surréalisme et l'après-guerre (Surrealism and the Postwar period*, 1947),[6] confirms the continued intensity of his intellectual involvement with the movement.

OTHER PRINCIPAL WORKS

Tzara's chief writings (poems except where noted) include: *La Première Aventure céleste de Monsieur Antipyrine* (play: Collection Dada, 1916); *Vingt-cinq Poèmes* (Collection Dada, 1918; reissued in *Vingt-cinq et un Poèmes*, (Ed. Fontaine, 1945); *Cinéma calendrier du coeur abstrait/Maisons* (Au Sans Pareil, 1920); *De nos oiseaux* (Kra, 1923); *Mouchoir de nuages* (play: Galerie Simon, 1925); *Indicateur des chemins de coeur* (Jeanne Bucher, 1928); *L'Arbre des voyageurs* (Ed. de la Montagne, 1930); *Où boivent les loups* (Ed. des Cahiers Libres, 1932); *L'Antitête* (Ed. des Cahiers Libres, 1933; reissued in three volumes, Bordas, 1949); *Max Ernst* (art criticism: Ed. des Cahiers d'Art, 1934; tr. by Ralph Manheim in *Beyond Painting*, Wittenborn, Schultz, 1948); *Grains et issues* (Denoël & Steele, 1935); *La Main passe* (G.L.M., 1935); *La Deuxième Aventure céleste de Monsieur Antipyrine* (Les Reverbères, 1938); *Midis gagnés* (Denoël, 1939); *Le Signe de vie* (Bordas, 1946); *Terre sur terre* (Ed. des Trois Collines, 1946); *La Fuite* (dramatic poem: N. R. F., 1947); *Arthur Rimbaud: Oeuvres complètes* (introduction: Ed. du Grand-Chêne, 1948); *Phases* (Seghers, 1949); *Tristan Corbière: Les Amours jaunes* (introduction: Club Française des Livres, 1950); *La Face intérieure* (Seghers, 1953); *Guillaume Apollinaire: Alcools* (introduction: Club du Meilleur Livre, 1953), *La Bonne Heure* (Jacquet, 1955). Selected volumes: *Morceaux choisis* (Bordas, 1947); *De la coupe aux lèvres: Choix de poèmes 1939–1961* (Ed. Rapporti Europei, 1961). Selected writings: *Tzara*, "Poètes d'aujourd'hui," No. 32 (Seghers).

THE DEATH OF GUILLAUME APOLLINAIRE

we don't know anything
we haven't learned one single thing about pain
that bitterly cold season
only leaves long streaks in our muscles
he especially would have loved the joy of victory
wise beneath peaceful sorrow   caged
unable to resist
if snow fell upward
if the sun rose in our houses in the middle of the night
just to keep us warm
and the trees hung upsidedown with their crowns
— unique teardrop —
if birds came down to us to find reflections of themselves
in those peaceful lakes lying just above our heads
THEN WE MIGHT UNDERSTAND
that death could be a beautiful long voyage
and a permanent vacation from flesh from structures systems and
skeletons

— M. B.

EPIDERMIS OF THE NIGHT-TIME GROWTH

Promenade of our waters
I am streaming forth in fingers of faded phosphorescent gloves
my muscles are aquiver with mercurial eagle flour
I'm enslaved with trembling should anyone lean against my cell
what a beautiful photo I would make splattered against the
    grillwork like a cake
I was with you and your eyes came along with us

we arrive by an intermediate route, limb after limb, and organ
    after organ.

— TIMOTHY BAUM and M. B

85

SALTIMBANQUES

brains inflate collapse
 big balloons deflate collapse
  (it's the ventriloquist's words)
inflate collapse inflate collapse
 collapse
   disintegrated organs
clouds too assume these same shapes now and then
  lonely widows get upset watching them
    now and then
  listen to all the vertigo
    in the acrobatics of the figures
    in the mathematician's head
    NTOUCA leaping
      jester
who is dada who is DADA
    so static poetry is our brand new invention
  MBOCO the asthmatic   HwS2
   10054   moumbimba
  there's a machine
  machine that is
      its white blood cells are vowels
and the vowels lengthen
    lengthen that is
we gnaw away at the clock
and so get caught up in it
AND JUST LOOK AT THE BRILLIANCE RUNNING THE WHOLE LENGTH OF
ALL THOSE ROPES
      smoke is billowing from the tightrope-walker's
      head
my aunt is crouching now in a trapeze in the gym
   her nipples are herring-heads
    she sports flippers
  and squeezes squeezes squeezes her bosom's accordion
she squeezes squeezes squeezes her bosom's accordion glwa wawa
 prohahab

86

while in the outlying areas the sunlight is sprouting beneath
    plowshares
        left parked before the bar at the inn
                                        nf nf tatai
all the little fellows fart as they watch the arrival of the circus
    trunks
full of lice
and all the grandmothers covered with soft floppy malignant
    tumors
        that is to say
with polypi

                                        — M. B.

BONITA

a e ou o youyou you i e ou o
youyouyou
drrrrdrrrrdrrrrgrrrrgrrrr
fragments of green time go drifting around my room
a e o ii ii i e a ou ii ii stomach
clock watch I want to grab its navel flab
cacrap crap crap and let go the center of the four quarter-hours
hey where are you going to now iiiiiiiiupft
sea that scene-shifter a o u ith
a o u ith i o u ath a o u ith o u a ith
glowworms within us
inside our intestines and our directions
but the captain studies the indications given by the compass
and the concentration of colors flies apart
stork snapshot in the drugstore now are my memory and an
    ocarina
horizontal silkworm propagation of oceanoscopic floating objects
the local madwoman is rearing all the jesters for the royal court
hospital becomes canal
canal becomes violin
and on the violin there is a ship
and on its port side the queen is there among the immigrants on
    the way to mexico

— M. B.

DRUGSTORE CONSCIENCE

the lamp of a lily will give birth to so great a prince
that fountainheads will flourish in factories
and the leech transform itself into a sickness-tree
I'm searching for the roots of things my immovable lord my
   immovable lord
why yes then fine eventually you're certain to learn
come spiraling toward some useless tear

wet parrot
lignite cactus swell yourself up between a black cow's horns
the parrot excavates the lofty babel tower that holy department-
   store dummy

in your heart there's a child — A lamp
the doctor declares he won't last out the night

then he sneaks off among short sharp streaking lines of silence
   siliceous rock formation

while the much-pursued wolf lies silhouetted against the
   whiteness
the chosen one tracks down its own fellow inmates
reveal the flora the growth from death itself and this will explain
   everything you need to know
and the cardinal of france will appear
the three lilies dazzling clarity electrical virtue
red long dry flashing fishes and letters under the colors

the landscape's leprous giant
hesitates between two towns
his footsteps are streams' cadences but then the turtles of the
   hills ponderously assemble
he spits out sand pummels his lungs to make them felt
the human soul and the nightingale whirl in his laughter-
   sunflower
he wants to pluck the rainbow now my heart is a starfish made
   out of notebook paper
in missouri in brazil in the greater or lesser antilles

if you meditate if you are happy Reader you become for just one
   instant transparent
your brain a transparent sponge
and in this transparency there will be another still more distant
   transparency
still more distant that is to say even when a completely new
   animal turns blue in this present transparency

— M. B.

EVENING

fishermen return with the stars of the waters
they pass out bread to the poor
thread beads for the blind
emperors stroll out into parks at this hour which is as bitter and
  precise as some old engraving

servants bathe hunting hounds
the light is putting on gloves
therefore shut the window
put out the light in your window as you would spit out the pit of
  an apricot
a priest from his church

good lord: weave soft wool for melancholy lovers
dip little chickadees in ink and clean the face of the moon

— let's catch beetles
and put them in a box
— let's go down by the riverside
to make earthen jugs
— let's hug
beside the fountain
— let's loiter in the public park
until cockcrow
and the town's up in arms

or in the granary
the hay prickles there we hear the cows moo
as they think about their little ones
let's make it

— CHARLES SIMIC and M. B.

HIGHWAY SINGLE SUN

the knives are on their feet
we need air
the crows have all left
future departures canceled
the year of the rock falls on us

I've watched so much smoke drifting off
from interrupted springtime
the necklace of the mist
shatters against hovels
and abandoned liberty

I walked over the moss
a deafened ear
a night entered into me
rounded as a chestnut-tree
high above silence

she spoke of a man
she acted out a dream
sown by the sun
for the poor people we are
though still richer than even our hills

and I've followed that star
I've sensed the joy
of words tightly curled in the herbs
what is this space
radiating within me

— CHARLES SIMIC and M. B.

92

THE APPROXIMATE MAN

PART I

Sunday solid lid above the boilings of bubbling blood
the whole week's weight squatting hard on its haunches
now collapses into the center of a rediscovered self
the bells toll on without reason and we do too
toll on bells without reason so much like us
we will celebrate with the sounds of the chains
we'll set rattling within us together with the bells

what is this language cracking the whip like this we somersault
    into light
our nerve-ends are the whips time holds in its hands
and doubt alights with its single pale wing
to be clasped crushed compressed down deep inside of us
like the crumpled wrapper of some package damaged in transit
gift passed down by one more age with its slitherings of the fish
    of bitterness

the bells toll on without reason and we do too
vegetables have their eyes on us
our actions are all controlled nothing is left concealed
the river has washed out her bed so much
she carries along the frayed threads of a vision which has
    dragged along too long
at the foot of tall walls licked up lives in bars
enticed the enfeebled intensified temptations evaporated ecstasies
dug down through the sediment of variations on tradition
to unlock the wellsprings of tears long emprisoned
wellsprings enslaved by banal quotidian suffocations
to break the grip of dim vision that had seized with desiccated
    hands
any lucid daylight creation or flickering apparition
able to elaborate the trouble preciousness of the smile
peering out like a flower through the buttonhole of the morning
those in quest of rest or lust

those who grasp electricity in both hands who seek somersaults
    sudden shocks
adventures conflagrations perfect certainty or slavery
pleading looks which have walked back and forth along the
    whole length of secret torment
worn down city sidewalks and expiated endless abasements by
    begging
follow in a row wrapped up in ribbons of water
and flow toward the ocean carrying as they come
human garbage and its steaming mirages of imagination

the river has washed out her bed so much
that even the light slides off these slippery waters
and sinks to the bottom with a heavy rattling like rocks

the bells toll on without reason and we do too
the cares we wear within us
which are our most intimate interior garments
which we don every morning
which are undone by night's dreaming hands
adorned with useless little metal emblems
polished clean in the whirlpool bath of the surrounding
    countrysides
in cities preparing for carnage for sacrifice
beside seas with their vast sweeps of perspective
upon mountains with their restless severities
in small towns with their painful nonchalance
the weight of the hand on the head lies very heavily
the bells toll on without reason and we do too
we depart with the people departing we arrive with the new
    arrivals
depart with the new arrivals arrive when everybody else has to
    leave
without reason a bit dry a bit hard severe quite crusty tough but
bread nourishment more bread to accompany
the savory song on the scale of the human tongue
colors fling down their weights and start to think things out
think things out and cry out and fall asleep and eat
fruits light as the smoke hovering in the air
thinking about the warmth from which all words are woven
and surrounding their very core and nucleus the dream called us

94

the bells toll on without reason and we do too
we stride on to escape the swarming of the highways
with a flask full of landscape one touch of ill-health just one
one single malady spreading in us its name is death
I understand that I carry its melody within me but proceed
    without fear
Yes I carry death now but when I die
I will be the one whom death must carry in his imperceptible
    arms
delicate and implicit as the fragrance of fresh grass
delicate and implicit as a departure without apparent cause
without bitterness without guilt without regret without
the bells toll on without reason and we do too
why seek the very link of the chain that links us to the chain
toll on bells without reason and ourselves as well
we'll set the shattered glass inside of us chiming as well
the silver coins together with the counterfeit
the remnants of festivals bursting into laughter a full-scale
    cloudburst a tempest
battering at the doors behind which chasms could open
ossuaries of atmosphere in which polar bones are ground down
    to bits
festivities which elevate our heads to the skies
and spit down on these haunches of ours with their own night of
    molten liquid lead

I speak of one who speaks who's speaking I'm alone
I'm only one small sound but I have a great many smaller noises
    inside of me
a frozen crumpled-down sound trampled down at the crossroads
    stamped into muddy sidewalks
here at the feet of a harried public all these men running with
    their deaths
around death himself who is holding out his arms
above the sundial of the sun's single solitary living hour

the dark breathing of the evening deepens
and the whole length of our veins echoes with oceanic flutes
transposed across the octaves of the strata of multitudinous lives
of lives ceaselessly repeated down to the infinite of the smallest
    atom of detail

but lofty so far aloft they go straight out of sight
and together with these lives all around us yet still invisible
the ultraviolet of so many other parallel paths
those we might have taken
those that might never have led us to this world
or by means of which we might have departed long ago so long
    ago
that by now we might have long since forgotten them together
    with our entire epoch and the earth that might have eventually
    sucked at our selves
those limpid liquid salts and molten metal lying still in the depths
    of wells

I think of the warmth from which all words are woven
and at its very core and nucleus this dream called us

— M. B.

TONIC

the boredom of seething crudities rises rancorously to your chest
landing-pier generously open to logical indecencies
paved with big chunks of sun
sunlight crushed at the crossroads of the waters

purer waters bubbling veins
veins of intermittent wind
masts are erected pointing at the flesh of clouds
made up of the multiform menacings that lie concealed beneath
    angelic togas

blue blue is the sky over the labors of sailors
the threads of the ages held tight between their hands
departures ventured toward stammering lisping languages
between their hands which light the first signal fires of strange
    new tongues

creak you winches you teeth in the mouths of the ocean
all along the anchor chain which ties us to the coast
for adolescent scents for products of export and love
I await at the entrance to laughter at the doorway of day

the light of day is lit upon your lips
tinted by the smiling ascendency of today
and your lips are aglow with the flarings of the syllables
freed through the luminous disentanglings of your lips

— M. B.

APPROACH

magical course of unending nights
nights swallowed in haste bitter mouthfuls taken in haste
nights trampled down beneath the muddy doormat of our
    sluggish passions
dry dreams suitable for the fixed stares of pecking crows

soggy soiled night-dark rags is what we have been constructing
yet in us in each one of us is a chromatic tower so lofty
that the view is no longer cut off by mountains and by rivers
the sky no longer turns away from our nets for catching stars
the clouds lie down at our feet like hunting hounds
and we can look into the sun until oblivion

and yet my satisfaction only finds its logical justification
in the nest of your arms which is the tide of night
after the outburst of shrieking storms streams down across death
it's a body uncased from its earthly suit of armor
unstringing one by one the beads from the necklace of our
    dreams of oblivion

— M. B.

FLUID

it is time to open the great door
it is a time to rebuild the ruins
it is a time for unraveling and cleansing
it is the time when the world is jeered at by its own guilt when
    the world is left dumbfounded
leaf of simplicity the sunshine is concealed from thee
you shed yourself upon the threshold among a thousand vigilant
    clusters
bolted down
you, there, eluding time sopped in its own servitude
nevertheless, awaiting it

hard life harsh life
the wind has vented its anger on the embers of your eyelids
and the flame has extinguished behind memory
its path void of any further hope
no more stars in its madness
only the solitary word
you concealed in the animal night
and you passing by

—— TIMOTHY BAUM

THE DOORS HAVE OPENED

The doors have opened without a sound they are wings
above the crushing countries with their clutching arms
the structures of fire give way to canals
strewn with the remnants of caravans lost in quests
bodies dangling down below the aerial highways
cremated in the throats of the cold crowd
a wild light streaking up the riverbed
cuts up the air with its transparent prow
ripening the eyes locked in the ocean prison
which fall asleep during enumerations
pebbles among the nourishing rays of light
no outcry stirs the waves of lips
boredom has run aground on a shoreline of primitive beachwear
and the hourglasses of bodies compacted of pure sunshine
stun time stop plows
smoke
straight furrow
acrid
a mist of impetuous rivers fills the arid mouth
nor does man confront man
nor have the stone pier and the ordinary glaciers of naked beings
    been near here
for these regions are truly wings
the doors have opened without a single sound
no one will ever even tremble — for such an outcry might irritate
    even woolen existences
and the terrible theatres of trumpets
stirrers-up of teapot tempests now they are wings as well
beneath the sheathings of roots some sun is rejoicing for the
    vultures which come after eternity
ringing out news of the light amid the fatigue of our waters

— M. B.

SONG V

if words were nothing but signs
postage stamps for all things
what would be the outcome of everything
dust
empty gestures
time wasted
neither agony nor joy would remain
in that odd world

— M. B.

MATURITY

In the profoundest depths the wind breaks every bell
all the crystals of the void with nobody there to hear
word your inner flavor has fled the human realm
and the wandering song I've followed up to the gates of this
    abyss

since joy has stopped rolling its wheel across the lips of the sun
the sun hatches its plots under ashes of solid rock
desiccation all is desiccation where once the tender bow of the
    water
the tender water drawn from language made the nights of
    mankind flower

listen can't you hear the glare of too many long nights' vigils
this winged name fluttering about from one branch to another
on the edge of every riverbank it always feels the same
I am fixed in position my footsteps alone depart

time has made its nest damped down with much sound-absorbent
    insulation
with sponges long extinct yet relentlessly ponderous
a long tearing sound takes the place of memory
and echoes of exhilaration smash to pieces against the
    windowpane

outside the landscape menacingly advances
the motions of the beech-elms come loaded with harsh reproach
flinging furious flailings against the window
silently you listen to desire enter the heart of winter

it's a fire kept in delicately sheltering hands
the haloed associations of words which once lit up have all faded
with the velvet forehead and its friendly eyes
yet there is nothing which lives untouched by the forgotten
    flarings of that flame

each shadow has a soul which still responds to that light
but that prize weighs next to nothing once the scales have been
    misadjusted

102

flickering from time to time is this forbidding vision
death staring straight out of the dark center of your laughter

— M. B.

THE WATER WAS CARVING OUT
TALL GRILLS OF GIRLS

The water was carving out tall grills of girls in the shadow of the sand.

We had encrusted ourselves during the night. No regret resisted the virulent mysteries. Far from the stones, at their very core. The thorns knew nothing nobler than self-denial. A fruit, remorse, like a tiny capsule of light. And the crown of the core joins the crown of thorns. Vast light flinging unfulfilled fruits on the shores — in bite-sizes, juicy foreshadowings of death. It's the sum of this countryside's poverty: Unfulfilled circumstances.

The absence of dreams, neither sad nor serious. But forever rockbound and veined with superannuated periods, winestained souvenirs and struggling plunges to the death. Immutable melancholy of the blankets of water which a sleeper in fossil coal pulls up to his neck. But, arm in arm, the waves flow out from the regions of thought; they deposit along the salty tang only their chilly memory of the sun.

Hideous, the face exchanged glaring glances with the lighthouse. And the monstrous creatures again assume their passive stances in the depths of forgetfulness. All the enormously phosphorescent desolation of a hand reaching out just as the tide begins to turn.

— M. B.

WAY

What is this road that separates us
across which I hold out the hand of my thoughts
a flower is written out at the very tip of each finger
and the very end of the road is a flower which walks along with
   you

— M. B.

PHILIPPE SOUPAULT

1897-

PHILIPPE SOUPAULT IS THE CO-AUTHOR with André Breton of the
first text to explore consciously the possibilities of "automatic
writing," *Les Champs magnétiques* (*The Magnetic Fields*, 1919).[1]
He is also the collaborator with Breton on one of the earliest at-
tempts at drama written according to its precepts, *S'il vous plaît*
(*If You Please*, 1920).[2] Between 1919 and 1923 he co-edited
Littérature, assisting with Breton and Aragon in its transforma-
tion from a general avant-garde periodical to one devoted to
Dada, and finally to a journal in which direct suggestions of
Surrealism were developed.

Soupault's earliest poetry is curiously unsuggestive of this
development. Its mood of gentle, wistful longing perpetuates
similar moods in Apollinaire, a personal friend; Reverdy is per-
haps present in its rhetoric-stripped, image-based texture. In-
creasingly, however, these characteristics take on Surrealist over-
tones, this transparency transmitting the desire to transcend the
processes and purposes of literary artifice, and the philosophical
corollary of this in the Surrealist context: the longing for a less
fixed existence and personal transformation. Far from assuming
a doctrinaire attitude toward these perspectives, the poetry is
determinedly intimate and more than willing to acknowledge
those moments of pathos in which change, even on the imme-
diate personal level, seems impossible.

Similar technical and thematic concerns prevail in the many
novels and tales Soupault wrote during the 1920's and 1930's.
Often they are outright adventure yarns in which the search for

a wider self is signified by external quests. Among the most intriguing of these is *Le Voyage d'Horace Pirouelle*,[3] a novel about a polar journey apparently inspired by Chaplin's film, *The Gold Rush* (1925). The poet's intense feeling of kinship with Chaplin's wandering hero, whom his own poetic narrator frequently resembles, is also expressed in his study *Charlot (Chaplin,* 1930).[4] His curiosity about contemporary American developments also extends to an essay written in English, *The American Influence in France* (1930).[5] In 1929 the poet spent some months in the United States conducting a course in French literature, an invitation extended mainly on the basis of articles about the French cinema the poet had been writing for the extra-Surrealist periodical *Europe Nouvelle*. Soupault's explorations of genres other than poetry include a series of essays on pre-Surrealist poets and painters, and on poetry in general.[6]

Soupault had already begun to withdraw from the movement in protest against what he felt was its increasing preoccupation with codification, especially on the political level. His activities in the next decade included the writing of a scenario at the request of the director Jean Vigo, just before the latter's death, and even wider travels as a journalist than those of the 1920's. In 1938 he helped found the anti-Nazi broadcasting station, Radio Tunis. In 1942 he was arrested by the Vichy government and imprisoned for six months; he escaped and in 1943 made his way to the United States, teaching a course in French literature at Swarthmore College, and living in Mount Vernon, New York. Upon his return to France in 1945 he was named Director of Foreign Programs for Radiodiffusion Française; in 1946 he was a press official for UNESCO. He continued to travel widely and to compose verse setting forth the theme of self-discovery, with endless journeying as its analogy.

OTHER PRINCIPAL WORKS

Poems except where otherwise noted: *Aquarium* (privately printed, 1917); *Rose des vents* (Au Sans Pareil, 1920); *Westwego* (Librairie Six, 1922); *Le Bon Apôtre* (novel: Le Sagittaire, 1923); *A la dérive* (novel: Ferenczi, 1923); *Les Frères Durandeau* (novel: Grasset, 1924); *En joue!* (novel; Grasset, 1925); *Le Bar de l'amour* (novel: Emile-Paul Frères, 1925); *Corps perdu* (novel: Au Sans Pareil, 1926); *Georgia* (Ed. des Cahiers Libres, 1926); *Le Coeur d'or* (novel: Grasset, 1927); *Le Nègre* (novel: Kra, 1927); *Les Dernières Nuits de Paris* (novel: Calmann-Lévy, 1928); tr. by William Carlos Williams as *The Last Nights of Paris*, Macauley, 1929); *Le Grand Homme* (novel: Kra, 1929); *Les Moribonds* (novel: Rieder, 1934); *Il y a un océan* (G.L.M., 1936); *L'Arme secrète* (Bordas, 1946); *Odes* (Seghers, 1946); *Message de l'île déserte* (A.A.M. Stols, 1947); *Chansons du jour et de la nuit* (Le Caire, 1949); *Chansons* (Eynard, 1949); *Sans phrases* (Girard, 1953). Autobiographical: *Histoire d'un blanc* (Au Sans Pareil, 1927); *Le Temps des assassins* (Ed. de la Maison Française, 1945; tr. by Hannah Josephson as *Age of Assassins*, Knopf, 1946); *Journal d'un fantôme* (Point du jour, 1956). Principal collected volume: *Poésies complètes 1917–1937* (G.L.M., 1937). Selected writings: *Soupault*, "Poètes d'aujourd'hui," No. 58 (Seghers).

ROUTE

I detected the memory of her voice as it alit and perched
My body cradled my thoughts
The telegraph wires were speeding away

The thud of a thrown stone struck noon

— M. B.

SUNDAY

The aircraft are weaving the telegraph wires
and the waterfall is singing the exact same song
At the coachmen's hangout the aperitifs are all orange
but locomotive engineers all have white eyes
the lady has lost her smile in the woods

— M. B.

SERVITUDES

Yesterday it was night out
still the advertising posters sing
the trees stretch out
the wax statue at the barber's smiles at me
No spitting
No smoking
rays of sunlight streaming from your hands you announced it to
    me
there are fourteen

I invent unmapped streets
several new continents flourish
the newspapers will be coming out tomorrow
Wet Paint
I'll go for a stroll naked except for my walking-stick

                                        — M. B.

SPORT ITEMS

Plucky as a postage stamp
he went he went his way
gently tapping his hands
to count his steps
his heart red as a wild boar
was throbbing throbbing
like a pink and green butterfly
From time to time
he set up a small satin flag
After a good deal of walking
he sat down to rest
and fell asleep
But ever since that day there have been a lot of clouds in the sky
a lot of birds in the trees
and a lot of salt in the sea
There are a lot of other things too

— JOACHIM NEUGROSCHEL

GOLD MEDAL

The night bangs around its stars
It's raining cotton and sand
It's so hot
but the silence is weaving sighs
together with the glory of summer
Almost everywhere
heat crimes are being reported
human storms that will overthrow thrones
and a huge light
in the west
and in the east
gentle as a rainbow
It's noon
Every clock
repeats
noon
A dull pause
like a huge animal
is pulling out its paws from every quarter
sticking out its quills
they are shadows and rays
The sky is going to fall on our heads
We're waiting for the wind
Which must today be pure azure
like a flag

— M. B.

GEORGIA

I can't sleep Georgia
I fire off arrows into the night Georgia
I'm waiting Georgia
I'm concentrating Georgia
Fire is like snow Georgia
Night is my next-door-neighbor Georgia
The slightest sound upsets me Georgia
I see smoke ascend then drift away from me Georgia
I flee like a wolf through the shadows Georgia
I'm running hard now this is the street these are the suburbs
   Georgia
It's a city like any other city Georgia
A place where I'm not in the least at home Georgia
I rush on the winds are coming Georgia
And cold and silence and fear Georgia
I'm running Georgia
I'm trying to escape Georgia
The clouds are low they are about to fall Georgia
I stretch out my arms Georgia
I refuse to close my eyes Georgia
I call Georgia
I cry Georgia
I call Georgia
I'm calling you Georgia
Will you come at last Georgia
Come soon Georgia
Georgia Georgia Georgia
Georgia
I can't sleep at night Georgia
I'm waiting for you Georgia
Georgia

—— M. B.

112

HORIZON

The whole town has come into my room
the trees have disappeared
and evening clings to my fingers
The houses are turning into ocean liners
the sound of the sea has just reached me up here
In two days we'll arrive in the Congo
I've passed the Equator and the Tropic of Capricorn
I know there are innumerable hills
Notre-Dame hides the Gaurisankar and the northern lights
night falls drop by drop
I await the hours

Give me that lemonade and the last cigarette
I'm going back to Paris

— ROSMARIE WALDROP

THE SWIMMER

Thousands of cries birds
the horizon draws a lifeline
And these waves these lost faces whisper
through gulfs stretching out like opened arms
At last I'm certain of being alone
North or West or wherever
the sun a-buzz with light
on Sky-and-Earth Street
I pause to discover whether summer is still red
in my veins
and my shadow revolves around me
like the hands on a watch
Sleep brings me insects and reptiles
pain and grimacing and lying
now the alarm-clock
I float face down at the dead center of the hour
with no help on the way without crying out for help
without conviction I go down endless aimless flights of stairs
and I continue without regret until sleep
in the eyes of mirrors and the laughter of the wind
I recognize a stranger who is myself
I won't move a muscle
I wait
I lock both my eyes tight
We'll never discover when the night begins
and where it ends
but on the whole that isn't important
tonight all the Black Eskimos in Kamchatka
will fall asleep with me
when fatigue settles on my cranium
like a crown

— M. B.

114

LIFE-SAVING MEDAL

My long nose sticks out like a knife
and my eyes are bloodshot from laughing
In the middle of the night I take in the milk and the moon
and run without turning about
If the trees are afraid behind me
Who cares
How beautiful indifference is at midnight

Where are all these people going
the pride of the city
streetcorner musicians
the crowd dances at top speed
and I'm just an anonymous passerby
or someone else whose name I've forgotten

— M. B.

CLASPED HANDS

Up in the sky big ships send out smoke
and on earth tonight a man is writing
beside a candle
with a Waterman pen
He thinks about gray birds
about slow waltzes which are gray birds
he thinks about a country he doesn't know about
as one dwells upon a dog that is drowsing
He knows a lot of things which have no names
on earth or in heaven
where the big ships fly
The trees insist on silence and rain
There is a man writing beside a candle
beside a drowsing dog
and thinking about the moon
and thinking about the Good Lord
There are also all these butterflies tiny advertisements for
   paradise
where the well-dressed angels dwell
the owners of elegant walking-sticks
and of big cars sleek subtle silent supple
The angels are friends
you ask their advice about choosing the right tie
and they answer sadly
Select the one the color of your eyes
The angels vanish into the candleflames
leaving only the trees
and of course animals which you forget
and which hide
These brave beings are aware that silence is *de rigueur*
at this hour of boldly approaching evening
at this hour when prayers descend
along with songs down cottonwool ladders
It's also the time when you see eyes
that don't want to be put out
stationary as seraphim

116

Angels of Paris lend me your wings
lend me your fingers
lend me your hands
Do I have to go on sleeping much longer
with my head heavier than sin
Do I have to die without crying out
in this silence insisted on by the trees
beside a candle
beside a sleeping dog

— M. B.

THE POET'S COUNSEL

Be like the water
the waters of streams and clouds
you can be all colors of the rainbow or no color at all
nothing should be able to stop you
not even time
There are no roads too long
nor seas too distant
Have no fear of the wind
and even less fear of the heat or the cold
Learn to sing
without ever wearying
murmur and slip yourself past
or push and shove
Leap or splatter

Be sleeping water
which runs which plays
water which purifies
water which is sweet and pure
because it's purification itself
because it's life for the living
and death to the shipwrecked

— M. B.

RIVER

Longitudinal corridor between vast subterranean foundations
dark inclination of parasitical lions
but oh frightening moon running like a great light
river
the furrows left by ships are your hair
night is your coat
the reflections that sleep against you are your scales
nobody wants to know you any more
you flow from the eyes of that unknown star
fructifying tears
but we'll never know your pale source
your adorable mouth
and your long wailing in the fields of your birth
You tell each tree that leans over you
Pass by my friend my brother and look where you're going
hope is mildewed
there's nothing left but that grand God of
mercy
and those great summons from the beyond so close to my heart
run there if you can
But don't you know the night would strangle you
with its bloody hands
Farewell my sea brother my deaf friend
I don't know if this stream your brother will ever see you
again
River sinuous like lips
and like the serpent asleep in this luscious lawn
maternal sheep
herd of lights

— ROSMARIE WALDROP

ANDRÉ BRETON

1896-1966

INSOFAR AS SURREALISM IS A GROUP MOVEMENT as well as a literary development, and insofar as Surrealism could consent to be led by one man, Breton was its director. The movement's birth in 1924 coincided with the publication of his first *Manifeste du Surréalisme (Manifesto of Surrealism)*[1] and was the direct result of Breton's pre-Surrealist organizational efforts.

Breton entered the Paris literary world during the final years of the World War I period with the publication of several poems in a somewhat Symbolist, Mallarméan mode, represented in the significantly entitled *Mont de Piété (Pawnshop*, 1919).[2] They attracted the attention of Mallarmé's chief living disciple, Paul Valéry; before long Valéry introduced Breton's work to other editors, and also to Proust, who gave the young poet a short-lived editorial job proofreading part of his great novel. Perhaps the relationship is not entirely as strange as it seems: albeit to different ends, and using dissimilar techniques, both Proust and Breton structure their work with special reference to the processes of "free" association.

It was as a young medical student with a special interest in psychology that Breton was mobilized early in 1915, serving as an intern in a series of military psychiatric wards. Later that same year he began to correspond with Guillaume Apollinaire, then also in the French army. By 1918 Breton was meeting with the older "younger" poet, in whose library he seems to have discovered for the first time not only De Sade but also the periodical *Dada*, edited in Zurich by Tristan Tzara. In 1919, Breton collaborated with Philippe Soupault in composing *Les Champs magnétiques* (*The Magnetic Fields,* published a year later),[3] purportedly the first text based solely on the psychiatric technique of free association; a prefatory note presented it as a text in psychic research and "spoken thought." Also in 1919, with Soupault and Louis Aragon, a fellow ex-medical student, Breton founded his own review, the "antiliterary" periodical *Littérature.* Although initially representing a broad range of avant-garde writers, it became dominated by Dada a few months later, around the time that Breton, at the head of an admiring group of writers, persuaded Tzara to come to Paris. Although it was in part due to Breton's assistance that Dada flourished in Paris for the next few years, it is generally agreed that it was Breton's 1921 call for a "Congress for the Directives and Defenses of the Modern Spirit" that produced the atmosphere of reevaluation and general questioning which made the death of Dada inevitable. Breton himself later remarked in an interview that he had realized that "the wide-open doors of 1918 led to a corridor that goes nowhere."[4]

The founding of the Surrealist movement occurred in 1924 with the publication of Breton's *Manifeste du Surréalisme* (*Manifesto of Surrealism*). Here, he described the technique of "automatic writing" in greater detail and espoused the technique of writing as pure psychic dictation which was to serve as at least a stimulus in much Surrealist work during the movement's early years. Breton also established the movement's philosophical coordinates, characterizing it as a quest for "the future resolution of those two states, dream and reality, into a surreality . . . ," and sounded the theme of revolt through recourse to "the marvelous" which is active throughout the movement's history. Moreover, Breton outlined what was to be generally considered the movement's legitimate ancestry, emphasizing such nineteenth-century writers as Baudelaire, Bertrand, De Sade, Rimbaud, Nerval, and Lautréamont, and the English "Gothic" novelist, Lewis. Also, he credited recent influences on his own thought: Apollinaire, Reverdy, Roussel, Jarry and the little-known Jacques Vaché — one of Breton's wartime military patients whose idea of "umore" became a prototype of what Breton was later to call "black humor." In another passage, Breton reasserted his feeling for the goals of socialism, while at the same time describing his own unwillingness to perform as a member of a gas workers' cell, concluding that Surrealism's path might be parallel to the Marxist path, but its means were not and could never be identical.

Although Breton was not a founding editor of the movement's first periodical, *La Révolution Surréaliste*, he assumed editorship with its fourth issue, subtitled *"And War on Work!"* (1925), and in the years that followed either had a direct hand in, or issued personally, most of the major manifestos, tracts, broadsides, handbills and open letters in which the Surrealist position was declared. Though anxious to develop associations with the Communist party during this particular time, Breton also asserted the need for the continued independence of the Surrealist position in such texts as *Introduction au discours sur le peu de réalité (Introduction to a Discourse on the Paucity of Reality,* 1927),[5] and *Légitime Défense (Legitimate Defense,* 1926).[6]

Many of Breton's best known extratheoretical writings also date from this productive early period. In addition to the prose poem appendix to the *Manifesto* (the "Poisson soluble," or "Soluble Fish," 1924),[7] these works include the novel *Nadja* (1928),[8] several plays in collaboration, and the first of the "poem-objects" — drawings or sculpture organized according to the same chance-based principles motivating the more "automatic" of his writings. In numerous introductions to catalogues, statements of support, and particularly in *Le Surréalisme et la peinture (Surrealism and Painting,* 1928),[9] Breton also set forth the Surrealist position with regard to painting, again affirming his faith in the psychic sources of art and his belief that the success of any work is more a product of the spontaneous energy of the individual artist's mind than the result of any calculated "skillfulness" or preconceived "technique." Breton also expressed this belief in the overall character of his individual works, which often resist characterization according to preconceived notions of genre.

In late 1929, Breton began to publish the *Second Manifeste du Surréalisme (Second Manifesto of Surrealism,* issuing it in abbreviated form in the final issue of *La Révolution Surréaliste,* then in book form in 1930).[10] Here he did not so much reaffirm the unity of the Surrealist position as assert the pressing need for an inner cohesiveness, even at the expense of excluding (as

Breton did with this document) several major figures who he felt had "strayed" — a roster which included, most notably, Robert Desnos and Antonin Artaud, as well as Philippe Soupault. It was an act Breton was to regret openly in later comments in which he himself reviewed, with full accountability, the loss to Surrealism represented by these "excommunications," as his opponents described them. In this Second Manifesto Breton also traced the philosophical roots of the movement to the ideas regarding the resolution of seemingly contradictory opposites — which is to say to the dialectics — of the German philosopher Hegel.

Despite the fact that he changed the name of *La Révolution Surréaliste* to *Le Surréalisme au service de la Révolution (Surrealism at the Service of the Revolution)* in 1930, he continued to defend the independence of the movement. In 1932, with the image of *Les Vases communicants (The Communicating Vessels)*,[11] he reaffirmed his faith in the interdependence of the two "vessels" of dream and reality and in the need for the governing of political reality by means of the individual dream rather than (as Stalinist Communism insisted) the opposite. That same year, in *Misère de la poésie (The Poverty of Poetry)*,[12] he rejected the purely realistic, externally oriented basis of the so-called progressive literature which had recently been espoused by one of his closest associates, Louis Aragon. In 1935, after the initial Moscow "purge" trials of dissident intellectuals, Breton broke definitively with the Communist party, collaborating in a group manifesto defining Surrealism's position, *Du temps où les Surréalistes avaient raison (On the Time When the Surrealists Were Right, 1935)*,[13] and *Position politique du Surréalisme (Political Position of Surrealism, 1935)*.[14]

During the late 1930's Breton traveled in Czechoslovakia and then in Mexico; in 1938 he co-founded with Leon Trotsky and Diego Rivera the short-lived "International Federation of Independent Revolutionary Artists," also co-authoring its program in a text which again asserted the necessarily independent nature of any truly revolutionary art.[15] Breton's later codifications include a *Dictionnaire abrégé du Surréalisme (Short Dictionary of Surrealism, 1938)*,[16] one of several works written in collaboration with other Surrealists, this with Paul Eluard; and, in 1940, an *Anthologie de l'humour noir (Anthology of Black Humor)*,[17] which was proscribed by the Nazi-controlled "French" Vichy government. In 1941, as a refugee, Breton came to the United States, where he worked as a broadcaster for the Voice of America broadcasts to Fascist- occupied countries.

Perhaps the most astonishing technical achievement in Breton's later years was the development of a prose form using the metaphorical and associative resources of poetry; or, as the form has been called by Balakian, "analogical prose." Works in this form include *L'Amour fou (Mad Love*, 1938)[18] and *Arcane 17* (1945),[19] written during a visit to Canada just before his return to France in 1945. Belonging to no known genre, they are perhaps the culmination of Breton's work exploring a psychologically directed esthetic. These later writings also underline the occultist, astrological and alchemical aspects of Surrealism.

In 1945, following a brief stopover in Haiti, during which a lecture on Surrealism is said to have intensified political demonstrations, producing widespread governmental reform, Breton returned to France. He organized a small group of writers around the banner of Surrealism, editing in succession a series of relatively short-lived Surrealist-oriented magazines, including *Néon*, *Medium*, *La Brèche*, and *Le Surréalisme*, *Même;* also directing an art gallery, L'Etoile Scellée. This activity notwithstanding, perhaps his most far-reaching work during these later years was the drafting of several texts which tended to consider Surrealism historically — as an enduring philosophy rather than as an on-going "movement." These include *Situation du Surréalisme entre les deux guerres (Situation of Surrealism between the Wars*, 1945);[20] the preface to a second edition of the Second Manifesto;[21] and *Prolegomènes à un troisième manifeste du Surréalisme ou non (Prolegomena to a Third Surrealist Manifesto or Not*, 1946).[22] Although through Breton Surrealism's influence extended by that time to writers indebted to Surrealist styles and themes yet indifferent to the idea of a Surrealist movement, Breton continued to identify himself closely with a relatively small circle of postwar writers in Paris who claimed adherence to group Surrealism; and he remained the undisputed leader of these remnants of the movement until his death.

Principal collections of poems: *Clair de terre* (Collection Littérature, 1923); *Le Révolver à cheveux blancs* (Ed. des Cahiers Libres, 1932); *L'Aire de l'eau* (Cahiers d'Art, 1934); *Fata morgana* (Sagittaire, 1941); *Pleine Marge* (Nierendorf, 1943); *Ode à Charles Fourier* (Ed. Fontaine, 1947; reissued by N.R.F., 1948; tr. by Kenneth White as *Ode to Charles Fourier*, Cape-Goliard, 1969). Principal volume of selected poems: *Poèmes* (N.R.F., 1948). Selections appear in *Young Cherry Trees Secured against Hares* tr. by Edouard Roditi, View Editions, 1946; reissued by University of Michigan Press, 1970); and in *Selected Poems*, tr. by Kenneth White, Cape-Grossman, 1969). Collections of essays: *Les Pas perdus* (N.R.F., 1924; reissued 1949; also by Livre de Poche, 1970); *Le Point du jour* (N.R.F., 1934); *La Clé des champs* (Sagittaire, 1952). Selected writings: *Poésie et autre* (Club Française du Livre, 1957); *Breton*, "Poètes d'aujourd'hui" No. 18 (Seghers). Works in collaboration other than those mentioned above: see introductory material on Soupault and Eluard.

EGRET

If only the sun were shining tonight
If only in the depths of the Opera House two breasts both glossy
and bright
Would contribute to the word "love" their most marvelous living
letter
If the worn wooden walkway opened out on the mountain peak
If the ermine cast a pleading glance
Toward the priest with his red ribbons
Riding back from the prison-compounds counting all the closed
carriages
If the luxurious echoes of the river waters I trouble so
Would only throw my body to the grasses of Paris
Why doesn't it sleet and hail in the jewelry stores
At least Springtime would be less terrifying for me then
If only I were a root of the tree of the sky
Or else the goodness in the sugarcane of the air
If we let women make ladders of our backbones
What do you see O so beautiful one one so silent
Beneath the Carrousel's arch of triumph
Should pleasure in the form of a perpetually perambulating
woman lead you on
The Chambers of Law no longer being filled with furrows except
for violet eyes of shaded promenades
What wouldn't I give for an arm of the Seine to slip itself
beneath this entire morning
Which in any case is not to be grasped
Nor am I resigned to rooms in lofty caressing halls
Where in the evening you receive penalizing phonecalls
When I leave I set fire to a little lock of hair which is also the
wick of a bomb
And that wick is hollowing out a tunnel under Paris
If only my train could enter that tunnel

— M. B.

ALWAYS FOR THE FIRST TIME

Always for the first time
I hardly recognize you by sight
Sometime during the night you come home to a building at an
    oblique angle from my window
An entirely imaginary structure
It is there that at any minute
In total darkness
I expect the incredible cleavage
Of the façade and of my heart
The closer I come to you
In reality
The more the key sings in the door of the unknown room
Where you appear to me and to me alone
At first you kept melting away into the dazzling light
The accidental raising of that curtain
Is a field of flowering jasmine which I once saw beside a highway
    at dawn one day just outside the town of Grasse
With its female fruit-pickers all balanced at exactly the same
    angle
Behind them the darkly fallen wings of the stripped shrubs
Before them the square of glowing light
The curtain imperceptibly raised
In one great rush all the flowers return
That's you there the person negotiating all the endless hours
    never sufficiently troubled by sleep
You as if you could actually be
The same person twice except that perhaps I'll never actually get
    to meet you
You pretend not to notice I'm watching
It's marvelous I'm not even sure you actually know I am
Your casualness brings me to tears
A halo of inexplicable interpretations surrounds your each and
    every gesture
It's a hunt for the dews of dusk!
There are rocking chairs on the overpass there are prickly
    branches which could catch at you in the forest

On rue Notre-Dame-de-Lorette there is a shop window
Featuring two lovely crossed legs sheathed in high silk stockings
Which flare out from the center of a great glistening cloverleaf
There is a silk rope ladder hanging down over the ivy
There is
(Making me lean far out over the precipice)
The definitive fusion of your presence and your absence
I've found the secret
Of loving you
For the first time forever

— M. B.

"THE MARQUIS DE SADE . . ."

The Marquis de Sade regained the interior of the erupting
    volcano
Whence he had come
With his beautiful hands still in ruffles
His eyes of a young girl
And that intelligence at the rim of panic that was
His alone
But from the salon phosphorescent with visceral lamps
He did not cease to hurl mysterious commands
That breached the moral night
Through that breach I see
The great creaking shadows the old sapped husk
Dissolve
So that I may love you
As the first man loved the first woman
In utter freedom
This freedom
For which fire itself was made man
For which the Marquis de Sade defied the centuries with his
    great abstract trees
With his tragic acrobats
Caught in the gossamer of desire

— KEITH WALDROP

127

VIGILANCE

The tower of Saint-Jacques in Paris totters
Like a sunflower
Bumps its brow a bit on the River Seine then its shadow goes
  slipping off subtly among the tugboats
At this moment on tiptoe in my sleep
I steal off to the room where I'm lying outstretched
To set it afire
In order that nothing more may endure of acquiescences which
  have been wrung from me
The articles of furniture give way to animals of exactly the same
  size who look at me in a friendly way
Lions in whose manes chairs disappear at last
Sharks whose white bellies incorporate the final shiverings of
  the sheets
During the hour of love and blue eyelids
Then in turn I see myself burning away I see that lugubriously
  solemn hiding-place of nothings
That was my body
Thoroughly probed by the patient beak of the fire-ibis
When it is done I enter invisibly into the Ark
Indifferent to the passersby of life whose pedestrian footsteps
  echo off in the distance
I see the skeleton of the sun
Through the flowering hawthorn of the rain
I hear the intimate human linen tearing like some vast leaf
Beneath the single nail of absence and presence conniving
All the mills of industry wither away only a single scallop-
  shaped piece of perfumed lace is left
A shell of lace in the perfect shape of a breast
I touch only the heart of things now I hold the thread

— M. B.

THE WRITINGS RECEDE

The satin of pages turned in books shapes a woman so beautiful
That whenever we hesitate in the midst of our studies we
    meditate longingly on this lady
Without daring to speak to her without ever daring to tell her
    she is so beautiful
That the knowledge about to become ours is invaluable
This woman passes us imperceptibly amid a sound like rustling
    flowers
Sometimes she turns back to us among the seasons of print
To ask what time it is or else she pretends to start staring with
    incredible fixity at jewelry
In a way real beings do not
And the world dies away a fracture opens in the ovals of the air
A rending in the region of the heart
The morning papers bring singing women whose voices are the
    color of sand on still untouched and perilous shores
And sometimes the evening news introduces very young girls
    leading animals on chains
But most beautiful of all is the space in between certain letters
Where hands whiter than the midday cornucopia of stars
Disconcert a nest of white swallows
So according to the omens it will never stop raining
Down low so low that wings are incapable of carrying them-
    selves there
There are hands from which you ascend to arms so delicate that
    the graceful intertwinings of the mists in the meadows above
    lakes is only their imperfect mirror
Arms joined to nothing except the exceptional peril of a body
    made to make love
Whose belly calls with the sighing plucked from bushes draped
    with veils
And about which the only earthbound thing is the great icy truth
    of sleds of stares on the pure white expanse
Of anything I'm not likely to see ever again
Because of the marvelous blindfolding bandage

Which is mine in this blindman's-buff of rendings and parting
wounds

— M. B.

A BRANCH OF NETTLE ENTERS
THROUGH THE WINDOW

The woman with the crepe paper body
The red fish in the fireplace
Whose memory is pieced together from a multitude of small
    watering places for distant ships
Who laughs like an ember fit to be set in snow
And sees the night expand and contract like an accordion
The armor of the grass
Hilt of the dagger gate
Falling in flakes from the wings of the sphinx
Rolling the floor of the Danube
For which time and space destroy themselves
On the evening when the watchman of the inner eye trembles
    like an elf
Isn't this the stake of the battle to which my dreams surrender
Brittle bird
Rocked by the telegraph wires of trance
Shattering in the great lake created by the numbers of its song
This is the double heart of the lost wall
Gripped by grasshoppers of the blood
That drag my likeness through the mirror
My broken hands
My caterpillar eyes
My long whalebone hairs
Whalebone sealed under brilliant black wax

— DAVID ANTIN

IN THE LOVELY HALF-LIGHT . . .

In the lovely half-light of 1934
The air was a splendid rose color the color of red mullet
And the forest when I began to enter it
Started out with a tree with cigarette-paper leaves
Since I was awaiting you
And since whenever you walk with me
Anywhere at all
How easily your mouth turns into the enamel tip of the axle-tree
From which the ceaseless diffuse blue wordy wheel climbs up
    and up
Only to pale away in the ruts
All allurements rush in to meet me
A squirrel came and pressed its white belly to my heart
I don't understand how he managed it
But the earth was full of reflections even deeper than those of
    water
As if metal had finally·split its shell
And you who were lying on a terrifying sea of jewelry
Turned
Naked
Under a great sun made of sky-rockets
I saw you taking down from among the radiolarians
The empty skulls of the sea-urchin I was there
But pardon me I was no longer there
I was raising my eyes overhead since the living casket of white
    velvet had abandoned me
And I was sad
The sky between the leaves glittered wild and hard as a dragon-
    fly
I was about to close my eyes
When the two wooden blinders which had flown apart suddenly
    snapped shut once again
Like the two inmost leaves of an immense Lily of the Valley
A flower able to contain the entire night
So I was there where you see me
In the perfume chiming out in great pealing waves

And before they had time to close once more as each day they do
    in this changing life
I had the time to place my lips
On your glass thighs

— M. B.

A MAN AND WOMAN ABSOLUTELY WHITE

In the depths of the parasol I see the marvelous prostitutes
On the side near the streetlamps their gowns are the color of
    polished wood
They are walking with a great piece of wallpaper
At which one cannot look without that choking feeling about the
    heart of ancient floors in buildings being demolished
Where a slab of marble lies fallen from the fireplace
And a skein of chains is tangled in the mirrors
A great instinct toward combustion rises from the street where
    they walk
Like scorched flowers
Their distant eyes raising a gale of stones
As they sink motionless to the center of the whirlwind
Nothing equals for me the sense of their useless thought
The freshness of the gutters where their little boots bathe the
    shadows of their beaks
The reality of their wrists of fresh cut hay into which they
    disappear
I see their breasts which seize a point out of this profound night
Where the time for lying down and the time for getting up are
    the only precise measures of life
I see their breasts that are stars over waves
Their breasts in which the invisible blue milk cries as ever

— DAVID ANTIN

FREE UNION

My wife whose hair is a brush fire
Whose thoughts are summer lightning
Whose waist is an hourglass
Whose waist is the waist of an otter caught in the teeth of a
tiger
Whose mouth is a bright cockade with the fragrance of a star of
the first magnitude
Whose teeth leave prints like the tracks of white mice over snow
Whose tongue is made out of amber and polished glass
Whose tongue is a stabbed wafer
The tongue of a doll with eyes that open and shut
Whose tongue is incredible stone
My wife whose eyelashes are strokes in the handwriting of a
child
Whose eyebrows are nests of swallows
My wife whose temples are the slate of greenhouse roofs
With steam on the windows
My wife whose shoulders are champagne
Are fountains that curl from the heads of dolphins over the ice
My wife whose wrists are matches
Whose fingers are raffles holding the ace of hearts
Whose fingers are fresh cut hay
My wife with the armpits of martens and beech fruit
And Midsummer Night
That are hedges of privet and nesting places for sea snails
Whose arms are of sea foam and a landlocked sea
And a fusion of wheat and a mill
Whose legs are spindles
In the delicate movements of watches and despair
My wife whose calves are sweet with the sap of elders
Whose feet are carved initials
Keyrings and the feet of steeplejacks who drink
My wife whose neck is fine milled barley
Whose throat contains the Valley of Gold
And encounters in the bed of the maelstrom
My wife whose breasts are of the night

And are undersea molehills
And crucibles of rubies
My wife whose breasts are haunted by the ghosts of dew-
moistened roses
Whose belly is a fan unfolded in the sunlight
Is a giant talon
My wife with the back of a bird in vertical flight
With a back of quicksilver
And bright lights
My wife whose nape is of smooth worn stone and wet chalk
And of a glass slipped through the fingers of someone who has
just drunk
My wife with the thighs of a skiff
That are lustrous and feathered like arrows
Stemmed with the light tailbones of a white peacock
And imperceptible balance
My wife whose rump is sandstone and flax
Whose rump is the back of a swan and the spring
My wife with the sex of an iris
A mine and a platypus
With the sex of an alga and old-fashioned candies
My wife with the sex of a mirror
My wife with eyes full of tears
With eyes that are purple armor and a magnetized needle
With eyes of savannahs
With eyes full of water to drink in prisons
My wife with eyes that are forests forever under the ax
My wife with eyes that are the equal of water and air and earth
and fire

— DAVID ANTIN

WORLD

In the salon of Madame des Ricochets
The mirrors are made of beads of pressed and processed dew
The console is constructed out of an arm among the ivy
And the carpet flows away like waves
In the salon of Madame des Ricochets
Moonlight tea is served in nightjar eggs
The curtains seduce the melting snow
And into this pearliness the piano and its vanishing-point sink in
    a single shape
In the salon of Madame des Ricochets
The lowered lamps beneath the leaves the flickerings
Struggle against the firelight in an anteater fuzz
When Madame des Ricochets rings
The doors burst open to make way for the servants upon their
    see-saws, sliding-ponds, and swings

— M. B.

IN THE EYES OF THE GODS

"Just before midnight down by the waterfront
If you see a disheveled woman coming after you pay no
    attention.
It's the azure. You have nothing to fear from the azure.
There will be a large blonde vase in a tree.
The steeple in the village of shiny melted colors
Will be your landmark. Take your time,
Remember. The brownish geyser flinging its fernlike sprays up
    through the air
Is there to greet you."

                        The envelope sealed on three corners with
                        a fish
Travels now beneath the suburban streetlights
Like a lion-tamer's sign.
                        Meanwhile
The beauty, the victim, the one locally known
As "The Little Mignonette Pyramid"
Was unstitching a cloud for the sake of her own amusement
Resembling a sachet of pity.

                        Later on the white suit of armor
The one responsible for performing various domestic duties as
    well as others
Taking things easier than ever,
The child in her shell, the being who was yet to be . . .
But silence for now.
                        Already a blazing fire in the hearth had
                        enkindled
A thrilling tale of cloaks and daggers
In her heart.

                        Meanwhile, on the bridge, at this very same hour
Just so, the cat-headed dew was swaying.
Nightfall, — and illusions would all be lost.

Now here come the White Fathers returning from their vesper
    ceremony

With the tremendous key suspended above them.
Here come the grizzled heralds; here finally is her letter
Or her lips: and my heart is a cuckoo for God's sake.

But even as she speaks, a wall is all that remains
Flapping in a grave like a yellowed veil or sail.
Eternity is in search of a wristwatch
Just before midnight down by the waterfront.

— M. B.

"THEY TELL ME THAT OVER THERE . . ."

They tell me that over there the beaches are black
From lava gone down to the sea
And unfold at the foot of a huge peak smoking with snow
Beneath a second sun made of wild canaries
What then is this far-off land
Which seems to draw all its light from your life
It trembles so real at the tips of your eyelashes
Gentle to your complexion as some immaterial linen
Just unpacked from the half-opened trunk of the ages
In back of you
Flickering its final sad flames around your ankles
The earth of lost paradise
A darkling glass a mirror of love
And further beyond toward your arms opened wide
Giving proof to the Spring
From which FOLLOWS
The non-existence of evil
All the flowering apple-tree of the sea

— M. B.

CURTAIN CURTAIN

The traveling theatres of the seasons will have played out my life
To my own catcalls
A little pit had been fitted out among the footlights from which
I might hiss
Hands clutching the grillwork I saw against a backdrop of dark
foliage
The heroine nude to the waist
She who committed suicide at the opening of Act One
The play went on inexplicably beneath bright spotlights
The stage slowly inundated in fog
And sometimes I cried out
I smashed the water pitcher I had been given and butterflies flew
out
Rising madly to the chandeliers
Pretending to be a ballet interlude drawn entirely from my own
thoughts
I attempted at once to slash my wrists with fragments of earthen-
ware
But they became countries in which I lost my way
Impossible to retrace the thread of those voyages
I was cut off by the shining loaf of bread of the sun
A character wandered around the room the sole ambulatory
personage
Wearing a mask with my features
Vilely he took the side of the ingenue and the villain
The rumor spread that it had all been settled on beforehand like
May June July August
Suddenly the pit sank down
Plunging through endless tunnels of bouquets held out at
shoulder-height
All wandering around of their own accord I scarcely dared slide
open the door
I had been granted too much freedom at once
Freedom to escape in the sled of my bed
Freedom to call back to life people I miss

The aluminum folding-chairs lined up in front of the ice-cream
    stand
Over which rose a dew-drenched curtain fringed with blood
    turned green
Freedom to drive actual appearances far ahead of me
It was marvelous there beneath the stage against a white
    backdrop appeared in fiery outline my own silhouette pierced
    to the heart by a bullet

— M. B.

GO FOR BROKE
For Benjamin Péret

In the heart of the Indian territory of Oklahoma
There is a man sitting
Who has the eyes of a cat circling a clump of couchgrass

A man encircled
Who sees through his window
The council of lying inflexible divinities
Rising every morning in greater number of fog
Shameful spirits
Spanish style virgins inscribed in a right isosceles triangle

The gasoline billows out over the continents
Like Eleanor's hair
And in his transparent skull
Out of sight
There are watchful armies
There are chants passing under the wing of a lamp
And there is the hope of traveling so fast
That the leaves and the lights will fuse on the surface of the
    glass

At the crossing of the nomad routes
There is a man they have drawn a circle around
Like a chicken

Buried alive in the reflection of the blue cloths
Piled up to the top of his closet

A man with his head wrapped in the stockings of the setting sun
And the hands of trunk fish

This country is like a huge nightclub
With its women from the ends of the earth
Whose shoulders roll the galleys of all seas
The American agencies have not forgotten to provide for these
    Indian chiefs
On these well pitted lands

Who are no longer free to move
Beyond the limits of the treaties of war

The futile wealth
The thousand eyelids of the sleeping water

The agent passes each month
Places his hat on the bed covered with a veil of arrows
And from his sealskin bag
Spreads the latest manufacturers' catalogues
Turned by the hand that opened and closed them when we were
   children

One time
One particular time
There was an automobile catalogue
Showing a wedding limousine
With fins extending ten yards
For the train
The car of a great painter
Cut into a prism
A governor's car
Like a sea urchin whose every spine was a flame thrower

But there was one
Fast
Black
Car
Crowned with mother-of-pearl eagles
Inscribed in all of its angles with rinceaux of salon fireplaces
Like waves
A carriage that could only be moved by lightning
Like the one in which the princess Acanthe wanders with shut
   eyes
A giant sedan chair of gray snails
And tongues of fire
Like those appearing at fatal hours in the garden of the tower of
   St. Jacques
A fast fish trapped in algae
Trying to free itself with pulsations of its tail
A great state or funeral limousine
For the last parade of a sainted emperor to come

Out of fantasy
That would outmode all life

His finger pointed without hesitation to the glazed image
And from then on
The triton crested man
Comes every evening
In a storm of pearls
To deck the bed of the corn goddess

I shall preserve for poetical history
The name of this dispossessed chief who is somewhat ours
Of this lone man superbly driven in his new machine
Flying the wind as his flag

He is called
He carries
The flamboyant name of Go-for-Broke
In life and death go running
Run the two rabbits together
Run your luck that is a volley of bells of celebration and alarm
Run the creatures of your dreams till they collapse spewing on
    their white collars
Run the ring without the finger
Run the head of the avalanche

— DAVID ANTIN

These no-man's-lands and the moon where I wander out-
run by the shadow tied down to the house of my heart

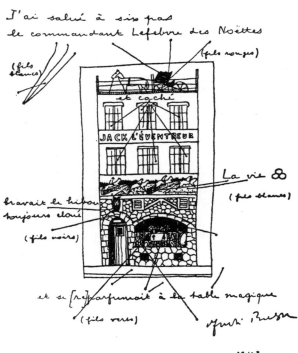

POEM-OBJECT

I salute from a distance of six steps away
Major Lefebre des Noëttes
(white lines)   (red lines)
                from concealment

                            Life
                            (white lines)
braving the owl
fixed forever
(black lines)
then refreshing oneself once more at the magic table
(green lines)

— M. B.

This work is a free improvisation around the decor of Jack Dele-
hanty's bar, located a few blocks from the Greenwich Village
apartment which Breton occupied for a time while in exile dur-
ing the war. Much of the decor alluded to here still exists, owls
and all. [Ed. note.]

ON THE ROAD TO SAN ROMANO

Poetry is made in bed like love
Its unmade sheets are the dawn of things
Poetry is made in a forest`

She has the space which she needs
Not this one but the other
    Governed by the hawk's eye
    The dew on the spindle
    The memory of a moist bottle of Traminer on a silver platter
    A tall rod of tourmaline over the sea
    A road of mental adventure
    Which climbs abruptly
    One pause and it's instantly overgrown

Don't shout that from the roof tops
It's not fitting to leave the doors open
Or go around calling for witnesses

    The shoals of fishes the hedges of small birds
    The rails at the approach to the great station
    The glow of two river banks
    The furrows on a loaf of bread
    Bubbles in a brook
    The days of the calendar
    Hog-wart

The act of love and the act of poetry
Are incompatible
With reading newspapers at the top of one's voice

    The way the sunlight falls
    The livid glitter which binds the ax-strokes of the
        woodcutter
    The string of a kite in the shape of a heart or a fish-trap
    The steady waving of the beaver's tail
    The perseverance of lightning
    The flinging down of sweets from the top of an old staircase
    An avalanche

The room of marvels
No gentlemen not the forbidden chamber
Nor the fumes of the barracks room on Sunday evenings

    The figure of the dance executed transparently above the
        marshes
    The body of a woman outlined by throwing knives
    The lucent rings of smoke
    The curls of your hair
    The twisting of a sponge from the Philippines
    The snakelike coils of coral
    The ivy's slitherings into the ruins
    She has all of time ahead of her

The embrace of poetry like the embrace of the naked body
Protects while it lasts
Against all access by the misery of the world

                    — CHARLES SIMIC and M. B.

LOUIS ARAGON

1897-

O NE OF THE MOST ACTIVE OF THE PARTICIPANTS in Surrealism's formative years, co-founder in 1919 with Soupault and André Breton of the antiliterary periodical *Littérature*, Aragon was also one of the first to explore the antitechniques of automatic writing, as texts finally published in 1969 indicate.[1]

Aragon brought to Surrealism a predilection for what he called "provocation," a taste formed during his association with Dada, to which he came at the bidding of Breton, a fellow military medic during the war. Two characteristic poetic provocations of the period (poems for which description will perhaps serve as quotation) are "Persiennes" ("Venetian Blinds"), consisting of the title repeated twenty times, arranged in several rows, and followed by a question mark; "Suicide," consisting of the alphabet in its ordinary sequence, broken up into five lines. Even during this time, when the poet in a Dada manifesto declared, "All that is not me is incomprehensible,"[2] this taste for the arbitrary had positive and Surrealist overtones. Echoing Rimbaud's assertion that "I alone hold the key to this savage sideshow," Aragon announced in the collection of his Dada period writings, which includes the two poems described above, *Le Mouvement perpétuel* (*Perpetual Motion*, 1925),[3] "I hold the key/ The bolt begins to twist like a tongue." The theme of psychic truth as the ultimate determinant for all things, attaining the proportions of the radical subjectivism which runs throughout Surrealism, reappears in his first collection of poems written during the Surrealist period, *La Grande Gaîté* (*The Grand Gaiety*, 1929),[4]

Aragon insisting in one poem, "The hand that dominates is *my* hand." Images of keys appear throughout the poet's early work, in a sense unlocking his approach to poetry.

The poetry is characterized by a refusal to be sentimental (even in love poems — since for this poet, as for most Surrealists, there is a sense that feeling is too real to require that); a directness of diction; and an angrily destructive attitude towards the conventionally accepted bulwarks of bourgeois — or, indeed, *any* — society. At this point the poet expressed outright contempt for the regimentations of Soviet Communism, referring in the second issue of *La Révolution Surréaliste* (1925) to "moronic Moscow," and replying to an angry response to his performance:

> You have chosen to isolate as an attack a phrase which bears witness to my lack of enthusiasm for the Bolshevik government, and with it for all Communism. . . . This is because I have always placed, and place today, the spirit of revolt far above any politics. . . . The Russian Revolution? . . . On the level of ideas, it is at best a vague ministerial crisis . . . it is only by a real abuse of language that this latter activity can be characterized as revolutionary.

One of the most active Surrealist theorists, Aragon's own informal "manifesto" of Surrealist practice is entitled (again with irony toward previous stylistic standards), *Traité du style* (*Treatise on Style*, 1928).[5] Aragon's more memorable statements on the movement occur, characteristically enough, in his novel, *Le Paysan de Paris* (*The Parisian Peasant*, 1926),[6] written shortly before *Nadja*, Breton's own novelistic attempt to localize the extraordinary through a recounting of chance encounters in the public streets of Paris. Surrealism is characteristically defined as "a vice, identical to the unreasonable and passionate employment of the stunning poetic image, both for itself and for what it brings along with it, in the realm of the representation of unforeseen disturbances and metamorphoses: because each image with a single gesture forces you to revise the entire Universe." Aragon also defines Surrealism as "the concrete form of disorder." In a 1930 essay on painting, Aragon made perhaps his most positively optimistic interpretation of the Surrealist concern for the extraordinary, declaring that "the marvelous is born of the refusal of one reality, yet also of the development of a new relationship, of a brand new reality which this refusal has liberated."[7]

Also in 1930, partly at the urging of Elsa Triolet — Mayakovsky's sister-in-law and the poet's future wife, as well as the subject of many later volumes of his poetry — Aragon attended the International Congress of Revolutionary Writers at Kharkov. Afterward, he published in the Soviet-controlled *Littérature de la Révolution Mondiale* (*Literature of the World Revolution*) his hortatory, "agitprop"-style poem satirizing the French rich and glorifying the Soviet regime, *Front rouge* (*Red Front*, 1930).[8] Attacked in the pamphlet *Misère de la poésie* (*The Misery of Poetry*, 1932),[9] by Breton, who saw in the poem a surrender of the imagination to the immediate imperatives of social propaganda, Aragon withdrew from the movement.

Except for political propaganda, Aragon wrote little further verse until World War II, in which he actively participated: first in 1940 as a combatant in the doomed French forces, then again as a Resistance worker. His wartime and postwar poems regain a certain measure of the earlier force, mainly by means of a delicately melancholy music harking back to the more lyrical side of Apollinaire, and a mythical imagery recalling the French poets of the distant past. Often the verse is composed in that most tradition-laden of all French meters, the alexandrine.

Aragon's later extrapoetic activity included the drafting of an essay on Soviet-oriented art, *Pour un réalisme Socialiste* (*Toward a Socialist Realism*, 1935)[10] and the initiation of a series of "Socialist Realist" novels under the (Surrealistically speaking) somewhat presumptuous general title, *Le Monde réel* — *The Real World*. In 1961 his historical novel *La Semaine sainte* (*Holy Week*)[11] became an international best seller. He continued his work within Party limits, remarking with respect to his Surrealist past, "I have always defended the skies of my youth."

OTHER PRINCIPAL WORKS

Short novels: *Les Aventures de Télémaque* (N.R.F., 1922; reissued 1966); *Le Con d'Irène* (1928, privately printed; reissued as *Irène* by L'Or du Temps in 1968, and confiscated). Plays: *Le Libertinage* (N.R.F., 1924; one play from this work, "L'Armoire à glace un beau soir" tr. by Michael Benedikt as *The Mirror Wardrobe One Fine Evening* in *Modern French Theatre: The Avant-Garde, Dada, and Surrealism* [Dutton, 1964]). Autobiographical: *J'abats mon jeu* (Les Editeurs Français Réunis, 1959); *Entretiens avec Francis Crémieux* (N.R.F., 1964). Poems: *Persécuté persécuteur* (Ed. Surréalistes, 1931); *Le Crève-coeur* (N.R.F., 1941); *Les Yeux d'Elsa* (Ed. de la Maison Française and Cahiers du Rhône, 1942; reissued by Seghers, 1957); *La Diane française* (Seghers, 1950); *Elsa* (N.R.F., 1959). Selected writings: *Aragon*, "Poètes d'aujourd'hui" #159 (Seghers).

SAFETY LOCK

My word
Hand caught in the door
Stuck tight old boy stuck tight
In other words
Or
The password please
Many thanks
Now I hold the key
The bolt begins to twist like a tongue
Therefore

— **M. B.**

DEFINITIVE DECLARATION

Let's have a hole in my poor
Pocket
But my dearest darling what about your big bunch
Of keys on their ring
Just let that vampire fall
Into the gutter the mud the dung
Too bad if the mechanical
Sweepers
Pass by scooping it all up in their passée
Skirts
If the upright uptight cops get screwed up and trip
Face down on their snouts
Feet caught in the keyring
All for the sake of the security of the aforementioned
Keys
Too bad if all those great matron ladies with their disapproving
Air
Bolt up their metaphysical doors
When I go by
Because
I love only you

— M. B.

THE BROTHERS LACÔTE
For Malcolm Cowley

The tidal wave entered the room
Where the entire little family was assembled
He said Greetings to one and all
And carried off the mother in the cupboard
The youngest son began to shout very loudly
He sang him a romance from his own home country
Telling of the edge of the forest
Of the very edge of the forest
Like that
The father said Kindly consider for just one moment
But the wave would not permit himself to be polluted
He put a little salty water in the mouth of that wretched
Progenitor
And the worthy soul passed away
God keep his soul
Then it was time for the daughters
In size places
The first on her knees
The next on her two cheeks
The third the third
Like the beasts believe me
The fourth likewise
The fifth I shudder in horror
My pen halts
And refuses to describe such abominations
Lord lord will you be less merciful than he
Oh I forgot the chicken in the pot
Was eaten in her turn
By the wave the mean tidal wave

— M. B.

DRINKING SONG

If glassware were really glassware
And not balloons
Floating across the night toward painted lips
Would hands still turn out to be birds

Hands which close around alcohol
Hands which cup the noxiousness and gas
Sheep which graze on the fields of the tablecloth
Have no fear of doves because
Of their whiteness
What a laugh

Doves you are not only a challenge
To the captive reconnaissance balloon which resembles me
Just like a brother but
Also to the lead soldiers down on the plain

Look look how the hands I adore
In the morning when the neon signs
Rival the very dawn looking as if
They might be capable of giving the very backbones of sheep a
    fatal twisting
Crack vertebrae!
Oho! Aha! that tinkling silver-plating was false
The teaspoons are made of lead just like those bullets

— M. B.

TERCETS

A bunch of keys the keys to such beautifully old-fashioned
   fantastic creatures
Hummed to themselves jingling
A song of the good old days

You poor maniac you haven't yet seen the ostrich
Who's getting herself all set once again to eat you up
Poor maníac

She's been preening with brilliantine
Her birdy fuzz
Yes with brilliantine

And now she puts on a really prepossessing look
Sharp eye
Foot planted like an educated person

Who would ever guess that in her own native land
Nobody paid the least attention to her
For her the Salons were completely pointless

But since she's been sleeping with Mr. Umbrella
People rush over and throw their arms around her neck
She smiles and simply oozes expensiveness

The umbrella twirls his moustache
And makes allusions to Josephine de Beauharnais
As a way of looking down his nose beak or handle

In some previous life
He would have fantasized endlessly about being Pasha of Egypt
Now all he wants to know is if

In such a situation
His harem would have consisted of houris or mummies
Since he's not too "up" about Egypt

— M. B.

POP TUNE

Cloud
A white horse stands up
And that's the small hotel at dawn where he who is always first-
    come-first-served awakes in palatial comfort
Are you going to spend your entire life in this same world
Half dead
Half asleep
Haven't you had enough of commonplaces yet
People actually look at you without laughter
They have glass eyes
You pass them by you waste your time you pass away and go
    away
You count up to a hundred during which you cheat to kill an
    extra ten seconds
You hold up your hand suddenly to volunteer for death
Fear not
Some day
There will be just one day left and then just one day more after
    that
Then that will be that
No more need to look at men nor their companion animals their
    Good Lord provides
And that they make love to now and then
No more need to go on speaking to yourself out loud at night in
    order to drown out
The heating-unit's lament
No need to lift my own eyelids
Nor to fling my blood around like some discus
Nor to breathe despite my disinclination to
Yet despite this I don't want to die
In low tones the bell of my heart sings out its ancient hope
That music I know it so well but the words
Just what were those words saying
"Idiot"

— M. B.

156

THE BEGINNINGS OF THE FUGITIVE

I abandoned hope next to a clockwork
As the ax chopped off the last minute
A large number of people had gathered for the execution
The children perching on shoulders
Made gestures of joy and fear

In another street at the seashore
The earth was turning in the sea air
A girl singing a nerve-wracking hit tune
Revealed a bit of her softer-than-life skin
There was hard killing everywhere
Horses escaping into elevators
Laughed like human people
It was a country of wounds where devouring winds blew
Jangled nerves were so widespread
That the trees shattered in the hands of men
Like so many matches
People left their homes no longer caring
How can you wear last night's clothes
Put your pianos on the sidewalk while waiting for rain
Wouldn't it be fantastic to die on a day like today
The city you live in is moving off
So tiny in your memory
Hand me the binoculars so that I can take one last look
At the laundry drying in the windows
Paradise everything's scattered Now is the time
When no one can speak the name of whoever he's touching
At least until the evening scent which is foreign to me
Like Armenian paper*
Or a new song that everyone knows already
Nothing binds me here not even the future
The artillery shell that could contain me hasn't yet been born
How small the sky can be at the end of a day
Its horizons are false its doors are boarded up

* Treated papers cut into thin strips which, when burnt, produce an incense
odor [Ed. note].

The moon truly believes that the dogs will bite it
I drive out the stars with my hand
Nocturnal flies don't pounce upon my heart
You can always shout Eyes Front! to me
Captains of habit and night
I break loose indefinitely under the hat of the infinite
Don't bother waiting for me at my illusory hang-outs

— JOACHIM NEUGROSCHEL

HOMELESS

This morning the rose wallpaper in my hotel room was replaced
By a frog paper   Though
No one came in except for
A memory wearing a very cool pure-white dress

Those batrachians have formed a league against
The luminous specter to drive it out of my mind
We no longer get on well   What an awful racket
Even the Toad Telephone that cro
Aks
My pencil hiding   However

I recall the deserted road between the strange gardens
Being demolished
No one would recognize the old Parisian neighborhood
White sphinxes have come cropping up from the moss toward
    the sky
Next in the alley
Like the postman's door-to-door race
Like resumptions of breathing in sobs
At our feet the Seine looked like
An overturned teapot

What looked like cherries on the hat
What looked like love in the eyes
Her two hands were flame and snow
And when she had poured the alcohol of the conflagration
On my mouth
I greeted her by name   Provocation
Let the wall marshes keep quiet
Mute lead make-believe bullrushes
No one would recognize this Parisian neighborhood
She said to me from the middle of her whiteness
This dress is thin enough why draw it
Aside   Can't you
Love me like this
Idol O true idol I rendered unto you

The requisite worship   I spunked your dress
One summer evening way way back
I'm probably addicted like no one else
To these devastations of my love
There is I'm sure of it a sexual abyss
Between decent folks and myself

All my life
I've gravely scattered my useless gyzm
Like a fire lit on board a boatless sea
Some sign in the stars may
Have occasionally responded to my squandered kisses
I'll never know   I retain only
Two or three convulsive images
Of women that I've loved mortally
Blundering castaway your wealth resides
In some scraps of furbelows considered worthless
Yet you still prefer these vacant lots
To happiness that eats its fill inside houses middle-
Classly lived in
You are nothing if not depraved

— JOACHIM NEUGROSCHEL

SPECIAL PREFERENCE

Over in the corner where the bishops sit stuffing themselves
The lawyers the Generals
Someone has written in red letters
OYSTER-BAR
Is that supposed to be some kind of a complex allusion

Everyone points out to me how pitiful all this is
This sort of joke
And also the sense of it seems all screwed up generally
And as for having anything to do with poetry
Well you know just what to think

But as for me I haven't finished with casting shadowy aspersions
On everything relating to the constabulary or the maul-it-ary
And above all with curetting curés with oyster-spoons
My appetite for iambics is not sufficient
For me to ask forgiveness with a bangety bang-bang-bang

But right here even if it is hard to tell from whence she comes
From comes she whence nonetheless Nonetheless
It delights me to oppose to those punchworthy worthies
A very lovely and completely nude woman
So very totally nude I can hardly believe my own eyes

Although it may possibly be the thousandth time
This apparition has appeared before my eyes
My eyes fall out flat at her feet
Her most humble servant

—— M. B.

TOO BAD FOR ME

Just like the heart that breaks at the onset of absence
the pit gas will blow up in Paris
with a long bang of shattered luxury
the children will stare at the last lay in the whorehouse
exploding like a grenade
then they'll play revolutionary and philosophical hopscotch
in which SKY will read RED FLAG
and EARTH EARTH as if nothing had happened

The children won't know a word of the language you use
to ask directions in the street
Monsieur will make them laugh and the Third Person
that domestic myth answering the doorbells
will astonish the memory as much as electric automobiles do
People will recall the everyday world
only because of those color prints of hunting scenes with
ladies in blue and pink marveling at a fox held up by a viscount
and the dead stag at the natural feet of the footman
in an emporium on rue de la Gaîeté

Just like the heart that breaks at the onset of absence
With no respect for love with no respect for fruit or flowers
the Revolution will trace somewhere on the window pane
the flash of diamond that will separate tomorrow from the day
   after
There'll be marvelous fringe
like the ruby of the lips on the lightning wound of life
There'll be clusters of disaster at the price
of the matchless conflagration
and if the eye of the dying caught in the hinge of the ancient
   universe
glimpses the springtime beyond the rifle shooting
let it regret that it won't live long enough with its body and its
   love
let it really feel regret while the bayonet of destiny
pierces it at the speed of light
The children will learn the incomprehensible words of history

162

The children will jeer at the Hotel Ritz and the fears of hunger
The children will sing age-old ballads   Ce n'est
que votre main
Madame*
They'll eenie-meenie-minie-mo whoever is "it" with secularized
    words
Clairvaux la Petite Roquette
la Santé le Cherche-Midi
Saint-Lazare
la Conciergerie

They'll eenie-meenie-minie-mo whoever is "it" with the name of
    god
They'll eenie-meenie-minie-mo whoever is "it" with pieces of
    silver and gold
They'll play pool with diamonds
with the heads of women who sold themselves for diamonds
They'll play with hoops made of the wheels
that crush today's poets
They'll play leapfrog over the rivers of tears
They'll play as we weep
when the heart that breaks at the offset of absence
no longer manages to hold back the rivers of tears over which
the future plays a horrible leapfrog

— JOACHIM NEUGROSCHEL

* "It's your hand and your hand alone, Madame. . . ." [Ed. note].

ONCE AND FOR ALL

What is it all language is attempting definitively to say?
— Sow white stones for the birds to peck at.
What frightens you worse than anything else in the world?
— A few slow-moving creatures which creep around after midnight beneath the trees of light; also around the buses.
Given the choice, what would you have preferred to be more than anything else in the world?
— The past, the present, and the future.
How would you describe virtue?
— A hammock of delight among the loftiest limbs of the forest.
What about bravery?
— Milk-splatters in my souvenir baptismal cup.
Honor?
— A prepaid round-trip ticket for a vacation in Monte Carlo.
What are your feelings regarding nature?
— Above my cradle occasionally a melancholy greyhound would come sniffing about, a creature as sad as precious stones sunken somewhere in the sea. Flickering flames fluttered above my forehead together with many necklaces made out of flowering marguerites. Bowing ladies dipped before the dwindling daylight. And one wandering evening not a soul was left beside the waters.
What then is love?
— A gold ring around the clouds.
What's death?
— A small fortress located upon a mountaintop . . .
.   .   .   .
— . . . a palace vegetation has overrun, an ice cube on some major city street, a peek in the direction of paradise.
— Oh, who was asking you, anyway!
Hmmm . . .

— M. B.

"I'LL REINVENT THE ROSE FOR YOU . . ."

I'll reinvent the rose for you
For you who are that rose which cannot be described
These few words at least in the order proper to her ritual
That rose which only words distant from roses can describe
The way it is with the ecstatic cry and the terrible sadness which
   it translates
From the stars of pleasure above love's deep abyss

I will reinvent for you the rose of adoring fingers
Which create a nave as they interlace but whose petals then
   suddenly fall away
I will reinvent for you the rose beneath the balconies
Of lovers whose only beds are their arms

The rose at the heart of sculpted stone figures dead without
   benefit of confession
The rose of a peasant blown to bits by a landmine in his field
The scarlet scent of a letter which has been "discovered"
In which nothing's addressed to me neither the insult nor the
   compliment

Some rendezvous to which no one has come

An entire army in flight on a very windy day

A maternal footstep before prison-gates

A man's song at siesta-time beneath the olive-trees

A cockfight in a mist-enshrouded countryside
The rose of a soldier cut off from his own home country

I'll reinvent for you my rose as many roses
As there are diamonds in the waters of the seas
As there are past centuries adrift aloft in the dust of earth's
   atmosphere
As there are dreams in just one childish head

As there can be reflections in one tear

— M. B.

DAWN

Who would ever have thought without this love from you
    Without this torment without this star
Like a black garnet at a woman's ear
    That there once was this fool in Granada
Without you I'd have been only this juggler of words
    This ball of sequins and fashions
A pebble the demon's feet kicked loose
    The toy of monsters and the world
My head was open to the wind's flights
    Like a house put up for sale
Inside me nothing but echo's dice rolling
    Educating me with their odds
When you appeared to me one night do you remember
    When our adventure started
You who taught me the meaning the taste of life
    Who returned sight to my empty eyes
You who turned my steps into the road of other men
    Who raised me from my ruins
Thanks to whom I have spent this time in wonder
    Not deaf to things
Thanks to whom I have taken my share of the burden
    That other men shoulder
In their hell my place and my pain and my fate
    And I have at least seen the breaking dawn

— LOU LIPSITZ and JEAN GILLOU

PAUL ELUARD

1895-1952

O NE OF THE MOST PRODUCTIVE of Surrealism's poets, Eluard was also exceptional for the duration of his association with the formal movement, in which he was one of Breton's closest associates. Eluard's first work possesses a quality evoked by the title of one of his collections, *Facile*[1] — reflecting as it does, in the best sense, a certain "facility." For all its magical, lyrical thrust, the work's language is simple and transparent: or, to use another word of which the poet was fond, "pure." Eluard's initial subject matter foreshadows this respect for archetypal essentials, his early titles suggesting a virtual revision of Genesis. They include *Le Devoir et l'inquiétude (Duty and Disturbance*, 1917),[2] *Poèmes pour la paix (Poems for Peace*, 1918),[3] *Les Animaux et leurs hommes, les hommes et leurs animaux (Animals and Their Men, Men and Their Animals*, 1920),[4] *Les Nécessités de la vie et les conséquences des rêves (The Necessities of Life and the Consequences of Dreams*, 1921),[5] *Répétitions (Repetitions*, 1922)[6] and *Mourir de ne pas mourir (Dying of Not Dying*, 1924).[7] Little influence of Dada appears in the poet's early volumes; from the outset, the language, tone, and intention are close to the mature work, which is usually constructive rather than nihilistic, inclusive of the reader of "good will" (an important value for Eluard) rather than exclusive.

Eluard's association with Surrealism began in 1920. Through his journal *Proverbe* he met André Breton, participating with the latter in Dada. This association seems almost fated: previously, Eluard had just missed encountering Breton at the 1918 première of Apollinaire's play *Couleur du temps* — a coincidence described in Breton's novel *Nadja* as contributing to the development of Surrealist optimism about the beneficial power of chance or hazard. It is curious, too, that during World War I Eluard served in the same branch of service — the Medical Corps — in which Breton and Aragon had also been active. He joined the Surrealist group immediately upon returning from a worldwide tour in 1924.

Eluard's writings as a Surrealist focus on a theme only vaguely suggested theretofore. The central motif of his mature work is the ability of Woman to act as the "Philosopher's Stone" — the reality-transforming, quasi-alchemical agent for which Surrealism is partly a quest. Woman is seen as Man's most intimate yet most mysterious equal, capable of revealing the best nature of individual men to themselves, as well as the best nature of humankind to itself. The bed of lovers is seen as the most likely locus of freedom on earth at present; one of the most frequent and striking images in this poetry is that of a road, running from the bedside and into the world. This too revises a Genesis myth: reversing the legend in which Woman is seen as only deriving from the side of Man, the beloved in Eluard is seen as the touchstone for the transformation of her lover, and also as a primary force for a change in the world beyond the bed.

Eluard's power as a love poet is reinforced by a technical approach which places great faith in the power of sight. As he suggests with his title, *Les Yeux fertiles* (*Fertile Eyes*, 1936),[8] there is or can be a productive mingling of what one desires to see, and what one "realistically" sees; the power of vision can influence or even improvise the reality it beholds in a process of creation in which what is seen and the "seer" combine. In turn, this is regarded as a process in which reader and poet can collaborate. Far from constituting what the Anglo-American "New Critics" were calling the "pathetic fallacy" during the years when Eluard was at the peak of his powers, any "confusion" is conscious and courted, the pleasure and delight of sight enabling transcendence of the all too earthly "capital of sadness," or *Capitale de la douleur*, as a work published in 1926 terms it.[9] The poet sums up this cultivation of a better vision than convention dictates in *Donner à voir* (*To Bring into View*, 1939),[10] a collection including, in addition to poetry, essays on Picasso and de Chirico, and also Max Ernst, whose collages the poet occasionally wrote poems to "illustrate." Here the poet confesses:

> I became a slave to the pure facility of sight, slave to my unknown and virgin eyes, innocent of both the world and of themselves. Tranquil power, I suppressed the visible and the invisible . . . indestructible, I was not blind. . . . When there is a total fusion of the real image and the hallucination it has provoked, no misunderstanding is possible. The resemblance between two objects comes as much from the subjective element contributing to establish it as from the objective relationship which exists between them. The poet is the supremely hallucinated man, the one who will establish resemblances consciously between the most dissimilar objects.

Eluard's commitment to a subjective idealism was absolute in several areas. Although by 1926 an enthusiastic Marxist, he withdrew from the Communist party a few years later, only to declare readherence in 1938, after he broke with Breton over the latter's anti-Stalinist position. His poetry directly following this event is frequently propagandistic, though remaining in distant touch with the lyricism of his earlier approach.

During World War II Eluard's poetry gained the acceptance of a worldwide audience. Still, that the poet intended to combine early and late interests, rather than (as in the case of Aragon, who also became a Communist in the 1930's) to submit to politically imposed ideals of "social realism," is made clear by the final work, in which the poet reasserts his faith in the all-embracing purity of his own idealism, dictated solely by the beloved.

OTHER PRINCIPAL WORKS

Collections of Poems: *Les Dessous d'une vie ou la pyramide humaine* (Cahiers du Sud, 1926); *L'Amour, la poésie* (N.R.F., 1929); *A toute épreuve* (Ed. Surréalistes, 1930); *La Vie immédiate* (Les Cahiers Libres, 1932); *La Rose publique* (N.R.F., 1934); *Nuits* partagées (G.L.M., 1935); *Les Mains libres* (1937); *Cours naturel* (Sagittaire, 1938); *Chanson complète* (N.R.F., 1939); *Poésie et vérité* (Ed. Baconnière, 1943); *Le Lit la table* (Trois Collines, 1944); *Au Rendez-vous allemand: 1942–1945* (Ed. du Minuit, 1944; reissued by N.R.F., 1945); *Le Dur désir de durer* (Bordas, 1946); *Corps mémorable* (Seghers, 1948); *Premiers poèmes: 1913–1921* (Mermod, 1948); *Poèmes politiques* (N.R.F., 1948); *Une Leçon de morale* (N.R.F., 1949); *Le Phénix* (Seghers, 1951). Principal collected volumes of poetry: *Oeuvres complètes*, Vols. I and II (N.R.F., 1968). Principal selected volume: *Choix de poèmes* (N.R.F., 1951). See also *Première Anthologie vivante de la poésie du passé*, Vols. 1 and 2 (an anthology of traditional French verse edited by the poet: Seghers, 1951); *Les Sentiers et les routes de la poésie* (five 1949 radio broadcasts: N.R.F., 1968). Other principle works, in collaboration (prose): *152 Proverbes mis au goût du jour* (with Benjamin Péret, Ed. Surréalistes, 1925); *L'Immaculée Conception* (with André Breton, Ed. Surréalistes, 1930); *Notes sur la poésie* (with Breton, G.L.M., 1938); *Dictionnaire abrégé du Surréalisme* (with Breton, Beaux-Arts, 1938); *Ralentir travaux* (with Breton and René Char, Ed. Surréalistes, 1930). Selected writings: *Eluard*, "Poètes d'aujourd'hui" No. 1 (Seghers); *Eluard: Selected Writings*, tr. by Lloyd Alexander (New Directions, 1948).

HEN

Oh yes, that the hen lays, befits;
Hen with its ripe fruit,
Hen with our profits.

— M. B.

PIG

Sun on its back, sun on its stomach
Head heavy and fixed
Like an artillery installation
The pig will function.

— M. B.

PAW

At night the cat goes out to cry out
Through the open air, through the night, the cat does cry out
And, from his human height, sadly, a man hears that cry.

— M. B.

WETNESS

The stone bounces off the water,
Where smoke can't penetrate.
The water, like some skin
Impervious to injury,
Is caressed by man and fish.

Trembling like a bow-string,
The fish, when caught by man,
Dies, unable to swallow
The light and air of this planet.

Still, man goes down into the depths
After the fish
Or the austere isolation
Of the water, pliant yet shut.

— M. B.

FEATHERS

Man would like to fly off
In a flurrying of wings
Overhead, the wind runs crying
Along the edge of a wing.

But the mother wasn't there
When this nest flew off,
But the sky beat down on this wing
When this nest flew off.

And, despair of the earth,
Man lies down outstretched among his words,
Beside the dead branches
In the old eggshells.

— M. B.

THE BELOVED

She is standing on my eyelids
And her hair is inside mine,
She is the shape of my hand,
She is the color of my eyes,
She is surrounded by my shadows
Like a rock by the sky.

Her eyes always opened
She never lets me sleep
Her dreams in broad daylight
Make sunlight evaporate,
Make me laugh, cry and laugh,
Speak without a thing to say.

— M. B.

ECSTASY

Before this feminine landscape I feel
As if I were a child standing before a fireplace
Full of delight with my eyes full of tears
Facing this landscape toward which everything in me moves
Where mirrors cloud over then become clear
Reflecting two nude bodies like season linked to season

I have so many excellent reasons to lose track of myself
On this pathless earth beneath this horizonless sky
Beautiful keys of staring eyes keys daughters ever descending
    from themselves
Before this landscape where in my hand I can capture an entire
    nature

Before this fire this very first fire
Sole good reason Mistress
Guiding star on which we are fixed
And across the earth and beneath the sky and beyond my heart
    and within it
A second flower and the very first green leaf
To be sheltered by the sea with its wings
And the sun shining down in the distance and all distance being
    generated just from us

Before this feminine landscape I feel
As if I were some green branch in a fire

— **M. B.**

TO LIVE HERE

I lit a fire, the blue sky having abandoned me,
A fire for a friend
A fire for a way to enter the winter darkness
A fire for an enhanced existence.

I fed to it what the days had fed to me:
Forests, foliage, wheatfields and vines,
Nests with their birds, houses with their keys,
Insects, flowers, furriness and feasts.

Once, I lived alone with the sounds of crackling flames,
Alone with the odor of their temperature;
I was like a boat slipping across impenetrable waters,
Like the dead I lived isolate with one single element.

— M. B.

FOR PABLO PICASSO

I

A good day's work I just met someone I can't forget
And will never be able to forget
And Women in Flight whose eyes
Made me two hedges a corridor of honor
Wrapped themselves up shyly in their smiles

A good day's work I went to see my carefree friends
The men didn't weigh too much
One who went by
His shadow changed into a mouse
And scampered away down a drainpipe

I've seen the sky an immensity
The lovely looks of men underprivileged in everything
Distant deserted shores

A good day's work starting out with depression
With deep shadows beneath dark trees
But which when dipped suddenly into dawn
Entered my heart by surprise.

II

Show me this man so gentle and eternal
Who said that fingertips can make the earth rise
And the knotting of the rainbow the coiling of the serpent
The mirror of flesh in which a child is pearled
And these calm hands going their way
Bare obedient and shaping all space
But heavily burdened with desires and imaginings
One hand following the next hand two hands on the same clock

Show me the sky cloud-laden
Reiterating the world hidden within my eyelids
Show me the whole sky with one star

I see the world lucidly without dazzlement
Mysterious stones phantom grasses
These great swallows of water these colossal blocks of amber
The play of dying ashes and embers
The solemn geography of human limits

Show me also the blackened bouquet
The drawn-back hair the lost eyes
Of these pure dark girls in flight at this moment but who are
    elsewhere at my will
Proud doors in this summer's wall
Curious vases without liquid but full of virtue
Uselessly made for simple rapports
Show me these secrets that unite their temples
To these absent palaces that make the earth rise.

— M. B.

WE ARE

You see the evening fire emerging from its shell
And you see the forest submerged in its dew and cool

You see the naked field at the flanks of a sky that cannot keep up
Snow high as the sea
And the sea sailing high in the sky

Impeccable stones pleasant woods vaguely veiled assistances
You see cities tinted with melancholy
Decorated with sidewalks crowded with I beg your pardons
A square where solitude has its smiling statue
And love its single house

You see animals
Such cleverly calculating counterparts with each species sacrificed
    to each
Innocent brothers with shadows confused
In a desert of blood

You see a charming child when he plays when he laughs
He is even smaller
Than the small bird far out at the tips of the furthermost twigs

You see a landscape flavored with oil and water
From which rock is exiled where the earth abandons
Her greenness to the summer which covers her from head to foot
    in fruits

Women stepping down from their ancient mirror
Bring you their youth and their faith with their own
And one her lucidity the sail which transports you
Secretly lets you see this world without you

Our life is the life all beings will live with

Animals my true gold standards
Fields my glorious adventures
Useful grasses sensitive cities
Humans will enter your head

Men from beneath beatings tears and sweat
But who will harvest the dreams they have cultivated

I see men true sensitive excellent and useful
Throwing down a burden thinner than death
To sleep with joy in the sound of the sunlight.

— M. B.

YOU ARISE . . .

You arise the water unfolds
You lie back down the water expands

You are water diverted from its abysses
You are the earth which takes root
And upon which everything will be built

You blow bubbles of silence in the deserts of noise
You sing hymns to the night stroking the rainbow's strings
You are everywhere at once you prophesy the end of highways

You sacrifice all time
To the eternal youth of the demanding flame
Which veils nature even while reproducing it

Woman you insert in the world a body always like
Your own

You are Resemblance

— M. B.

179

OUR MOVEMENTS

We live in the oblivion of our metamorphoses
Daytime is very lazy but night keeps busy all the time
Nighttime shakes the midday sieve of air until it sifts down and
  disappears
Nightfall lets no dust fall on us

Still this echo thundering around us all day long
This echo external to our hours of embracing or anguish
This too sudden fusion of sensitive
And insipid realities in reality its two suns are separate

Are we close to or far from our consciousnesses
Where are our boundaries our roots our true aims

But always this endless pleasure in our metamorphoses!
Skeletons coming to life in collapsed decaying walls
Rendezvous arranged with inanimate objects
With clever flesh and with the blindmen of great vision

Appointments are scheduled by the full face with the silhouette
By suffering with good health in broad daylight
By the forest with the mountains in the valley
By mineshafts with flowers by a pearly glow and bright sunlight

We are cheek by jowl now we are common as dirt
We are born on all sides of us we exist without boundaries

— M. B.

AGELESS

We approach each other
Through forests
Take the street of the morning
Mount the steps of the mist

We meet each other
The heart of the earth is shriveled dry

Once again a new day to insert in the world

◢

The sky will become wider
We have had enough
Of living in the debris of sleep
In the low shadows of repose
Weariness and indifference

The earth will take on the shape of our living bodies
The wind will submit to us
Sunlight and nightfall will pass across our eyes
Without altering them at all

Our determined space our pure atmosphere is firm enough
To fill in the hesitations excavated by mere habit
Together we will reach a resurrected memory
And speak in a sensitive tongue

◢

O my perverse brothers you who hoard in your eyes
The confusions of night and its horrors
There where I left you last
With your heavy hands dipped in the old idle oils
Of your past acts
With so little hope that you make death look correct
O my wandering brothers
I move in a straight line toward life I look like a man
Who must prove that the world is made to human measure

Nor am I alone
A thousand reflections of me multiply my light

A thousand similar perspectives equalize our flesh
It's the bird the child the stones the distantmost fields
Coming together with us
Gold giggles to see itself excavated from its abysses
Water and fire strip bare for the present
The eclipse is stripped from the forehead of the universe.

Hands recognized in our own hands
Lips melted into our own
The first floral warmth
Mixed in with the freshness of our blood
The spectrum breathes deeply as we do
Overflowing dawn
At the tip of each blade of grass a sovereign queen
Atop all mosses at the tips of the snow
From waves of sands overturned
From childhoods extended
Beyond all caverns
Beyond ourselves.

— M. B.

PAINTED WORDS
For Pablo Picasso

To understand everything
Even
The tree with the eyes of a prow
The tree beloved of lizards and lianas
Even the blazing fire even the blind man

To unite wing and dew
Heart and cloud day and night
Window and landscape of everywhere

To abolish
The sneer of zero
Which tomorrow shall roll on gold

To sever
the petty proprieties
Of giants fed only on themselves

To see all eyes reflected
In all eyes

To see that all eyes are as beautiful
As what they are able to see
An absorbent sea

So that we may laugh lightly
About having been hot at having felt cold
About having been hungry and thirsty

So that speaking
May be generous
As kissing

To merge bather and river
Crystal and dancer of the storm
Dawn and the bosom's season
Desire and the proverbs of childhood

To give to woman
Meditative and private
The precise shape of the caresses
Of which she has been dreaming

So that deserts may fall into shadow
Instead of establishing sites
In my own
Shadow

To give
My own
Good

To give
My own
Right.

— M. B.

MAX ERNST

In one corner agile incest
Hovers about the virginity of a small frock
In one corner the abandoned sky
Releases white balls to the thorns of thunder.

In one corner that all the eyes have made brighter
They are expecting the fishes' anguish.
In one corner the carriage of the foliage of summer
Immobile, glorious, and forever.

By the light of the youthfulness
Of lamps ignited extremely late
The first to come shows her breasts which the scarlet insects
are killing.

— ROBERT BLY

184

YVES TANGUY

One night all nights and tonight like every other night
Outside the hermaphroditic night
The proliferation of which is not in the least inhibited
The hunters' flashlights and their venison both are sacrificed
But deep inside the glazed eyes of lynxes and owls
The endless enormous sunlight
The heartbreak of the passing seasons
The crow of the family circle
All the power of vision surrounded by earthly reality.

There are stars on the icy water thrown into relief
Blacker than any night
And exactly on schedule like a last ray of sunset
All illusions fall into memory's flower
And all leaves beneath the shadows thrown by odor.

And all these girls try in vain by using their hands
By arching their backs by opening the anemones of their breasts
    to seduce me to sleep
I catch nothing at all in these nets of shuddering and skin
From the ends of the earth to the twilight of the present
Nothing resists the dismalness of my visions.

Disguised as wings silence has frozen fields
Which the gentlest gesture of desire breaks open once again
Then revolving night catches them up
And flings them to the rim of the horizon.

You and I had decided that nothing could ever be defined
Except according to the pressure of a single finger placed by
    chance on the controls of a broken-down machine.

— M. B.

THE END TO EVERYTHING

Feet in fancy gold slippers
Legs in icy clay
Upright the walls covered with useless flesh
Upright dead beasts
Here an agglutinous whirlwind
Fixes wrinkles and grimaces for all time
Here coffins give birth
And drinking-glasses are full of sand
And empty
Here drowned men sink
Blood destroyed
In the unfathomable waters of their own past hopes

Dead leaf weak distraction
In opposition to desire and ecstasy
Repose has discovered its master
On beds of spikes and stone

The plow of words is rusted now
No furrow of love approaches the flesh
A melancholy act is flung into the pasture
Before devouring misery
Down with walls covered with torturesome arms
Which can penetrate men
Men blackening in shame
Others celebrate their own shit
The best eyes are abandoned

Even dogs feel awful.

— M. B.

FROM OUTSIDE

The night the cold the solitude
They locked me in taking the most scrupulous pains
But the branches found their way into prison
All around me grass found sky
They bolted out the sky
My prison crumbled
The living cold the burning cold had me well in hand.

— M. B.

LIBERTY

On my school notebooks
On my desk and the trees
On the sand on the snow
I write your name

On all the pages that have been read
On all the pages that are blank
Blood paper stone or ash
I write your name

On the gilded images
On the arms of the warriors
On the crown of the kings
I write your name

On the jungle and the desert
On the nests on the bushes of broom
On the echo of my childhood
I write your name

On the marvels of the nights
On the white bread of the days
On the betrothed seasons
I write your name

On all the rags of azure
On the pond that mouldy sun
On the lake that moon full of life
I write your name

On the fields on the horizon
On the wings of the birds
And on the mill of shadows
I write your name

On every breath of dawn
On the sea on the boats
On the demented mountain
I write your name

On the foam of clouds
On the sweat of the storm
On the thick tasteless rain
I write your name

On the sparkling forms
On the bells of the colors
On the truth of bodies
I write your name

On the wakened paths
On the unfurled roads
On the overflowing market-places
I write your name

On the lamp being lit
On the lamp going out
On my houses all together
I write your name

On the fruit cut in two
My mirror and my bedroom
On my bed empty shell
I write your name

On my dog greedy and tender
On his trained ears
On his clumsy paw
I write your name

On that springboard my door
On the familiar objects
On the flood of blessed fire
I write your name

On all flesh that says yes
On the forehead of my friends
On each hand that is held out
I write your name

On the window of surprises
On the attentive lips
Far above silence
I write your name

On my demolished refuges
On my crumbled lighthouses
On the walls of my boredom
I write your name

On the absence without desire
On the naked solitude
On the footsteps of death
I write your name

On health that has returned
On the risk that has vanished
On hope without memory
I write your name

And through the power of a word
I start my life over
I am born to know who you are
To give you your name

Liberty

— W. S. MERWIN

MEDUSAS

I

She is about to awaken from a black and blue dream
She is about to arise from an ash-gray night
Her leg is slender her foot is bare
Audacity attempts its first step

At the sound of a well-rehearsed musical phrase
Her body passes by in reflections in bright light
Her body paved over with the rains fully armed with sweet per-
    fumes
Unwinds the morning spindle of her life.

II

Standing on the highest arching of a huge bridge
With pride adrift out to sea
I await all that I have ever known
Overflowing with sparkling space
My memory is immense

Generosity dances along my lips
Warm rags illuminate me
A road departs from my forehead

Close by and far away
The sea leaps up to greet me
It has the shape of a hanging grape-cluster
Of ripe pleasure

Yesterday I loved I shall love today as well
There is nothing I shy away from
My past is faithful to me still
And time runs in my veins.

III

Beneath outworn rafters beneath sterile ceilings
In a large room very severely furnished
These bound knees confer a certain quality
On miserable straight lines

Her hair trapped in a cracked mirror
Water warbles among the mosses of her forehead
The evasive drifting of a smile evaporates
The last of her illusions into a vanished sky.

IV

Earth paces restlessly through the regions of her bed
Beasts of the earth and men of the earth
In the regions of her bed
There are only wheatfields
Vineyards and fields of flowering feelings
The road is laid out without equipment
All hands all eyes lead to the bed
To the passionate secret revealed
To shadows structured upon dreams

Released by the fingers of the air in ascent
The golden vase of a kiss

Her throat so heavy and so slow
But weighted down with thousands of ripened sheaves
Arrives at her fall festival of flowers

She brings hunger and thirsty desire

Her body is a naked beloved
It leaps forth from her eyes
And its light knots up night and flesh and the earth
The infinite light of a body in abandonment
And of two eyes reiterating themselves over and over again.

V

My sisters capture in their nets
Howls and cries of dogs
As for me I prefer to feed myself
On the hope of a perpetual passion
Black orangeblossom bough blonde armor
Delirious bees laughter bursting
Laughter invisibly incognito
Bark of dawn dizzy dazzling wing
Nestful of debauched leaves
Innocent young poison mountain liana
Sweat of swimming cold smoke
Giant step steadily pounding dance
Perpetual brow perfect palm
Mineshafts aloft in the open air axle of the wind
Monument turned misty gone flaming mad
Game lacking losers health without holes
Water a torch afire each tower a mixture
Martyr radiant among sharp angles
Eye shining through shame and mist
First snow ever to celebrate
Accomplishment of solitude
Exile to the springs of strength.

VI

Where are you now can you see me hear me
Will you recognize me
I the most lovely and alone
I hold back the river-flow like a violin
I let the days go by
I let ships and clouds go by
Tedium lies dead by my side
I hold all the echoes of childhood my treasures
With this laughter in my throat

193

My landscape is an enormous happiness
And my face a lucent universe
Elsewhere they weep black tears
They wander from cavern to cavern
Here you can never be lost
And my face sinks in pure waters I can see it
Singing a single tree
Softening stones
Reflecting the horizon
I lean against trees
Sleep on stones
With waters I applaud the sun and the rain
And the serious wind

Where are you now can you see me hear me
I am the creature behind the curtain
Behind the very first curtain to rise
Mistress of the green countryside against all the odds
And of the plantlife of nothingness
Mistress of waters mistress of the air
I dominate my own solitude
Where then are you
By dreaming about me inside the walls where you are
You can see me hear me
And yet you would alter my heart
Rip me from the very bosom of my eyes

I have the power to endure without destiny
Between frost and dew between oblivion and presence

Coolness or warmth they mean nothing to me at all
I shall scatter across your desires
The image of myself you offer me
My face has but one star

You must submit to loving me in vain
I am the eclipse the dream of the night
Forget about my crystal curtains

I shall remain in my own leaves
I shall remain in my own mirror
I mix together the snow and the fire

194

My stones possess my sweetness
My season is for all time.

VII

And so by the grace of your lips arm mine.

— M. B.

"POETRY OUGHT TO HAVE A
PRACTICAL PURPOSE"
For My Exacting Friends

If I tell you that the sun in the woods
Is like a belly carried away in a bed
You believe me you approve of my desires

If I tell you that the crystal of rainy days
Echoes forever in the laziness of love's ecstasies
You believe me you draw out the duration of your loving

If I tell you that in the branches of my bed
A bird is nesting that never says yes
You believe me you share my own distress

If I tell you that at the bottom of some stream
A river's key turns like an overture to verdure
You believe me still more you can follow

But if I sing to you of my whole long highway with no detours
And my enormous countryside like a footpath unending
You give up on me you depart for the wilds

For you only wander aimlessly without recognizing that men
Have the need to hope and to struggle
To explain the world and to change it

With one step of my heart I shall lead you
I've lived without power for a long time it's the way I live now
But I'm amazed to hear you say I speak to you just to delight
    you
When I would free you to unite you
As much as with algae and the reeds of the dawn
As with our other brothers creating their own daylight.

— M. B.

SOME WORDS WHICH,
UP UNTIL NOW, HAD REMAINED
MYSTERIOUSLY FORBIDDING FOR ME
For André Breton

The word cemetery
For some men a dream of glorious interments

The word cottage
You find it frequently
In classified ads and pop songs
It's wrinkled a little it must be an old man in disguise
It has a thimble on its finger it's a sheathèd pet parrakeet

Gasoline
Known thanks to the examples
Of the fingers of flame

Neurasthenia a word lacking all shame
Blackberry jelly fleck between two staring eyes

The word Creole all clad in cork but lying on satin

The word bathtub drawn
By a pair of thoroughbred horses uglier than crutches

Here beneath my lamp tonight the word arbor is a first name
And mastery is a mirror in which everything is frozen

Lacemaker delicious melting word hammock trellis ransacked

Olive-tree tall chimney inside a tambourine of light
The keyboard of sheep muffled in the field

Fortress malice in vain

Poisonous mahogany curtain

Coffeetable elastic grimace

Hatchet unfortunate bet on the dice

Vowel vast tintinnabulation
Pewter tear laughter from this good earth

Safetycatch radiant rape
Ephemeral azure in the veins

The word meteorite geranium by the open window
Overlooking a palpitating heart

The word broadshouldered block of ivory
Petrified bread moistened pens

The word frustration evaporated alcohol
Doorless stairwell poetic death

The word for male infant like an islet

Myrtle lava gold braid cigar
Lethargy cornflower circus fusion
And how many other words there are besides these
Words to take me everywhere and nowhere
Words just as marvelous as all other words
O my human empire
Words which I write out here
Against all the odds
Taking care
To tell all.

— M. B.

"THE EARTH IS AS BLUE
AS AN ORANGE . . ."

The earth is as blue as an orange
No there's no error here words never lie
There's no chance at all of your merely writing a rhapsody
Now its time for kisses to comprehend
Madmen and passions
That lady with her wedding-ring mouth
Every secret and smile
And what indulgent vestments are involved
In conceiving of her totally naked

Whatever the color was of wasp-waisted beings now they
    blossom into green
The dawn light slips over your neck
A necklace strung from windows
Wings cover over leaves
You have every solar joy here
All the sun in the world
On the pathways of your beauty.

                              — M. B.

ONE MOMENT'S MIRROR

It diffuses daylight
It holds up to men the images of appearance unbound
It presents to men the possibilities of abstraction.
It is hard as rock,
Rock still shapeless,
The rock of shifting and vision,
And its radiance is such that all external armor, all masks, seem
    false when seen in its shine.
What was formerly grasped by the hand refuses to take the
    form of a hand,
Everything it embraces ceases to be,
Birds mix in with the wind,
The sky with its own solidity,
Man with his own reality.

— M. B.

JEAN (HANS) ARP

1887-1966

EQUALLY GIFTED AS POET, PAINTER, AND SCULPTOR, Arp brought an exceptionally flexible spirit to Surrealism.

Born in the much-contested territory of Alsace-Lorraine between France and Germany, the poet had intellectual ties with both countries. From 1912 to 1914 Arp was a member of the "Blue Rider" group of expressionist painters, whose other members included Kandinsky, Franz Marc, and Paul Klee. In the early months of the war Arp's travels included a stay in Paris, where he became acquainted with Picasso and Apollinaire; in 1915 he settled in Zurich. With his wife-to-be, the painter Sophie Tauber, he participated in literary and artistic soirées at various cafés, including the historic ones at the Cabaret Voltaire, cradle of the Dada movement. Arp was among those present at Tristan Tzara's celebrated random selection of the name "Dada" from a dictionary. However, he was a somewhat less ferocious Dadaist than the latter, remaining relatively aloof, evidently preferring private experiment to public manifestation. It was around this time that Arp's work became by and large abstract, the artist executing collages which stretched the bounds of the figurative to the limit; also during this period Arp inaugurated his series of abstract drawings to accompany books of poetry, among them works by Tzara,[1] Péret,[2] and, of course, Arp himself.[3] His previous work in this medium, illustrations published in 1914 for the Bhagavad-Gita, had been loosely figurative.[4]

Arp's first works to appear under the auspices of Dada were visual rather than verbal. Sketches reproduced in various Dada journals, several dating from the 1917–1918 period, were presented under the title "Automatic Drawing." Like the series of sculptures in wood relief with which Arp had been simultaneously experimenting, the sketches were "arranged according to the Law of Chance," since chance "embraces all laws and is unfathomable like the first cause from which all life arises; and can only be experienced through complete devotion to the unconscious." This, Arp claimed, was "creating pure life." Such a positive identification of Dadaist spontaneity with "creation" was of course unusual among members of that movement, perhaps making Arp's later transition to Surrealism that much more natural.

Arp's first collection of poetry, published in 1920 in Hanover, Germany, and in German, bears the somewhat Tzaraesque (or perhaps Duchampesque) title *Die Wolkenpumpe* (*The Cloud-Pump*).[5] Soon after its publication, translations by Tzara and André Breton appeared in *Littérature*. The work is characteristic of Arp: lucid in language, playful and almost childlike in tone, but with a scarcely disguised bite. Already, nature is seen as a creature with a will of its own, overcoming that of rational man whenever possible. As he says in one of the many essays on the nature of creation that he wrote and revised throughout his life:

> art is a fruit growing out of man like the fruit out of a plant like the child out of the mother. while the fruit of the plant grows independent forms and never resembles a balloon or a president in a cutaway suit the artistic fruit of man shows for the most part a ridiculous resemblance to the appearance of other things. reason tells man to stand above nature and to be the measure of things. thus man thinks he is able to live and to create against the laws of nature and he creates abortions. through reason man became a tragic and ugly figure. i dare say he would create even his children in the form of vases with umbilical cords if he could do so. reason has cut man off from nature.[6]

In 1920 Arp collaborated with the painter Max Ernst — himself an exponent of chance in the visual context, and a future Surrealist — in the latter's neo-Dadaist "Fatagaga" photo collage and other activities in Cologne. In 1921 Arp, Tzara, and Breton collaborated in assembling what was to be the final issue of *Dada*, that movement's literary organ, in the Tyrol; later that year Arp rejoined Tzara once more, this time in Paris.

Arp never officially "broke" with Dada but participated in the first Surrealist visual arts exhibition, held at the Galerie Pierre in 1925. After 1926, when he moved his household to the French capital, he began to publish work in *La Révolution Surréaliste*. In 1927 he signed two of the movement's "open letters": "Permettez!" ("With Your Permission!") and "Hands Off Love" (the title in English since its subject was the paternity suit against Chaplin, in which the Surrealists took the part of the actor).

With its simplicity of shape and color, Arp's visual work is a close visual counterpart to his poetry. The latter's clarity of language is echoed in shapes simplified in the extreme, and in the use of only two or three colors — a radically different approach for its time, yet greatly influential in later years (for example, in the work of the American "minimalists" of the late 1960's). A more specific, iconographic, connection was emphasized after 1930, when Arp began working in a biomorphic style, the work, according to Marcel Duchamp, resembling "how the body would have looked had it been redesigned"; the poems and plastic works share images such as mouths, moustaches, navels, and so forth, all intermixed with and even transposed with symbols drawn from the nature of which the body is a part. Arp named his one-man art movement "Concrete Art," also noting that "certain Surrealist objects are also concrete works. Without any descriptive content, they seem to me exceedingly important for the evolution of concrete art, for, by allusion, they succeed in introducing into this art the psychic emotion that makes it live."

Predictably enough, Arp's contacts with the Surrealists decreased during the late 1920's and early 1930's. His concern with "Concrete Art" aside, he seems to have resented the increasing involvement with party-line politics on the part of certain Surrealists (some of whom were about to desert the movement themselves). He summed up the spirit of all his work when he wrote in retrospect:

> Some old friends from the days of the Dada campaign, who always fought for dreams and freedom, are

now disgustingly preoccupied with class aims. . . .
Conscientiously they mix poetry and the [Soviet] Five-
Year Plan in one pot; but this attempt to lie down while
standing up will not succeed. Man will not allow him-
self to be turned into a scrubbed, hygienic numeral
. . . which, in its enthusiasm for a certain politician's
portrait, shouts yes like a hypnotized donkey. Man
will not permit himself to be standardized.[7]

Principal works in the French language (verse unless otherwise noted): *Des taches dans le vide* (Les Feuillets de Sagesse, 1937); *Sciure de gammes* (Parisot, 1938); *Poèmes sans prénoms* (privately printed, 1941); *Le Blanc aux pieds de nègre* (prose poems: Ed. Fontaine, 1945); *Trois Nouvelles exemplaires* (short novels with Vincente Huidobro: Ed. Fontaine, 1946); *Le Voilier dans la forêt* (Broder, 1957); *Vers le blanc infini* (Lausanne-Paris, 1960); *Soleil recerclé* (Broder, 1960); Selected poems: *Le Siège de l'air: 1915–1945* (Vrille, 1946); Selected writings: *Jours effeuillés: 1920–1965* (N.R.F., 1966, the basis for *Arp on Arp*, ed. Marcel Jean, tr. Joachim Neugroschel, Viking, 1972).

I AM A HORSE

I'm riding in a train
that's absolutely packed
in my compartment
every seat is occupied by a lady
holding a man on her lap
the air is intolerably hot
the atmosphere is stifling
all the passengers
have gigantic appetites
they eat nonstop
suddenly the men begin to whine
they want to be breast-fed
they want to be suckled
they want to be nursed
They unbutton the women's blouses
and clasp their breasts
They fill themselves with nice fresh milk
Only I do not suckle on anyone
nor am I suckled by anyone
nobody sits on my lap either
for I am a horse
I sit up straight and solid
with my hind legs
on the railroad train seat
and prop myself up snugly
using my forelegs
I neigh energetically heeheehee
and on my chest shine
all nicely aligned
the six buttons of sex appeal
just like bright buttons on a uniform
O how small this world is
how big cherries

— M. B.

A DROPLET OF MAN

a droplet of man
a soupçon of woman
complete the beauty of the bouquet of bones
it's time now for an aubade
in the fur of fire
the wind arrives running on the soles of its feet
like the horse on its four wheels
space has a vertical aroma

space has a vertical aroma
the wind arrives running on the soles of its feet
it's time now for an aubade
in the fur of fire
a droplet of man
a soupçon of woman
complete the beauty of the bouquet of bones

— M. B.

WHAT VIOLINS ARE SINGING IN THEIR BEDS OF LARD

the elephant's in love with the millimeter

the snail dreams of some victory over the moon
its slippers are as pale and as pure
as the gelatin rifle of a neo-soldier

the eagle has all the gestures of some much-rumored realm of
   void
its underbelly is swollen with lightning

the lion sports a moustache in pure flamboyant gothic
its skin is calm
it chuckles like an inkspot

the deep-sea lobster has the bestial growl of a raspberry
all the good breeding of an apple
all the compassion of a plum
and all the lecherousness of a pumpkin

the cow takes the parchment road
the one which vanishes in a volume of flesh
the hairs of this book have tremendous volume

the snake sneaks sneakily very sneakily
around the washbasins of love
which are filled with hearts pierced by arrows

a butterfly if stuffed becomes a big fat stutterfly
a big fat stutterfly becomes a stuttering stupendous stentorian
   stutterfly

the nightingale starts all stomachs watering also all hearts brains
   and guts
that is to say lilies roses violets and lilacs

the flea sticks its right foot behind its left ear
its left hand in its right hand
and jumps with its left foot over its right ear

— M. B.

SAWDUST FROM THE SCALES

While I lick my body
as the day licks its own body
somewhere between the sky and a lunch-break
a cannon fires point-blank at somebody's verdant soul
a rooster on crystal crutches
hops along behind a mammal bell
which soars through the stiffness of the air
whinnying like feminine firewood.

The tongue is useless for talking
it's better to use your feet to speak
than that bald old tongue of yours
it's better to use your navel for talking
what the tongue is good for
is knitting up monuments
is bowing away on an ink violin
is washing up whales covered with seaweed braid
is fishing around for the roots of the poles
but above all the tongue is good
for letting hang out of your mouth
and letting flutter around in the wind

— M. B.

INFINITE MILLIMETER MANIFESTO

First we have to let forms, colors, sounds sprout
and then explain them.
First we have to allow legs, wings, hands to grow and then fly
    sing form manifest themselves.
I'd be the last to draw up a plan as if I were involved with a
    timetable or a mathematical calculation or a war.
The art of stars, flowers, forms, colors overlaps with the infinite.

— M. B.

DOMESTICATED STONES

stones are stomachs
bravo bravo
stones are torsos of the air
stones are limbs of the waters
on the stone that takes the place of the mouth
a fish bone grows
bravo
a stony voice
is having a tête-à-tête
toe to toe
with a stony stare
stones are tormented as flesh
stones are clouds
since their second nature
dances around on their third nose
bravo bravo
when stones scratch each other
toenails sprout among the roots
since stones have ears
to eat the right time

on the cloud that takes over for the head
a natural nose grows
the toenails of the eyes scratch around at the very roots of nature
stones sprout and dance around on clouds
bravo bravo
ears sprout among roots
the third stone sucks away on air-flesh
the second stone eats feet
bravo bravo bravissimo
for herring bones have a harbor
when feet dance on heads
nails sprout on stones
hours scratch each other
bravo
guts in stomachs are roots

stones are heads
how orderly nature is
the feet dancing around among the tree-limbs of flesh
have a tormented stare
a stare of hours and bowels
in place of all you called natural sprouts a foot
o bravo bravo bravo bravissimo
ears noses mouths heads feet are all stones now

— M. B.

WHITE BLOCKS

the blocks of dawn crumble
accompanied by the ravenous cooing
of the turtledove of mystery
of its six red breasts summer shows me
the very top two
a long mane of multiple organs takes its place upon my head
my back is covered by bleached-dry phrases
when I pull on my fat little foot skates
the vegetable people all applaud me
an oral star sprouts in my mouth
it tastes like the cracked and sun baked tears
of the accidental roses of the asphalt
it purrs like a brood just born from a stone's stomach
the globular air balances upon its stem
clouds sprout in my hands
I caress my clouds
and fall asleep
I sleep as snug as in an egg
I sleep and wait for leaves to grow all over me

mystery's chubby globularity balances on my head
clouds of stone come and cover the asphalt's phrases
I crumple down on the blocks of dawn
dawn coos now
the organ of the air accompanies the red tears
on the stems of the stars
which are the reeds of summertime
I caress the bleached-dry back of mankind
I raise my head high
purring like some starved stone
the turtledove offers me all its six vegetable breasts
tiny hairs of snugness grow

— M. B.

THE FEET OF MORNING . . .

the feet of morning
the feet of midday
and the feet of night
walk around continuously
among pickled bottoms
the feet of midnight
on the other hand stand firm
there in their snoods
of knitted echoes

as a result of which
a lion is a diamond

upon the canopies of bread
sit those who are dressed
and those undressed
whose undressed hold between their toes
swallows made of lead
those who are dressed hold between their fingers
birds' nests made of lead
and every hour
those who are undressed get dressed
and those who are dressed get undressed
to exchange the lead swallows
for lead nests

as a result of which
the tail is an umbrella

coats with swallow tails
and swallow heads
stand coats with their tails
and heads
on their tails
and heads

as a result of which
the tongue is a chair

child feet
fall from the ceiling
ladies of high society
wear them instead of gloves
proud as if their leather skin had been suntanned by the moon

as a result of which
love is a comb

in one mouth
opens another mouth
and in this mouth
opens another mouth
and in that mouth
opens another mouth

and so on and so on
endlessly
it's a melancholy prospect
which goes on adding one "certain indefinable something"
to another
"certain indefinable something"

as a result of which
the tongue is a pillar

— M. B.

THE TYROLEAN ELEPHANT

It squeaks, it creaks. Together, the Tyrolean elephant and the rubber grandmother bang on the piano of death. Over and over again they bang, without respite and with a vengeance. They foam at the mouth, they perspire. Their hands transform the piano of death into scrap iron. When at last nothing is left of the piano beneath their hands, they rub on the zillions of time, they make neat piles out of electric innards inside zeppelins, conduct coronations for flies, and dine on salted infants, phosphorous oranges and marmalade made out of aircraft. The rubber grandmother smokes a cigar as grand as a grandmother. She utters joyous cries. The rubber grandmother has sex appeal and when she appeals, the fiendish and fragrant mushroom throws itself with a terrible energy upon the rubber grandmother whom it licks without respite from top to bottom. Haven't you got anything else there inside your mouth? The pleasure is certainly grand. The grandmother grows even grander. Keep on, fiendish and fragrant mushroom. Keep on! Outdo yourself, you terrible luscious crocodile! The ecstasy is certainly enormous. The Tyrolean elephant is diplomatic. All he says is honk, honk, honk. But since the fiendish and fragrant mushroom refuses to outdo itself, the rubber grandmother flings it like a fly without feet into a lake of foul old oil all the while squeaking: Marmalade, marmalade, all is marmalade. Only the heavy plop of an expeditionary navy into sugary milk tarnishes the pure nudity of this majestic dance.

— M. B.

214

THE WHITE ETC.

The white cathedral changes into white gloves. White, white, white. The white elephant currycombs the hair of the air in the white froth of the void. White, white, white. Eyes hurl milky objects onto electric railway tracks and stack up white shrieks around rubber-covered pianos. White, white, white. White time licks hands, gloves, women, faces, hair. White, white, white. White hands come to tear out the teeth of the lake. White, white, white. Little stars of light dance around on big glossy oranges to the great delight of billions of tiny white children. White, white, white. Whiteness is changing itself into a sugary death which pleads: please, white, white, more white.

The monuments sweat marmalade. Great iron feet go stamping along beneath a rainfall of teeth beside the cathedral made of mushrooms at the white woman's place. The white woman eats a faded dry old scalp or two now and then. Down at the lake, the white woman's face dumps a dance of phosphorus with long legs of air. Now the elephant rubs down the white woman, rubs down hard. The air disappears and the magnificence of existence throws the sugary and the salted over all the quick and the dead.

— M. B.

SEASONS THEIR ASTERISKS
AND THEIR PAWNS

you're so very blue my dear springtime
yet you've done rather well for yourself
too bad for summer if summer doesn't get a little something out
    of it
all the green wigs are ringing now
what time is it
it's a quarter to summer
the stars are unlacing their bodices
and peeling open their lecherous roses
the dials of the day read july
here comes winter again late again as usual
over its shoulder is slung a man who is pale as snow
a man who succumbed to the succession of daily wintry summers
too many summers can even square the circle circle the square
it's winter every monday
winter saws the whiteness of blackness into two exactly equal
    parts
separating the two sections neatly with a nice sharp knife
while the master of the realm snoozes on resting on the laurels of
    his perfumed roots
not even the challenge of the clanking armor paraphernalia
    seething up from black coffee can bring him to his feet
nor the snow falling so early this year
on scowling leprechauns fairies and sprites
while the chain-mesh of the human breast bursts
and the set cycle of days turns on its faucets full force
letting the waves of human leaves rush out
we've become very small once more
and we follow a procession of ants in deep mourning
all with torches in their hands
and mice in their mouths
beneath the umbrellas of numbers
the crucified food has approximately the same shape as autumn

— M. B.

BLACK VEINS

in my heart among the clouds of fog
the specters of roses expire
a star settles down on the edge of my bed
it's quite old quite wrinkled

gray spiders move off in single file
toward the black-veined horizon
they tread on as if to some fairy's final burial
the very void heaves a sign

my poor dreams have lost their wings
my poor dreams have lost their flames
they lean their elbows
on the coffin of my heart
and dream of tiny gray bits and pieces

day dawns once more
but my strength has gone
the sky comes down and covers me completely
I open my eyes for all time

— M. B.

BLACK JOY

flowers are blackened with joy
the sky is beautiful as flame
i'm transported by just one day's worth of flower-labor
how would you like to fly away with me

how would you like a day's worth of lightning-flashes
how would you like a flower identical with heaven
how would you like several flowers like lightning-flashes
how would you like a fiery sky

hovering just beyond my head
is you my lovely flower-labor
hovering just beyond my head
is you my lovely black flame of joy

—— M. B.

BENJAMIN PÉRET

1899-1959

Péret's poems are increasingly regarded as among the purest Surrealist creations. In addition, he played a crucial role as the co-founder and editor for three numbers of the first of the movement's periodicals, *La Révolution Surréaliste*, was an active theoretician and anthologist and one of André Breton's closest associates, remaining a self-proclaimed Surrealist to the end of his life.

Péret came to Paris in 1920 after the acceptance by the editors of *Littérature* of one of the first of his poems to break out of his early, Symbolist style. He was brought by Breton to the initial Dada spectacles in Paris in 1919; his disaffection from that movement soon followed, Péret issuing in *Littérature* the anti-Dada tract *A travers mes yeux* (*Through My Eyes*, 1920).[1] Here, he accused Dada of already having become as "old-fashioned" as "Cubism or Futurism," and he announced his departure from Dada with resounding definitiveness.

For nearly two decades after his first published collection, tales in a genre somewhere between the prose poem and prose fiction, *Au 125 du boulevard Saint-Germain* (*125 Boulevard Saint-Germain*, 1923),[2] Péret published verse almost exclusively. Editorially, in addition to work for *La Révolution Surréaliste,* he issued with Breton and Eluard *152 Proverbes mis au goût du jour* (*152 Proverbs Revised for Our Times*, 1925),[3] and with Breton, Eluard, and Aragon, the important broadside *Au grand jour* (*Into the Light of Day*, 1927),[4] a tract asserting the need for Surrealism to surface and reach a wider public.

219

Péret's poems exist almost entirely in terms of classic Surrealist poetic techniques. Concerned with the fusion of the most disparate imagery, they employ as premises analogies and associations having scant objective confirmation and often more conceptual than visual. The poems establish their own interior logic as sole reference point, their flavor deriving from the rigorousness with which this logic is pursued. The question in "Just Now" ("what voice . . . will dare to speak like an equation") is answered by the poet himself, who in rejection of prior logic, creates a virtual mathematics of analogy. Dissimilar objects are relentlessly compared, the word *comme* — "like" or "as" (as in Lautréamont's formula, "as beautiful as the chance meeting of an umbrella and a sewing-machine on a dissection table") functioning as equating link.

One by-product of Péret's technique is that the objects of which he speaks seem to become endowed with a vitality surpassing that usually associated with them. The poet sees things as participating in an all-but-secret existence, one perpetually blighted by the definitions common to humans, which conventionally relegate such "subhuman" representatives to an inferior status. By implication, such definitions are seen not only as destructive with regard to life on earth generally, but also as limiting to the human imagination and its potentialities. Péret's thorough intransigence with regard to traditionally self-righteous ideas of the human may well have been a major psychological factor in preventing his poetry from achieving a currency equal to other Surrealist work.

In 1926, at the height of Surrealism's political involvement, Péret joined the Communist party. He became active in party organizing in Brazil in 1931, and fought during the Spanish Civil War. Mobilized in France in 1939, he was arrested in 1940 for "subversive" activities, but escaped to Mexico just before the installation of the Nazi-dominated Vichy government. After the war he returned to Paris. His later writings include *Le Déshonneur des poètes* (*The Dishonor of the Poets*, 1945),[5] an attack on the simpleminded realism to be found in the work of the wartime propaganda poets, poets of the Left not excluded. The poet's concern for the theoretical and historical aspects of Surrealism also developed into several later critical anthologies of its works, including the *Anthologie de l'amour sublime* (*Anthology of Sublime Love*, 1956),[6] *Anthologie des mythes, légendes et contes populaires d'Amérique* (*Anthology of the Myths, Legends and Folk Tales of the Americas*, 1959),[7] and (for an Italian publisher) *La Poesia surrealista francese* (*French Surrealist Poetry*, 1959).[8] His own later poems continued in an energetic Surrealist mode.

OTHER PRINCIPAL WORKS

Collections of poems: *Le Passager du transatlantique* (Collection Dada/Au Sans Pareil, 1921); *Immortelle Maladie* (Collection "Littérature," 1923); *Il était une boulangère* (Sagittaire/Kra, 1925); *Dormir, dormir dans les pierres* (Ed. Surréalistes, 1927); *Et les seins mouraient* (Ed. des Cahiers du Sud, 1928); *Le Grand Jeu* (N.R.F., 1928); *De derrière les fagots* (Ed. Surréalistes, 1934); *Je ne mange pas de ce pain-là* (Ed. Surréalistes, 1936); *Je sublime* (Ed. Surréalistes, 1936); *Dernier malheur, dernière chance* (Ed. Fontaine, 1945); *Air mexicain* (Ed. Arcanes, 1952); *Les Mains dans les poches* (Fata Morgana, 1965). Tales: *La Brebis galante* (Ed. Premières, 1949; Ed. du Terrain Vague, 1959); *Mort aux vaches et au champ d'honneur* (Ed. Arcanes, 1953); *Histoire naturelle* (privately printed, 1958). Selected tales: *Le Gigot, sa vie et son oeuvre* (Le Terrain Vague, 1957). Selected poems: *Feu central* (Editions K, 1947). Principal collection of poetry, in progress: *Oeuvres complètes*, Vol. I, 1969; Vol. II, 1971 (Eric Losfeld). Selected Writings: *Main forte* (includes the prose *Au 125 du boulevard Saint-Germain* [Ed. Fontaine, 1946]); *Péret*, "Poètes d'aujourd'hui" No. 78 (Seghers).

HELLO

My airplane in flames my Rhinewine-flooded castle
my ghetto of black iris my crystal ear
my rock slipping off a cliff to crush the local police-chief
my opal snail my mosquito made out of air
my bird-of-paradise mattress my hair of black foam
my exploded grave my rain of red grasshoppers
my flying island my turquoise grape
my collision of wise and foolish autos my wild flower bed
my dandelion pistil stuck in my eye
my tulip bulb in the brain
my gazelle wandering through a moviehouse at midnight in the
    midtown area
my cashbox of sunlight my volcanic fruit
my laugh of a secluded lake where absent-minded prophets
    always remember to come and drown
my high tide of black-currant my mushroom butterfly
my waterfall as blue as the ground-swell that begins the spring
my coral revolver whose mouth attracts me like the eye of a
    glistening wet well
as glazed over as the mirror in which you contemplate the flight
    of the hummingbirds of your own eyes
lost in a display case for white linen whose frame is made
    entirely out of mummies
I love you

— M. B.

WHERE ARE YOU

I'd like to speak to you cracked crystal crying like a dog in a
   night of wind-whipped laundry
like a dismasted ship into which the foaming sea-moss is
   beginning to creep
in the very midst of which a cat is mewing because all the rats
   have already left
I'd like to speak to you like a tree uprooted in a windstorm
which has shaken the telegraph wires so much
they look like a scrub-brush for mountains closely resembling the
   lower jaw of a tiger
which is gnashing away at me with the disconcerting sound of a
   bashed-down door
I'd like to speak to you like a subway-train broken down in front
   of the entrance
to a station
into which I stride with a splinter in one toe like a bird in a vine
which is no more capable of yielding the desired wine than a
   closed-off street
where I wander footloose as a wig in a fireplace
which has not warmed anything for so long
it thinks it's a snack-bar counter
on which the rings left by glasses form a long long chain
So I'll simply say to you
that I love you as the kernel of corn loves the sun rising high
   above its blackbird head

— M. B.

WHO IS IT

I term tobacco that which is ear
and so maggots take advantage of this opportunity to throw
   themselves on ham
causing an incredible combat between the fountains
gushing forth from gingerbread
and the eyeglasses that prevent blind men from having 20–20
   vision
Even if the woman facing me ate a dissecting table
roulette would still bring a sense of loss to the Chinese overlord
who is hiding in a suitcase
in which a tramp heavily gloved and booted
just like a penholder
might easily recognize the rainbow that appears above the vines
   after harvesttime
the time when wine refuses to become either red or white
and forswears forever looking the future directly in the face
for fear it's going to turn its back on it
humming a yodeling-tune
all about blonde hair
unless of course it turns out to be about brown hair
or about the rabbits that go around assassinating partridges
so that your day's catch will be good
and so that the wind whistling around chimneys
will keep the rivers from sleeping too deeply in their beds

— M. B.

IT KEEPS GOING ON

An old suitcase a sock and an endive
have arranged for a rendezvous between two blades of grass
sprouting on an altar draped in drooping bowels
This has resulted in the founding of a bank specializing in
    mortgage loans
which lends onions in order to earn armchairs
And so this world goes on
A little cupful of sand here
a broken bedspring there
A missing ear finds itself again
as a sticky beard
in a Louis XVth living-room
And obstacles are really opportunities in this dog's life of ours
    which is certainly a bitch
which licks its own ass and walks on its own four feet
And we're never licked as long as we can still communicate
about all the buttons on the door which throw up whenever the
    human hand throws a punch at them
and all the steep staircases which plug up the nose
because of the corpse of wearing ties
and goldfish all dying of shyness
and all the pigeons which refuse to alight on noses
which all fell far too long ago
into that gutter where none dare venture
for reasons of either youth or age
or because a man might miss his train
which anyway is happily bound to be derailed

— M. B.

A THOUSAND TIMES

Among the gilded debris of the gasworks
You will come upon a bar of chocolate which flies off as you
approach
If you run as fast as an aspirin-bottle
you will find yourself somewhere far beyond the chocolate
which upsets the landscape so
just like an open-toed sandal
over which one throws a traveling-cape
so as not to terrify passersby with the spectacle of all this nudity
which makes teeth chatter before their boxes of rouge
and leaves fall like factory chimneys
And so the train goes chugging by without stopping at the little
station
because it is neither hungry nor thirsty
because it is raining and it has no umbrella
because the cows have yet to come home
because the road isn't level and it doesn't like to have to meet
miscellaneous boozers crooks or cops
But if swallows formed a line at the kitchen door
to await their turn to be cooked
if water refused flat to cut the wine
and if I had five francs
There would be something new under the sun
there would be long loaves of bread on wheels to batter down the
doors of police-stations
there would be nurseries for the incubation of beards in which
sparrows could devote themselves to raising silkworms
there would be in the hollow of my hand
a small cold lamp
glazed as an egg on a plate
and so light that the soles of my shoes would fly off like a false
nose
as a result of which at the bottom of the sea there would be a
telephone-booth
from which nobody could ever complete a call

— M. B.

226

TWINKLING OF AN EYE

Waves of flapping parrots pierce my head whenever I see you in
   profile
and the fatty sky becomes striated with long veins of blue light
which spell out your name wherever I look
Rosa coiffed with an African tribe arranged in a series of tiers on
   a staircase
the staring breasts of whose women see through the eyes of
   whose men
Today I stare through your hair
Rosa of morning opal
and I awake myself through your eyes
Rosa of armor
and I think thanks to your detonating breasts
Rosa of lake turned green by its frogs
and I sleep in your navel of Caspian Sea
Rosa of sweetbriar during the general strike
and I wander between your shoulders of Milky Way fed by
   comets
Rosa of jasmine in the night of bleaching operations
Rosa of haunted house
Rosa of black forest inundated by green and blue postage stamps
Rosa of toy kites above a vacant lot where children battle it out
Rosa of cigar smoke
Rosa of sea-foam become crystal
Rosa

— M. B.

JUST NOW

Through the fault the last earthquake just exposed
escape many birds all shaped like pipes
cats leap up because their tails are all ascending
and enormous fountains of champagne
foaming so much that their bubbles block the sun
turn it green as an old roastbeef
and blue as a vine in the spring
where once opened
one by one
the shy pheasants of eyes
which are fixed on me now like a red banner on a barricade
I come like a waterfall over a lantern
like a bullet through a fascist chest
But whenever two eyes added to the fixed stare of nipples call
like a jonquil among hot rattling saucepans
the red bouncing ball
the red lantern of the street barricaded by kisses
burns lower to let me pass
tell me squirrel of the first street-sounds of the day
what cry of a cigar being eaten by rats
what brain made out of a flaming pheasant-full field of heather
    will flutter in the air like a fan
and what voice from a cork-tree turned bottletop
will dare to speak like an equation

—— M. B.

228

AND ON THE VERY FIRST DAY . . .

In the inside of the letter *a* there sprouts a finger placed on lips
because *b* came down hard on the head of *c*
which bursts wide open giving off a resinous stench
from which escape sighs scrambling on all fours higher and
    higher up the rope ladder of desire
even as the drunken *d*
staggers around only to finally topple down a long steep staircase
at the foot of which once again it encounters *j* kissing the empty
    slippers of *g*
which naked yet covered with hair from head to foot
liked to bathe in the gentle river *q*
paying no attention to the various hypocritical waterlilies which
    were only watching and waiting
for the opportunity to throttle it like some innocent *f*
whose disappearance might pass completely unnoticed
until an *i* with outstretched wing comes fluttering along from
    buttercup to buttercup
thereby creating one of those radiant spring evenings
bringing the *e*'s out to loiter before their doors
and echoing the thousand hunting-calls of the *n*'s which keep
    clawing and clawing away
at one long soft feather disappearing down its usual homey hole
where awaiting it are a smiling *l* with breasts like sharpened
    arrowheads
keeping time in a gradually diminishing rhythm
in a cradling hollow of rocks all encrusted with bloodsucking
    seashells
which occasionally *r* sends creeping out at him like a bridge
    stretching out across some gorge
haunted by fearful phantoms who flatten the earth underfoot as
    they flutter
one of whom snatches up a flaming torch
carried away by an *h* foaming at the mouth with bestial fury
to vast deserts carpeted with skeletons which suddenly rise to
    their feet in whirlwinds

since *p* is gasping like the sparkling of some furtive eye in the
   direction of some random female passerby
whose figure so suggestive of such soft sweet caresses has already
   vanished
between the pages of some old-fashioned romantic novel
whose pages are being hastily thumbed in the very shadow of *t*
who will not see the horror which is eternally anticipated
yet never reduced
of the churning masses of *k*'s who lie bleeding at his feet
daytime like an hysterical spiral and nighttime built like a trunk
   just about to burst
both begging an implacable *o* to spare them the dreadful shame
of the springtime's first flowers and fruits
swarming with voracious *m*'s whose poisonous bites
produce a slow death agony
where numb before the red-hot pin-pricks of various *v*'s
which slowly but surely come shooting through for their reunion
   at their annual festival
beneath the shelter of enormous *s*'s which smile down upon their
   partying
while in the distance a *u* armed from head to foot
is dueling to the death with an *x* which he's on the very verge of
   slaying
despite the bitter remonstrances of a *w* blinded with rage
but a self-possessed *y* with wise old eyes holds him back
Just in the nick of time too because *u* suddenly spins around and
   begins threatening
Cut it out now *w* or I'll have to *z* you

— M. B.

230

SONG IN TIME OF DROUGHT

Sky of a hanged man, is it going to rain?
if it rains I'll eat watercress
unless it rains lobsters

Sky of a heel, is it going to rain?
if it rains you'll have fried potatoes
unless it rains jail

Pigs-gut sky, is it going to rain?
if it rains you'll have an onion
unless it rains vinegar

Policeman sky, is it going to rain?
if it rains you'll have a donkey
unless it rains skunks

Cuckold sky, is it going to rain?
if it rains I'll have a wife
unless it rains your girls

Parson sky, is it going to rain?
if it rains you'll be butchered
if it doesn't rain you'll be burned

Stable sky, is it going to rain?
if it rains you'll have stones
unless it rains flies

Sky of a witch, is it going to rain?
if it rains you'll get a comb
if not a shovel

Sewer sky, is it going to rain?
if it rains you'll have a flag
if it doesn't rain a crucifix

Is it going to rain, sky of ashes?

— JAMES LAUGHLIN

TO PASS THE TIME

In May or else in September
the teeth of kitchen utensils start chattering
and all their hair falls out since hats are losing theirs too
And so smoke comes out of a dresser drawer
shaped just like an airplane
located somewhere between a poplar-tree and a diving-bell
gulping up the the same dust that he spat back out before
and that gives us all a big laugh
the way a melon might
the way a frankfurter might
the way a whipped-cream cupcake might
the way a Leyden-glass jar might
the way the opening of the fishing-season might
the way a sack of wheat might
the way, etc.
which dances through closets in which sleeps the roasting pan
dented in the war of 1870
and which insists in various tones of voice
that someone give him a brand new tie made out of corrugated
    iron
which will serve as a rabbit hutch
or shock-absorbing springs
which would become white bread bright
as a pearl-oyster hung at the neck of a naked woman
hairless and voiceless
yet so radiant that a person might very well be reminded of an
    entire forest of evergreens
in a keyhole

—— M. B.

TO BE CONTINUED

Nothing much to say about the jonquil smiling at me like a garlic
    clove
Nothing much to say about the jonquil with its squirrel's head
which is slowly swallowing the mad alarm-clock ringing at the
    top of its lungs breathtakingly inside the prison of my ribs
it's only a mere flower just as a stone is but a toy
but then there is this sausage inhabited by billions of eels
as covered with fuzz as moldy cheese
which rows up the Loire when the flies begin to leave the sausage

Nothing much to say about the squirrel-headed jonquil
except that I love it
as a sea serpent loves the siesta time
which he will never experience

tulips more vicious than spoiled liver

you are my sister tear from a green ear

She will always be for me the first growth of any given year
she who circles the sun who is hotter than any mayfly
like an uncut diamond
whose veins even now are already giving off the odor of
    hawthorn before the descent of wings to it
as thrown into obvious relief as a fist in a cow's face
as a mosquito in the cell of my skull

— M. B.

ON ALL FOURS

Wiped out by the hugeness of the big electric crane
the fly's leg nevertheless goes traveling through my eye as no
    traveler ever managed to before
Though it may rain sardines
or blow hard enough to unscrew Mt. Blanc
it travels without stopping to consider the temptation of closed
    umbrellas
of ancient sabers hung from old suits of armor
which now only know how to blow their noses and sneeze
Sneeze and blow
it's a life no self-respecting carrot in white sauce would envy
nor the grass peeking from in between the pavement-cracks
    fringed by lace-making establishments
sly as an eye behind a pince-nez
as a railway signal which changes from red to green
without announcing a stop at the next station
like a metropolitan park in which a satyr is hiding
But still the fly's leg asks no questions of anyone
because the professors take only the rickety staircase seriously
where the gas at times succeeds in killing its enemy the rat
by throwing stones as if at a fleeing cop
and the stars that terrify goldfish
are neither for sale nor for lease
for the truth is they are not even stars but simply apricot tarts
which have forsaken the pastry shop
and now stroll along aimlessly like a traveler who's missed his
    train at midnight
in a deserted town where the gas lamps whine because their glass
    has all been smashed
Even if that same traveler should encounter a naked lady
walking along the furthermost edge of the pavement
because a silent procession is making its way between her and
    the houses
of old crocodiles terrified by the hellfires rising from their own
    pipes
each searching for a church with a vast supply of holy water

Even if that same traveler should meet this girl
he won't be able to escape the fumes of a burning candy-store
a million fleas jumping out of it will later be held responsible for
    the disaster
but if the stone burns like a lamp to guide the pigeons home
our traveler will feel consoled
and wait
contented
stupid
passionate
courageous
sad
or somewhat lazy
for his beard to grow long enough to be shaved
leaving a deep gash near the ear
a small troubled and cautious lizard
will creep out of it
which will have no luck at all in finding its master's lizard again
and will lose himself somewhere in the vicinity of the fireplace
There waiting to play a dirty trick on him
are the hair-pin the hat-pin the tie-pin the napkin-ring
and that brute of brutes the broken salad-bowl
clenching its fist

— CHARLES SIMIC and M. B.

ROUND OF THE SIDEWALKS

THE storm breaks in the bureau-drawer
And it's a fight to the death
Between the comb and the salsifis
The comb has teeth made of salsifis
And the hair of the salsifis falls to its heels
They stare at each other like china dogs
The dogs that break like glass
Because they wanted to bark
And the china wouldn't let them
Goodbye china dog, salsifis and comb
My waistcoat buttons are singing like mad
And the top one takes a streetcar
He goes to la Villette
He walks down the Rue de Flandres
There he buys some wooden shoes
And the streetcar tracks applaud
He says hello to the steaming horse turds
Over which the sparrows flutter
What horsemanship cries a little old woman
Who wears a pair of sugar tongs in her hair
And her little grandchildren who limp
(The ones born in the even years
Limping with their left legs
And the others on the right)
Follow a pair of mating dogs throwing stones at them
It's raining
And the old woman's hair melts into the sugar tongs
Her head is just a huge beet
The children have eaten its leaves
The beet trembles
And the houses trickle away like melting butter
Spread out like parachutes
But my waistcoat buttons go off down the street
Arm in arm like drunken sailors

— JAMES LAUGHLIN

236

NEBULOUS

When the night of butter just emerged from the churn
inundates the moles of railway stations announced by the
    trumpets of eyes
and enlarges like a subway platform coming closer and closer
only to obliterate your image
which revolves in my brains like a heliotrope in the grip of a bad
    case of seasickness
then collar buttons leap into the air like lambkins formerly
    perched upon a powder keg
thereby flinging into the distance tremendous fountains made
    out of neckties
But you pass like a current of dew-drenched air across the wings
    of a smoking lantern
and you close that door which makes the same sound as a shovel
    burying a potato
the door of the mine shaft
the door of the contested territory along the border
where I wander around among the tornadoes of your staring
    eyes
which grow green again among the trees and so glow bluely there
    in the wood
and which keep founding dynamite factories in the depths of
    the forest
there where the most beautiful breasts in the world stand ajar a
    little only to cry out No through the open space
as they shake out their hair which is like the black sun
shining on a downpour crossing the sidewalk
when the droplet of water of your feet stands there
like a busy-signal in a person's ear
but which expectation has long since seen terminated since by
    now it has become inhabited by rats which gnaw holes in it
before it becomes a floating laundry barge run aground on a
    deserted isle
or a sailboat lost in a railroad carriage
No it's only a bundle of radishes which is drying out like some
    incumbent President

before turning itself into a deserted pale city square
over which glowers a palace of fluorescent mica
where
in the midst of some rusty old battering rams
and devoured by flowering honeysuckle
a column of blood and forget-me-nots having the shape of your
    hands will suddenly spurt into the air flinging forth several
    phosphorescent Yesses
which will eject around themselves vast aurora borealises of
    ostrich-feathers and peaches
swelling like a sea you'll never want to cross
and which hums at your feet like some small seashell
where once again the echo of your voice can be found

— M. B.

SOMEONE'S KNOCKING

A flea's leap like a wheelbarrow dancing along the kneecaps of
    old cobblestones
A flea which melts away on a staircase in the place where I live
    with you
and the sun like a bottle of red wine
all turn to black
a black flogged slave
But I love you the way a seashell loves the sand
from which someone digs it up as the sun takes on the shape of
    a kidney-bean
which begins to expand like a pebble whose heart is being
    stripped bare by the rain
or an overturned can of sardines
or a sailing-ship whose jib-sail has been ripped

I want to be the fragmented projection of sunlight on the
    ivy-covered wall of your arms
this tiny insect which tickled you when I knew you better than I
    do now
No
this mite made out of iridescent sugar no more resembles me than
    mistletoe does an oak
of which nothing is left except a crown of green branches in
    which a couple of robin redbreasts are nesting

I am yet to be
because without you I'm not even the small space between the
    old cobblestones of future barricades
I have your breasts in my chest so much
that two smoking craters stand out there like a reindeer in a cave
in hopes of embracing you the way an old suit of armor might
    hug some naked lady
it has been awaiting down to the deepest depths of its rust
even as it softly melts like the windows of a house afire
like a chateau in a chimney
like a ship adrift
without either anchor or helm

toward a desert isle covered with blue trees which make an
    individual dream of your navel
an isle where I'd like to sleep with you

— M. B.

LOUIS XVI GOES TO THE GUILLOTINE

Stink stink stink
What's that stink
It's Louis XVI that bad egg
and his head drops into the basket
his rotten head
since the cold is terrific this 21st of January
It rains blood it rains snow
and all sorts of other filth
that flourishes out of his ancient corpse
like a dog croaked on the bottom of a pail
in the midst of dirty laundry
who has had plenty of time to start decomposing
like the fleur-de-lys on the garbage can
which the cows refuse to nibble
for they give off an odor of true divinity
god the father of all mud
who gave to Louis XVI
the divine right to croak
like a dog in a laundry-pail

— CHARLES SIMIC

240

MY FINAL AGONIES

To Yves Tanguy

270 The birches are worn out by mirrors
441 The young father lights a candle and gets undressed
905 How many have died in sweeter morgues
1097 The eyes of the strongest
1371 Maybe the old people have forbidden the young ones to
go into the desert
1436 First memory of pregnant women
1525 My foot's asleep in a brass bowl
1668 My heart exposed to the aorta moves from East to West
1793 A card looks on and waits
For the dice
1800 Polishing, that's the least important
1845 Stroke the chin and wash the breasts
1870 It's snowing in the devil's stomach
1900 The children of the invalids
have had their beards trimmed
1914 You'll find some gasoline but it won't be for you
1922 They're burning the social register in the Place de l'Opéra

— JAMES LAUGHLIN

NORTH WIND

At midnight down by the rivulets of asphalt
I've seen the shadow of a wooden sun which was whistling the
    song of untillable soil
while tilting a bit
to the right of her locomotive pulling out of the station
and to the left of her fishing-fleet returning empty to port
I pursued her across the underbrush of adverbs which had
    returned to the state of nature
stumbling against the monuments erected in the suburbs to the
    memory of boxes of candy
whose eyes sparkled like those of prostitutes
Sometimes a pair of suspenders worn bishop-style or several
    violently trembling soup-plates
made me pause by posing a question relative to the destiny of
    modern man
I responded politely with a smile and a sweep of my scythe
biting my tongue to keep the pathway in sight
and took up the pursuit again in the midst of many conversations
    in German
which came out of molehills where one detected the blooming of
    forget-me-nots
Brains petrified and barely breathing the moss-infused air
on cliffs of lips cleverly painted to imitate kisses
the quaking shadow of the Queen of Clubs washed over by
    waves of moonlight adrift among the clouds
from which she held forth her two arms made of telephone wires
    dotted with swallows
which were playing a scene from *La Traviata*
with her body a bayou trapped by a fire on the far horizon
led me by leaps and bounds of such a size and shape
as to cause me to break out from the hatch of my head
one thousand small compartments
now filled with flour over which were sliding decapitated swans
    all carrying open umbrellas
now filled with widows' weeds where squid were navigating

which darted about in fright at the sounds of doors banging as
they blew back and forth in the wind
a short a complete preadolescent evening
Reaching as far as the beaches where chemists in a line as long as
a ball which will not roll
were añalyzing a sea pregnant with a shirt embroidered with
wine-dark scarlet fungi
inflated to the bursting-point with enthusiasm
regarding the shadow of the Queen of Clubs which was only
slightly visible
in the light of seven suns which were ringing out the breakfast
hour
by slowly opening their corollas to full intensity
flying away in the wind escaping from chestnut-trees in flower
walking back and forth around a corkscrew

— M. B.

CLUBS ARE TRUMP

Assemble the stone fragments from the shattering of forward
   dashes and the mistake made by twigs floating away on the
   water
Doubt from the horizons on the other side of your eyes
and set out across white mountains of fernleaves
which slowly fray away the restraining wires of mad passion
The thighs of the sky circle around you
and shadows slam their door without locking it
since the lock doesn't work because of various malefactors
   shaped like tunnels
But because of the incomparable environment of sheer cliffs
— and whenever the necklaces of illusion shatter like the crystal
   of tears
so that the brook suddenly drains away like an emptied cup —
the wretched shellfish of the winding road unfolds abruptly as a
   life jacket
a life jacket which is only good for saving the suicides with
   flaming hands
standing on the laughing hillsides
because the hillsides of suicides laugh with a laugh like waterfalls
with curlicues in their smoking voices
and endless staircases and banisters in their gestures
which wander off in all directions among the blue bubbles of lost
   time
A person who has not let his days drain away through the
   sewerpipes of the snow
knows nothing of the dissolving-power of flowering hawthorn
   taking a bath in blond sand
nor the desperate courage of little trickles of pure water crossing
   whole arsenals of swamps
And he who has not felt the prismatic eyes of palmtrees
falling on the dorsal fin of oatfields
whose downfall corresponds exactly to the degree to which black
   coffee has been roasted
such a man will never know the meaning of Lost Wind
and can only lay claim to forgetfulness

to the most definitive forgetfulness of fluttering eyelashes
unless his breath leaps up
at the mad passage of walls undermined by falling strata
set in motion by the anger of obstacles being overcome

— M. B.

SLEEPLESS NIGHTS

Having passed by the carton of Camembert cheese
the little mayfly's become lost in the exact same desert
where the ham nearly perished from hunger
He darts to the right he darts to the left
but left and right he sees only tomatoes whitewashed with spray
He looks overhead and sees nothing except a coatrack
making mock of him
O varnished coatrack so brightly polished by the lobsters
have mercy on a little mayfly playing on his flute
to try and charm you
since he always did see you as some kind of snake
So why weren't you the kind of snake supplied with eyeglasses
    or else the one with rattles
in that case the mayfly wouldn't have chewed upon his flute
in his despair
and he wouldn't have waited for death
somewhere in back of a necktie
And death wouldn't have come to him
like a set of crystal teeth
and death wouldn't have plucked him up
like an old cigarette butt

— M. B.

ROBERT DESNOS

1900-1945

ALTHOUGH ONE OF THE ORIGINAL PARTICIPANTS in the Surrealist movement and one of the most effective practitioners of Surrealist techniques, Desnos was also one of its most devotedly independent spirits. On several levels the poet had, as he once claimed, "a mind full of metamorphoses."

Desnos' first extant poetry dates from 1919. It was first published in *Littérature* during the movement's so-called "laboratory," or incubational, period. In a highly serious, not to mention instructional, form of wordplay, the early poems are often structured according to experiments with language, including puns, interchange of syllables, and the deliberate mishearing of homonyms; the resulting combinations produce imagistic juxtapositions which are "marvelous" in the sense about to be codified in the first Surrealist Manifesto. Breton singles out Desnos for particular praise in both the Manifesto and the autobiographical *Les Pas perdus* of 1924, and also in the novel *Nadja* (1928), where he describes with some awe Desnos' ability to write and speak automatically, under almost any circumstances, to "fall asleep" and enter states of trance at will.

During the later 1920's Desnos' interest in possible metamorphoses slowly began to extend to Surrealism itself. Though he was one of the movement's most prolific poets of desire, his love poems are unpredictable, even in the Surrealist context. Whereas certain Surrealist love poets tend toward a certain lofty romanticism, the fulfillment of desire practically constituting a moral imperative in a writer such as Eluard, Desnos frequently con-

246

siders the possibly beneficial relationship to feeling of desire deferred. Desnos' lyrical yet curiously antirhapsodic outlook is frequently evinced in "asides" that take the reader into his confidence, such as the one in "The Spaces inside Sleep," where he speaks of wishing to see his beloved with a clarity perhaps lying beyond all literary images, Surrealist imagery not excluded; to see "You, despite a facile rhetoric in which tides expire on sandy beaches, in which crows flutter through ruined factories, in which whole forests rot and crackle beneath a leaden sun"; or the aside in his novel, *La Liberté ou l'amour* (*Liberty or Love!* 1927),[1] in which the poet interrupts a paean to the beloved to question himself:

> The woman whom I love, the woman, ah! I was about to write her name. I was about to write "I was about to speak her name."
> Count, O Robert Desnos, count the number of times you've used the words "marvelous" and "magnificent" to describe her.

Desnos' production violates expectations in genre as well as style. While Breton and others were warning against the excessive popularization of Surrealism, Desnos was writing film criticism for three successive Parisian newspapers. Also, he wrote film scenarios[2] and one of the best theatre pieces to come directly from the movement, *La Place de l'Etoile* (1927; revised 1944).[3] Subtitled "antipoem," the play, like the poems, is a mixture of romantic vision tempered with humorous, hilariously incongruous detail, producing an overall effect which is "marvelous" in the Surrealist sense and magical in the extreme.

Attacked in the Second Manifesto of Surrealism both for his journalistic work and for being what Breton called too "talented" — that is, too eclectic — a writer, Desnos' response was the so-called *Troisième Manifeste du Surréalisme* (*Third Manifesto of Surrealism*, 1930),[4] actually a counterattack on Breton. Also, beginning in 1932 his activities included association with Radiodiffusion Française. This gave rise to a longish, relatively regularly metered poem based on a character in popular French detective fiction, "Complainte de Fantômas" ("Complaint of Fantômas"),[5] which was set to music by Kurt Weill and broadcast in 1934. Desnos' later works include many other experiments in strict forms, including the sonnet. However, in 1936, in an experiment recalling his earlier automatic writing, he undertook to write one poem a day for an entire year.

During the Nazi occupation Desnos was one of the editors of the clandestine publishing house Les Editions du Minuit, and, in addition, he published poems of his own with other houses using various pseudonyms. The day after the première of a film based on one of his scenarios, *Bonsoir Mesdames, bonsoir Monsieurs*, the poet was arrested. Deported first to Buchenwald, then to a concentration camp in Czechoslovakia, he died of typhus in 1945, just a few days after the camp's liberation.

In the late essay *Réflexions sur la poésie* (*Reflections on Poetry*, 1944),[6] Desnos characterized the general direction of his ever-evolving interests as an attempt to

> fuse popular language, even the most colloquial, with an inexpressible "atmosphere"; with a vital use of imagery, so as to annex for ourselves those domains which — to this very day — remain incompatible with that fiendish, plaguing poetic dignity which endlessly oozes from tongues once ripped from that scabrous Cerberus still blocking the gateway to the domains of poetry. . . .

In 1946, in the preface to the new edition of the Second Manifesto, Breton regretted his own and Surrealism's estrangement from the poet.

OTHER PRINCIPAL WORKS

Poetry: *C'est les bottes de 7 lieues cette phrase "Je me vois"* (Galerie Simon, 1926); *Corps et biens* (N.R.F., 1930); *The Night of Loveless Nights* (privately printed, 1930); *Les Sans Cou* (privately printed, 1934); *Fortunes* (N.R.F., 1942); *État de veille* (Godet, 1943); *Contrée* (Godet, 1943); *Le Bain avec Andromède* (Ed. de Flore, 1944); *30 Chantefables pour les enfants sages* (Libraire Gründ, 1944); *Les Trois Solitaires, Nouvelles inédites,* and *Oeuvres posthumes* (Les Treize Epis, 1947); *Calixto, suivi de*

248

Contrée (N.R.F., 1962). Selected poems: *Choix de poèmes, L'Honneur des poètes* (Ed. du Minuit, 1946); *Domaine public* (N.R.F., 1953). Other principal works: *Le Vin est tiré* (novel: N.R.F., 1943). Also essays: introduction to *Tihanyi: Peintures 1908–1922* (Ed. Arts, 1936); contribution to *Les Problèmes de la peinture*, ed. by Gaston Diehl (Confluences, 1945); introduction to *Picasso: Peintures 1939–1946* (Ed. du Grand-Chêne, 1946); *De l'érotisme considéré dans ses manifestations écrites et du point de vue de l'esprit moderne* (Ed. Cercle d'Art, 1953). Selected writings: *Desnos*, "Poètes d'aujourd'hui" No. 16 (Seghers).

ARBITRARY DESTINY

For Georges Malkine

Once again the great days of the crusades return!
Through this sealed window the birds refuse to speak
Like fish in an aquarium.
In the display window
a pretty woman smiles.
Everyday happiness you are a lump of sealing-wax
while I go traveling on like some mist.
A great many ushers anxiously pursue
a perfectly inoffensive butterfly escaping down an aisle.
Beneath my cupped hands it becomes a pair of lace panties
and your eagle flesh
O my dreams while I hold you in my arms!
In the world of tomorrow they will bury you for free
nobody will catch cold anymore
people will speak in the language of flowers
and shine with a glow previously unexperienced.
But today is still today.
I feel my commencement ceremonies coming
the way wheatfields feel in June.
All right officers just slip those manacles on me.
The statues refuse to obey they turn their heads away.
Across their pedestals I'll scribble insults then sign my worst
    enemy's name.
Far off across the seas between two tides
a lovely woman's body scares off sharks.
They rise to the surface to admire themselves there in the clear
    air
but dare not nibble at those forbidden bosoms
such tasty tasty bosoms, too.

— M. B.

250

NIGHTFALL

You'll depart when you feel like it
The bed closes in on itself and comes undone with delight like a
black velvet corset
And a radiant insect settles on your pillow
Sparkles then returns to darkness
The thundering surf comes rolling in then suddenly it falls silent
Picturesque Samoa is snoozing inside the softness
Underground tunnel what are you doing with all those national
flags? you're getting them all covered up with mud
Beneath its guiding star and beneath all the mud and the muck
The shipwreck accentuates itself beneath the eyelid
I spin yarns to invoke sleep
I gather up night's little bottles and set them in a sequence on a
shelf
The plumage of the woodland singer becomes confused with
fragments of cork which take on the shape of a single staring
eye
Don't go there it will be the death of you isn't joy much much
too omnipresent
One additional guest at the round table in the realm of green
emerald and reverberating steel helmets there beside a stack
of battered old ancient armor
One single filament one nerve in the passionate extinguished
lamp of sunset
I sleep.

— M. B.

THE SPACES INSIDE SLEEP

Here in the night are the seven wonders of the world, grandeur
and tragedy and crime.
Here forests combine to mingle with their own legendary beasts
hidden in the thickets.
You are here.
Here in the night are the steps of a man strolling by, steps of the
assassin, steps of the night watchman, the light from a
lamp-post and also the light from some ragpicker's flashlight.
You are here.
Here in the night trains and boats travel by together with the
mirages of landscapes lit by the light of day. The last breath of
dusk and the initial shivers of the dawn.
Notes from a piano, fragments of some voice.
A door slams. A clock.
Moreover not merely material things and beings and their
sounds.
But myself as well, chasing myself and then running on endlessly
past myself.
Here you are, the chosen one — you, the one I await.
Sometimes at the moment of slumber strange faces appear, then
disappear.
When I close my eyes, phosphorescent blossoms flourish and
fade and flare up again like the fires of some carnal or conjugal
conjuring.
Undiscovered landscapes across which I travel in company with
the creatures I have created.
You are here, I'm sure, discreet and exquisite spy.
And Emptiness itself, the soul of which I touch.
All the perfumes of heaven and the stars and the cock-crow
2,000 years ago and the cries of peacocks in parks filled with
fire and kissing and squeezing.
Hands which wring themselves sinisterly in the pale wan light
and axles which creak along snakily twisting roadways.
You are here, no doubt — you, the one I never quite recognize,
and who therefore I recognize perfectly well
And who, though present in all my dreams, persist in permitting

yourself to be sensed in them while never actually appearing.
You who cannot quite be grasped either in dreams or in reality.
You who belong to me by virtue of my desire to possess you in
fantasy but whose face never draws closer to mine except when
I close my eyes tight against both dreams and reality.
You, despite a facile rhetoric in which the tides expire on sandy
beaches, in which crows flutter through empty factories, in
which whole forests rot and crackle beneath a leaden sun.
You who are the solid base of all my dreams yet who jolt and
upset all my metamorphosis-laden soul and you who leave
behind your glove upon my fingertips whenever I bend to kiss
your hand.
Here in the night there are stars and the shadowy motions of
oceans, those of rivers, of forests, of cities, of the grass, of the
lungs of millions and millions of beings.
Here in the night are all the wonders of the world.
Here in the night there is *no* guardian angel — but there *is* sleep.
Here in the night are You.
In the daytime, too.

— M. B.

IDENTITY OF IMAGERY

Furiously I battle against animals and bottles

In such a short time perhaps ten hours have gone right by me
one after the next

The beautiful swimmer who was once so fearful of coral wakes
up this morning

Coral crowned with holly knocks at her door

Oh! carbon again it's always carbon

I call on you O guardian genius of dreams and of my solitude let
me speak once more of the beautiful swimmer who was once
so fearful of coral

Oppress no more this most seductive subject of my dreams

The beautiful swimmer was resting on a bed strewn with laces
and birds

The garments spread upon a chair at the foot of the bed were
illuminated by the flickerings of coals by the final flickerings
from coals

And this particular creature come from the depths of the sky of
the earth and of the sea was proud of his coral-colored beak
and his great crêpe wings

He had spent the entire evening following various funeral
. processions toward assorted suburban cemeteries

He had attended formal balls in embassies and stamped with his
fernleaf emblem innumerable white satin gowns

He had reared up horribly in front of fleets and their vessels had
never been seen again

Crouched now in the fireplace he awaits the awakening of the
foam in the song of the boiling kettle

His sonorous footsteps had troubled the silence of the night in
streets with echoing pavements

O tell me where is she now that beautiful swimmer that swimmer
who was once so fearful of coral?

But the swimmer herself had once again fallen asleep

Leaving me here alone standing face to face with fire where I will
remain all night to question the carbon with its shadowy wings
which continue to fling upon my monotonous progress the

shadows of its smoke and the terrible reflections of its embers
Carbon sonorous carbon merciless carbon.

— M. B.

THE VOICE OF ROBERT DESNOS

So like a flower or the flowing of the air
like the running of a rivulet among the flickering shadows in its
  glare
like a smile just barely glimpsed that celebrated midnight eve
so much like all of happiness and so much like sadness too
here comes midnight now hoisting its naked torso aloft above the
  church steeples and poplar tops
now I summon to me all things lost out in this landscape
crumbling corpses oak-trees become sawn-off stumps
remnants of old rags rotting underfoot as well as bedlinen drying
  on fences around farms .
I summon to me tornadoes and hurricanes
tempests cyclones typhoons
the tidal washes too
the tremors of the earth
I summon to me the smoke from volcanoes and also that coming
  out of cigarettes
the smoke-rings of expensive cigars
I summon to me all lovers and love-affairs
I summon to me the quick as well as dead
I summon gravediggers I summon assassins
I summon executioners I summon ship-pilots construction-
  workers and architects
I summon assassins
I summon human flesh
I summon the one whom I love
I summon the one whom I love
I summon the one whom I love
triumphant midnight unfolds its satin wings and stands there
  just beyond my bedstead
church steeples and poplar tops both bend to my desire
one set collapses while the other sinks more slowly
the lost wanderers of the countryside find themselves once again
  in finding me
crumbling corpses resurrect at my voice
the young sawn stumps grow prolific with bright green

the ragged remnants which were rotting both in and on the earth
flap before my voice like banners of revolt
the bedlinen drying on fences around farms now garbs the most
    adorable women whom I do not adore
but who follow me still
obedient to my voice and adoring me
tornadoes whirl around in my mouth
hurricanes bring if such a thing is possible color to my lips
tempests purr at my feet
typhoons if such a thing is possible start to paint my portrait
I accept the drunken kisses of cyclones
raging tides crash forward before my feet
the tremors of the earth make me tremble not at all but cause
    carnage at my call
volcanic smoke clothes me in wisps
and that from cigarettes becomes my cologne
while the smoke-rings from cigars create my crown
love-affairs and even long-sought love itself take refuge here
    with me
lovers hearken to my voice
the living and the dead yield to me and greet me the first quite
    coldly the second with familiarity
gravediggers abandon their half-finished holes to announce that I
    alone can command their nocturnal labors
assassins salute me
executioners cry for revolution
cry my voice
cry my name
ship-pilots take their fix from my eyes
construction-workers suffer vertigo as they hear me
architects depart for the desert
assassins give me their benediction
human flesh pulsates at my call
the one whom I love cannot hear me
the one whom I love will not listen
the one whom I love never answers.

                                — M. B.

IDÉE FIXE

I bring you now this tiny piece of seaweed which once mingled
  with the sea-foam together with a comb
But your hair is more perfectly plaited than the clouds with the
  winds with the heavenly beamings and thus it is with the
  throbbings and sobbings of life pulsating here beneath my
  hands they die away as do the waves amid the reefs along the
  shoreline yet in such rich abundance that a long long time will
  have to pass before one can be dissuaded of their perfumes and
  their dwindling into this twilight region wherein this comb is a
  motionless marker indicating without shifting the stars lost in
  their silken trajectories but traversed by my fingertips which
  still invoke deep in their hollow interiors the humid caress of
  the ocean but an ocean more perilous still than that ocean from
  which this piece of seaweed once was plucked together with
  the scattered flocculence of a squall at sea
A fading star is like your lips
They turn bluish as wine spilled upon a tablecloth
A moment passes with all the depth and profundity of a mining
  operation
Anthracite sighs softly then showers in great snowflakes upon
  the town
It's so cold now in the little dead-end street where once I knew
  you so well
A forgotten house number on a building now in ruins
The number 4 I think.
I will find you again after a few days beside this little pot of
  flowering marguerite.
The mines are muttering to themselves
The rooftops are thickly coated in anthracite.
Within your hair which is like the absolute end of the world this
  comb
The mist the weary bird and the loud bluejay
All fade away and die away there all roses and emeralds too
Every bloom and gem.
The earth falls apart shatters like a star with the earsplitting
  sound of steel scraping pearl

258

Still your perfectly plaited hair has exactly the same shape as a
hand.

— M. B.

REMARKS FROM THE ROCKS

The queen of the azure and the fool of the void go past you in a
    taxicab
At each window heads of hair are leaning out
And the heads of hair say: "See you soon!"
"See you soon!" say the jellyfish
"See you soon!" say the shining silks
Says the mother-of-pearl, say the pearls, say the diamonds
Soon there is a night of nights moonless and starless
A night made out of forests and deserted shores
A night made out of love and all eternity
In the window that was being stared at, a pane of glass shatters
Over the tragic landscape, a strip of cloth flaps about
You will be alone
Among the fragments of mother-of-pearl and diamonds
    definitively carbonized
Inert pearls
Alone among silks which will become the empty shells of dresses
    as you approach
Among the trails of jellyfish which vanish as soon as you look up
Perhaps only the heads of hair will not escape you
Will obey you
Will curl around among your fingers like irrevocable
    condemnations
Short hair of little girls who loved me
Long hair of women who loved me
And whom I did not love too much
O remain there at that window a long, long time!

A night made out of nights of deserted shores
A night made out of luminousness and funerals
A staircase unfolds beneath my feet but daylight reveals only
    shadows and disasters as my destiny
Only the colossal marble column of doubt holds the sky above
    my head
Empty bottles which I smash into glittering smithereens
Odor of cork thrown back by the sea

Ship riggings as imagined by very young girls
The remains of mother-of-pearl which is gradually grinding itself
    down to powder
An evening of evenings made out of love and all eternity
Deep endless sadness desire poetry love revelation
    miraculousness revolution love deep infinity surrounds me
    with these chattering shadows
Eternal infinitudes are smashed into fragments O heads of hair!
It was it will be on a night of nights with neither moon nor pearly
    glow
Without bits of broken bottles, even.

— M. B.

SUICIDED BY NIGHT

Green boughs bow down low when the dragonfly appears at the
    turning in the footpath
I'm traveling toward a tombstone more translucent than snow
    white as milk white as quicklime shining as the ramparts
The dragonfly splashes around in milk-puddles
The glassware suit of armor shudders shakes begins to walk
    away
Rainbows tie each other up into knots resembling Louis XVth
    furniture ornaments
And just look at that! Already the ground trampled down by our
    passing dares to raise its hand
Whacks the glass armor
Rings doorbells
Flies through the air
Screams groans oh! oh! oh! oh! Ship-wake you're all broken
    down now by this blue boulder's sound
Gigantic sponge fragments falling from heaven are inundating
    the cemeteries
Wine is flowing with the sound of thunder
The milk and the trampled ground and the armor are battling it
    out on the grass which is turning from white to red
Thunderclap and lightning and rainbow
Oh! Ship-wake how you crack wide open now you sing!

The little girl on her way to school recites her lessons.

— M. B.

CUCKOO-CLOCK

Everything was as if in a child's drawing.
The moon had on a top-hat the eight highlights of which skipped
off across the surface of a pond,
A ghost in a handsomely cut shroud
Was smoking a cigar at the window of his apartment,
Located on the lowermost story of a dungeon
Where the wise old crow was telling the fortunes of several cats.
There was a child in a nightgown lost among snowbound
roadways
Because she went out in her slippers to seek the missing silken
fan and high-heeled formal pumps.
There was a huge fire above which, gigantically,
The shadows of firemen floated.
But, above all, there was the fleeing thief, a big sack on his back,
On the road lit up by the moon,
Surrounded by the barking of the watchdogs in nearby villages.
And the cluckings of upset chickens.
I'm not a wealthy man, said the ghost tapping off his cigar ash,
I'm not a wealthy man
But I'll bet you five bucks
That boy will go far if he keeps at it.
Vanity, all is vanity, answered the crow.
What about your sister? asked the cats.
My sister has beautiful jewels and beautiful spiders
In her castle of darkness.
A crowd of countless servants
Comes every night to carry her to bed.
When she wakes up, she has a basket of goodies, a soft grassy
spot, and a little trumpet
To toot into.
The moon set its top-hat on the ground.
And that made a pitch-black night
Into which the ghost dissolved like a sugar-cube in a cup of
coffee.
The thief kept trying to find his way
And finally fell asleep

And nothing on earth could be seen
Except a smoke-blue sky and the moon cleaning its face with a
    washcloth
And the lost child wandering among the stars.
Here is your pretty fan
And here your fancy dancing slippers
Your grandmother's old corset
And some rouge for your lips.
You have permission to dance among the stars
Yes you may dance for the lovely ladies
Across mountains of heavenly floating roses
From which one drops every night
To reward the sleeper with the most beautiful dream of all.
So slip on your shoes and lace up these stays
Put one of these red roses in your bosom
Some pink on your lips
And then flutter your fan
So that on earth there still may be
Nights to follow the days
Days to follow the night.

— M. B.

IF YOU ONLY KNEW

Far from me as the stars, the sea, and the other traditional
trappings of poetical mythology,
Far from me, yet present nonetheless since you are so unaware
of it,
Far from me, and even more silent than you are distant, since I
think about you all the time,
Far from me, my gorgeous mirage and my perpetual dream, in a
way you'll never know.
If you only knew.
Far from me and perhaps all the more so because you are
completely unaware of me and grow still more unaware of me
every day.
Far from me because you can't possibly love me or what amounts
to the same thing, because I can't imagine such a thing.
Far from me because you methodically ignore my every desire.
Far from me because you are so cruel.
If you only knew.
Far from me, O ecstatic as a flower dancing in the river at the
end of its underwater stem, O melancholy as seven hours of
evening in the mushroom cellars.
Far from me, still more silent than if you were present and still
more ecstatic than the hour that comes tumbling toward us
out of the sky, in the shape of a stork.
Far from me at that moment when the crucibles sing, at that
moment when the silently foaming sea folds back upon the
pillows.
If you only knew.
Far from me, O my present present torment, far from me and
lost in the noise of oyster shells crushed beneath the
somnambulist's feet at false dawn as he passes before the
doors of deserted harborside seafood restaurants.
If you only knew.
Far from me, my persistent, substantial mirage.
Far from me there is an island turning to observe the passage of
ships.

Far from me a docile herd of cattle wanders off the path the edge
of a cliff, then pauses obstinately there, far from me, O cruel
one.
Far from me a shooting star lands in the poet's nightly bottle. He
puts back the cork and, while staring at the fallen star through
the glass, also sees constellations rising along the far walls,
far from me, you are that far from me.
If you only knew.
Far from me a building under construction is completed.
At the top of a scaffold a bricklayer in white overalls sings a sad
song to himself and then, in the leftover cement, sees the
entire future of the house: the kisses the lovers and the suicide
pacts, the nakedness in the beds of beautiful strangers together
with their midnight meditations, and various voluptuous
secrets discovered in the polished parquet.
Far from me,
If you only knew.
If you only knew how I love you and, even though it's true that
you do not love me, how happy I've become, because I'm
stronger now, being proud to step ahead with your image in
my mind, and to step out of this entire universe.
How happy I am to be dying of this.
If you only knew how I've conquered the world.
And you, so beautiful, so unconquered too, if you only knew
how completely you've become my prisoner.
O you who conquer me from so far away.
If you only knew.

— M. B.

FOR A DAYLIGHT DREAM

The murder of the customs inspector was magnificent what with the blue circles around his wide-open eyes and the quacking of ducks beside the pond

The murder was magnificent but soon the sun had transformed itself into a great black crêpe mourning cape

Which is the god-child of golden-brown and an exact portrait of the depths of the sea

The swan stretches out on the grass and thus we have the poetry of metamorphosis The Swan which becomes a matchbox and the matchtip disguised as a tie

Melancholy finale Metamorphosis from silence to silence and drinking-song of a crackling fire on a Sunday evening in the suburbs of Neuilly lightning-bolt which burns itself out struggling against the fatal attractions of the magnetic north and so lacking in the capability necessary to comprehend that never from the depths of shadowy consciousness exploding in a sudden flurry consisting of wings and lightning-rods and concerned lest that fiery staircase be wholly transformed into waters amongst the strange undersea growths which ofttimes fishermen would pull up in their nets plaited of curls and pearls to the great horror of the redskins of the Great Plains and the fatal emblem charged with the responsibility of discovering the exact speed and velocity which sobs and palpitates thanks to the interruptions from doorbell buzzers which which which well what which?

Gather gather the rose and forget your fate for a little space gather now gather now the rose and the palmtree frond and slowly lift the tiny eyelids of your outstretched little girl so she may stare at you ETERNALLY.

— M. B.

I'VE DREAMED OF YOU SO MUCH

I've dreamed of you so much that you have lost your reality
Is there enough time left on earth to ever reach that actual
    physical body and to kiss on that mouth the birth of that voice
    which is so dear to me?
I've dreamed of you so much that my arms, which by now have
    become accustomed to embracing your shadow and then
    folding back across my own chest, might not be able to bend
    around to the literal shape of your form, perhaps.
So much that to once actually stand before the living illusion of
    what has haunted and possessed me for so many days and
    years, could very well transform me to shadows.
Oh equilibriums of the emotional scales!
I've dreamed of you so much that it might already be too late for
    me to ever reawaken. I sleep on my feet, body able to be
    swayed by all the usual illusions of life and love but as for
    you — the only being who matters to me anymore — I would
    probably be able to touch your face and lips even less than the
    face and lips of the next passerby.
I've dreamed of you so much, walked and talked so much, and
    slept so much with your phantom presence that all I can do
    now, and perhaps all I can go on doing, is to remain forever a
    phantom among phantoms, a shadow a hundred times more
    shadowy than that shifting shape moving now, and which will
    go on moving, stepping lightly across the sundial of your life.

— M. B.

THE ROSE OF MARBLE AND
THE ROSE OF IRON

The enormous white rose of marble towered alone above the deserted square where the shadows stretched out to the infinite. And the single marble rose stood aloft beneath the sun and the stars and was queen of the solitude. And although odorless the rose of marble atop its stiff stem atop the granite pedestal was dampened by the dews of the heavens. The moon paused with a pensiveness in her glacial heart and the goddesses of the gardens the goddesses of marble there beneath its tall petals came to feel all the chill of their icy bosoms.

The glass rose resonated with all the sounds of the seacoast. There was not a single sob in all the breaking waves which did not send her into vibrations. Around her fragile stem and her radiant heart the rainbows revolved with the stars. The rain ran in delicate pellets down its leaves which sometimes the wind made tremble to the horror of drainpipes and glowworms.

The rose of coal was a black phoenix which facepowder had transformed into a rose of fire. But ceaselessly drawn from the shadowy corridors of the mine where miners pluck her with all due respect in her natural anthracite setting in hopes of transporting her intact into the light of day issues forth the rose of coal to keep watch at the doorways of the desert.

The rose of pink blotting-paper bled sometimes at twilight when the evening came to kneel at her feet. The rose of blotting-paper guardian of all secrets yet unreliable confidant bled a blood thicker than ocean foam yet which was not its own.

The rose of the clouds appeared above doomed cities during the hour of volcanic eruptions during the hour of flash-fires during the hour of riots and over Paris also when the 1871 Commune mingled its prismatic gasoline veins with the odor of gunpowder and the rose of the clouds was sweet on the 21st of January sweet in the month of October in the cold wind of the steppes sweet in 1905 during the hour of miracles during the high hour of love.

The wooden rose presided over scaffolds. She flowered in the
heights of the guillotine then fell asleep in the small moss
beneath the immense shadows of mushrooms.
For centuries the rose of iron had been beaten by the blacksmiths
of lightning. Each of its leaves was as vast and forbidding as
some unknown clime. At the last touch it gave off the sound of
thunder. But how gentle to true lovers was this rose of iron.

The rose of marble the rose of glass the rose of coal the rose of
blotting-paper the rose of clouds the wooden rose the rose of
iron will go on flowering forever but today they are leafless
and flat upon your carpet.

Who are you anyway? you who crush beneath your naked feet
the scattered debris of the rose of marble the rose of glass
the rose of coal the rose of pink blotting-paper the rose of
clouds and of the wooden rose and of the rose of iron.

— M. B.

ONE DAY WHEN IT WAS NIGHT OUT

He escaped under the river. Pebbles of ebony golden steel cables
and the armless cross.
All or nothing.
I hate all love as if it were a single person.
Death inhales with great lungs of vacuum.
The compass drew squares and five-sided triangles.
At midday the stars shone.
The hunter with his fishing-creel full of fish was dreaming on the
riverbank at the very center of the Seine.
An earthworm marks off the center of a circle on its
circumference.
In silence my eyes utter ardent exclamations.
Then we went off together into a deserted alley where crowds
pressed in on us tightly.
When the stroll we were taking had sufficiently relaxed us we
finally found strength enough for our repose but then just as
we awoke our eyes locked tight and dawn poured over us all
the reservoirs of night.
The rains dried us off again.

— M. B.

HALF WAY

There is a precise moment in time
When a man reaches the exact center of his life,
A fractional section of a second
A fleeting fragment of time more abrupt than a darted glance
More sudden than the peak of love,
Faster than light.
And a man is aware of this moment.

Long avenues stretch out between tall walls of foliage
Leading to the base of a distant tower in which a lady lies
    sleeping
Whose beauty resists kisses, resists passing seasons
As a star the wind, a rock the waves.

A ship, shaking and trembling, sinks to the bottom, weeping.
A flag flaps at the top of a tree.
A well-groomed woman, but with stockings falling over her
    shoetops
Appears at a streetcorner,
Excited, shaking
Hand shielding a lantern extinguished but still smoking.

And once again a drunken dockworker sings at the far end of a
    bridge
And once again a girl nibbles the lips of her lover,
And once again a rose-petal drifts down into an empty bed,
And once again a trio of grandfather clocks chime the same hour
At intervals of several minutes,
And once again a man passing in the street turns around
Because someone has shouted out his name,
Except it turns out he wasn't the one the woman was calling to,
And once again a government official in full regalia
Disagreeably discountenanced by the tension of his shirt-tail
    caught between his trousers and his shorts,
Inaugurates an orphanage,
And once again, after bouncing out of a speeding vehicle,
A marvelous tomato rolls around in the gutter,

272

To be swept up again later on,
And once again a fire breaks out somewhere on the sixth floor of
   a building
And burns at the heart of a silent, indifferent city,
And once again a man suddenly hears a song
Long forgotten, and forgets it again,
And once again a great many things,
Many, many other things that a man notices suddenly in that
   moment at the exact center of his life,
Many, many other things unfolding at great length in this
   briefest of earth's brief moments.
He savors for a while the mystery of this moment, of this
   fractional section of a second,

After which he says: "Let's get rid of all these black thoughts!"
And so he gets rid of all these black thoughts.
And what could he say
And what could he do
That would be better?

— M. B.

EBONY LIFE

A dreadful dullness will characterize the coming day
And the shadows thrown by streetlights and fire-alarm boxes will
　weary the light
Everybody will fall silent even the most taciturn even the most
　talkative
Finally all wailing babes will die away into absolute silence
Tugboats locomotives the wind
Will slide by without a sound
You will hear the overwhelming voice coming from very far away
　passing through the city
It will have been expected for a long long time
Then drawing nearer to the Castle Keep of Sunlight
When the dust and the stones and the absolute absence of tears
　unite in the deserted public places to weave daylight's brand
　new royal dressing-gown
Finally you will be able to hear this voice invading
It will growl at great length before all portals
It will pass through the city tearing down flags and breaking
　windows
You will be able to hear it
What silence reigned before it came but greater still is the
　silence which this voice will not exactly disturb with its
　presence but which it will openly accuse of a forthcoming
　homicidal act which it will attack which it will denounce
　soundly
O day of misery and joy
And on the day on the coming day after this voice goes to
　town
A ghostly seagull will have whispered to me that she adores me
　just as much as I adore her
That this tremendously terrifying silence had truly been my love
But that the wind which carried this voice to me was the great
　revolution of the world
And that this voice would be favorable to me.

— M. B.

274

DESPAIR OF THE SUN

What strange sound was slithering along the length of the
staircase at the foot of which dreamt the radiant apple.

The orchards were finished for the year and far off the sphinx
stretched out in sands crackling with heat among the fragile
veils of evening.

Would this sound endure until the awakening of all the tenants
in the neighborhood or would it slip away into the shadow of
morning twilight? The noise went on. The sphinx with its
watchful eyes had been sensing it for centuries and was
wishing that at last it could experience its actual impact by
hearing it. That is why no man should be astonished to see the
supple silhouette of the sphinx among the shadows of the
staircase. The beast was leaving clawmarks with his paws
upon the polished passageways. The shining buttons on each
apartment door threw their effusions down the elevator shaft
and the persistent sound sensed the approach of the One
long-awaited throughout millions and millions of shadow-
flickers seizing him by the scruff of the neck but then suddenly
the shadow faded.

It's the poem of the morning beginning while in her humid bed
with undone hair coming down over her eyes and her
bedclothes even more wrinkled than her eyelids the wayward
adventuress awaits the moment when her door which is still
locked before the onslaught of the flowing of the heavens and
of the evening opens onto a vista of agate and gum.

It's the poem of the daylight in which the sphinx lies down in the
bed of the wayward adventuress and despite the persistent
sound swears to her an honorable and eternal love.

It's the poem of the daylight beginning with the fragrant fumes
of chocolate and the monotonous clickety-clack of the floor-
polisher astonished to observe upon the staircase the
clawmarks of the night-wanderer.

It's the poem of the day beginning with match-sparks to the
great horror of the pyramids who are astonished and saddened
not to find their majestic companion still crouching at their
feet.

But what was this sound, anyway? Reiterate this inquiry while
the poem of this day is beginning while our dear beloved
wandering sphinx meditates on the convulsiveness of this
countryside.
This sound was not the sound of the clock nor that of footsteps
nor even that of some coffee-mill creaking.
What was this sound? What's going on here anyway?
Will the staircase plunge ever deeper? Will it climb ever higher?
Dream accept the dream it's the poem of the day just about to
begin.

— M. B.

AT THE WORLD'S LAST OUTPOST

They're mouthing things down in the dark street at the far end
of which the river waters go trembling by the barges.
This cigarette butt flipped out the window makes a star.
Now, down in the dark street, they're mouthing some more
mouthings.
Oh, shut your mouths already, will you!
Thick, constricting evening, evening too heavy to inhale.
A cry comes in our direction, nearly touches us,
Then gives out just before it gets here.

Somewhere in the world, at the foot of some embankment,
A deserter is trying to negotiate with several sentinels who can't
understand a word he's saying.

— M. B.

THE GREAT DAYS OF THE POET

The disciples of light have never invented anything except a
somewhat less dense form of darkness.

The river rolls along the tiny body of a woman, and this
signifies that the end is near.

The widow in a wedding-gown gets into the wrong train.

All of us will arrive late for our own funeral.

The ship of the flesh runs aground upon a small seashore. The
navigator requests that the passengers all keep quiet.

Patiently, the waves wait. Nearer, my God, to Thee!

The navigator requests that the waves start to speak. They speak.

Night seals up all her bottles with the stars and makes a killing
in the export trade.

Enormous department stores are built for nightingale sales. But
they will never satisfy the Queen of Siberia who wants a white
nightingale.

A British Commodore swears he'll never again be caught
plucking sage by night from between the feet of the statues of
Salt!

In response to this a small Cerebos salt-cellar leaps weakly to
attention on its delicate little legs.

On my plate it sprinkles what is left of my life.

Just enough to salt the Pacific Ocean.

You will place a life buoy on my grave.

Because one never knows.

— M. B.

ANTONIN ARTAUD

1896-1948

INVENTOR OF THE TERM "Theatre of Cruelty," and exerting profound influence on contemporary theatre even today, Artaud was also one of the key figures at the start of the Surrealist movement and the director of its so-called Central Bureau for Surrealist Research.

It was in 1920, as a young actor-poet who confessed quite frankly to having spent several of the war years in a psychiatric sanatorium, that Artaud came to Paris to begin a career in the theatre. In 1921, he acted at the Théâtre de l'Oeuvre of Lugné-Poë (the original director of Alfred Jarry's *Ubu Roi*, the play which seems also to have instigated the theatrical career of Apollinaire). The next year he was accepted as a student in Charles Dullin's Théâtre de l'Atelier; in 1923 he was engaged by Georges Pitoëff to play at the Comédie des Champs-Elysées. In the same year he began to participate in the activities of the pre-Surrealist circle, becoming one of the most frequent contributors to the initial issues of *La Révolution Surréaliste*, for the most part editing its third number, consecrated to "The End of the Christian Era" — a new attack on one of the favorite subjects of Surrealist disgust.

Artaud's attachment to Surrealism seems identical with his enthusiasm for its acceptance of the unconscious and its apparent approval of all forms of subjective vision. The initial broadside Artaud composed in 1925 to explain the purposes of the Central Bureau declares Surrealism's chief aim as "the readjustment of all external thought . . . in the name of . . . inner liberty.

278

It applies to the spontaneous reclassification of things according to a profounder and finer order, an order impossible to detail by means of the ordinary functioning of reasoning."[1] The statement paraphrases with dignity Breton's first Manifesto, to be sure, but it is only fair to recognize its personal urgency.

Artaud broke with Surrealism in 1927, partly over a pamphlet whose authors included Aragon, Eluard, Péret, and Breton, and which declared that henceforth Surrealism would not only concern itself with psychic and other inner redefinitions, but would attempt to operate more publicly (in the words of its title), *Au grand jour* (*In Broad Daylight*), perhaps involving political explorations. Artaud's disagreement was expressed in the pamphlet *Au grand nuit où le bluff Surréaliste* (*In the Middle of the Night or the Surrealist Bluff*).[2] In it, he declared in favor of inner liberty against all external imperatives, including political imperatives, concluding: "I know that in the present debate I have on my side all free men, all true revolutionaries who feel that individual liberty is far superior to that which might result from any conquest obtained along the scale of social adjustment."

Another factor provoking the schism was Artaud's founding in 1927 of the Théâtre Alfred Jarry with another former Surrealist, the playwright Roger Vitrac. Breton saw the move — somewhat shortsightedly, it would now appear — as threatening to Surrealism's independence, and even as an attempt to commercialize the movement. With his countercriticisms of Artaud's pamphlet and criticisms of his theatre interests in the 1929 Manifesto, Breton made Artaud's separation definitive.

Despite the conflict, Artaud's declaration in an early Central Research Bureau pamphlet that Surrealism represented "a new kind of magic," is reflected in his later writings on and for the theatre. He himself wrote only one play in conventional theatre format, the brief *Jet de sang* (*Jet of Blood*, ca. 1927),[3] one of the productions given on opening night at the Théâtre Alfred Jarry. A broader sense of his dramatic techniques may be seen in his various adaptations of texts by others, and in his two scenarios for the stage, *La Pierre philosophale* (*The Philosopher's Stone*, 1930–1931)[4] and *Il n'y a plus de firmament* (*The Sky is Empty*, 1931),[5] as well as in his theoretical writings, the most important of which is *Le Théâtre et son double* (*The Theatre and Its Dou-*

ble, 1938).[6] Derived from Surrealism is perhaps this text's central tenet: that it is vital to violate occidental rationalism by "de-Western-culturalizing" art. Artaud's recommendations to this end included the study of Eastern models of theatre, the use of marvelous and magical spectacle, the enrichment of poetic language by juxtaposition with specifically theatrical styles of gesture and movement, and the consequent suppression of all but essential textual material, this better to serve the purposes of spectacle. His recommendation that the physical barriers between players and audience be abolished, not only in theatre seating but even to the point of holding performances in such patently noncultural surroundings as the street, probably prefigures contemporary developments in "environmental theatre." Yet this also parallels the use of the street as setting for the portrayal of "quotidian magic" in many of the characteristic Surrealist poems and novels of the 1920's.

Artaud's sense of the difficulty of bringing his deepest esthetic ideals to the stage is perhaps reflected in his interest in the cinema. In 1926 he appeared as Marat in Abel Gance's *Napoléon*; in 1928 he played a monk in Carl Dreyer's *The Passion of Joan of Arc*. Also, he composed the scenario for the short film *La Coquille et le clergyman* (*The Seashell and the Clergyman*, 1928).[7]

Artaud's poems are at one with the impulses of his theatre, despite what at first may appear to be a certain traditionalism of format. A central theme, especially in those written during the Surrealist years, is yearning for a change towards openness, towards acceptance of the inward man. At first this is recommended in the interest of transforming reality into a realm of the marvelous, even to the point of invoking (in the words of one of the poems) "a sexual festival"; later, this rejection of physical externals extends to the poet's own body, insofar as it fails to signify a fusion with the spirit. In the most intransigent of his "post-surrealist" poems the body is seen as a living mummy, serving solely as a dead weight to the spirit.

In simultaneous pursuit of esthetic and personal renovation, Artaud spent several months in Mexico in 1936, during which time he participated in peyote rituals, an experiment which is described in one of his last major prose texts, *Au Pays de Tara-*

humaras (*In the Land of the Tarahumaras, 1937*).[8] A year after returning, he suffered a severe nervous setback, and was confined; he remained institutionalized until 1946, partly to keep him out of the hands of the occupying German military forces. In 1946, in the preface to a new edition of the second Manifesto, Breton regretted their separation; that same year, Breton organized a theatrical soirée in homage to Artaud, beginning the resurrection of Artaud's reputation.

OTHER PRINCIPAL WORKS

Together with his other works, Artaud's Surrealist-period texts are numerous enough to be scattered throughout the seven volumes of the *Oeuvres complètes*. His books of verse also collected in this volume: *Tric-trac du ciel* (Galerie Simon, 1923); *L'Ombilic des limbes* (N.R.F., 1925); *Le Pèse-nerfs* (Collection "Pour vos beaux yeux," 1925), and many uncollected earlier and later poems appear in Vol. I of the *Oeuvres complètes*. Selected writings: *Artaud Anthology* (City Lights Books, 1965; tr. by various hands, ed. Jack Hirschman); *Artaud*, "Poètes d'aujourd'hui," No. 66 (Seghers).

POET OF THE BLACK

Poet of the black, a virgin's bosom
still haunts you,
bitter poet, life's ended for you,
the entire town's afire
the sky's being drained away by the rain
and your pen goes gnawing away at the heart of life.

Forest, forest, eyes swarm on
over the proliferating pinecones;
hairs of the storm, poets
ride off on horses, on dogs.

Eyes rage, tongues twist,
the sky flows into nostrils
like a nourishing blue milk;
I dribble down now from your mouths
women, harsh and vinegar-hearted.

— M. B.

TREE

This tree and its trembling
forest dark with calls,
with cries,
gnaws at the hidden heart of night.

Vinegar and milk, the sky, the sea
the heavy burden of the heavens,
all conspire to create this trembling
which lives on and on, intact at the heavy heart of shadow.

A heart which breaks in two, a hard star
dividing and dissolving in the sky,
the clear lucid sky that cracks
at the call of the clanging sun,
make the same sound, make exactly the same sound
as night with this tree at the center of the storm.

— **M. B.**

ORGAN AND SULPHUR

The times are right for the organ
The one the winds scatter through the night
The organ fills up the whole little square
With its ice that turns into bone

You, you sneaky little city
Put out all your women on every balcony
This manna slowly rising from the rocks
Is better than all your trembling ecstasy

I invite to the black feasts of love
Where the sour wine of noises spurts
The wanderer who chases across the night
And the adolescent without any memory

And anyone who finds his phrases
In the labyrinths of his dream
And also anyone who looks for his mother
Lying down close beside him

Town with your sperm and your shoulderblades
Town with your beds stretched out across the very sky
I invite you all to the sexual festival
Down to the angels of your churches

— M. B.

GERMAN ORGAN

The German Organ moves the monkey
In the square with the narrow pavements
And the besieging surrounding Fair
Unfolds itself like one great banner

The old fair borders the sky
At the very edges of town
While the organ keeps exploding and exploding again
With the noises of the organs of heaven

An accelerating waltz
Sets fire to the lacework of the city
Set off in the organ's belly
Is some bomb nobody can understand

O secret, false
Town covered with scales, town with all your roofs
The only music you do admit
Which makes you the least bit tipsy, you empty

You digest, without absorbing
O music, slicing music
With your marble harmonies
Which crush the frozen sky

— M. B.

ROMANCE

Music emerges from the windows
Melt, O marrow of our bones
The whole town falls upsidedown
In a delightful spasm

In the black town the sound
Made by several hidden organs
With harsh-handled thrusts
Heightens, heightens with each push

Oh the town is loaded to the bones
By this unparallel liquor
Which pours in through its ears
Piercing their central crystals

Still a silence dwells deep within
This intoxicating tune
The whole town waits to be drawn
From the very heart of the organ

And the expectation recurs again
In the pause between each turn
That the falsehearted handle
Imposes on the lucid music

What Africa or what Arabia
Contains the refrain we listen for
O break the frozen glass of our foreheads
Music, O wounding music

— M. B.

SNOW

Obsession of the snow, pearl,
Branches fire rock stage-setting
Marrow of the white elder tree, virgin candle
And sperm finally closing the circle

Protests of the spirit old chariots of fire
Window of flesh road of souls
Bellies of embers and breasts of flame
Husbands of virgins also beard of God

Precocious laughter, naïvetés
Frozen flames, detachment
Standardized restitutions
Inexpressible purity

Whirlwinds of souls white atoms
And once again we see the landscape
Burning silver souls of the magi
Stolen stars soaring souls

Piercing sighs voracious lips
Delicious inflammation
Purged lilies snow of the years
And this wheel whirring in ecstasy

— M. B.

PRAYER

O give us skulls of hot coals
Skulls burnt up by heaven's thundering
Lucid skulls, real skulls
Crossed back and forth by your presence

Allow us our birth under inner skies
Sifted out from voids in downpours
And let Vertigo cross over us
With incandescent fingernails

Satisfy us we have a hunger
For universal disturbance
O pour out an astral lava
For us in place of our blood

Detach us. Divide us
With your hands of amputating coals
Open up burning roads for us
Where dying can outdo mere death

Intoxicate our brains
As we drink from the breasts of your pure Science
And tear away our intelligence
In the claws of some new typhoon·

— M. B.

TRAPPISTS

Trappists, Trappists cheat the sky
Swine Brother since you shit
Your pigs achieve a state of grace
Revealing themselves angelic

A spirit breathes among the dunghills
A breeze come from one knows not where
So that all the cabbages are transformed
In this little garden without one lawn

Among all the earthly palaces
Full with their humility
The monks lay down their dusts
They are so low, they are luminous

Dirt seals off the secret
Of the planetary membrane
Where the substance is assembled
For their overreaching dreams

So here we have a hyperspace
The sanctified cripple
The floozy in a state of grace
And the widow with icy belly

— M. B.

MOON

With a bitter flavor tonight, jealous
Of some obscure whore
Cavernous, black, weighted down by the pollution
Drifting between the moon and ourselves

Splenetic moon upon the sea
She was an aggravated moon
Like the thoughts of somebody extremely sick
Of the essence of the universe

In the incredible obscurity
Where this moon was rising
The summer calm
Held out its cloudy boughs

— M. B.

THE BAD DREAMER

My dreams are above all a liquor, a sort of effluvium of nausea into which I plunge and which is littered with bloody bits of glass. Neither in my Dream-Life nor in my Life-Life do I attain the exceeding loftiness of certain images; I do not set myself up or hold myself up as a continuous being. All my dreams are without connections, without county seat, without capitol, without maps of the metropolitan environment. A certified autopsy of severed members!

Besides that, I am too committed to my own ideas to permit anything actually occurring to arouse my interest: I only ask one thing, which is that I be locked up definitively inside my own thought.

And as for the physical appearance of my dreams, I've already described it: a liquor.

— M. B.

THE NIGHT WORKS

In the wineskins of full-blown sheets
where this whole night breathes so deeply
the poet feels his hairs
grow and multiply.

Over all the earth on counters
uprooted glasses pile sky-high
the poet feels both his thought
and his balls say bye-bye.

For here life with the very belly
of thought are on trial
bottles bang the brains
of this assembly of the aerial.

The Word curls forth from sleep
flower-like or like a cup
with forms and fumes inside.

Glasses and asses collide
life is clarified
in brains become crystallized.

The passionate poetic court
convokes at the lofty heights of green baize;
around the void revolves.

Life flits through the thought
of our thick-haired poet:

Just one window commands the street
while cards flap on;
in that window a very vaginal woman
places her belly under consideration.

— M. B.

WINDOWS OF SOUND

Windows of sound where stars turn,
showcases in which brains burn,
the sky seething with immodesties
gobbles up the nudity of the stars.

Bizarre violent milk
bubbles up from the depths of heaven;
A snail climbs up and throws into disarray
the complacency of the clouds.

Delights and rages, the entire sky
flings itself on us in one cloud
a whirlwind of primitive wings
torrentially obscene

— M. B.

ADDRESS TO THE DALAI LAMA

We are your most faithful servants, O High Lama, give us, grace us, with your illumination, in a language our diluted European minds can understand; and, if need be, transform our beings, create for us a mind turned entirely toward those perfect heights where the spirit of man can be finished with suffering.

Create for us a Mind beyond habits, a mind truly frozen in the Mind; or else a mind with purer habits, your own habits, if they truly relate to liberty.

We are surrounded by bellowing popes, versifiers, critics, dogs, our true Mind has gone to the dogs utterly, the dogs who think in terms of earthly immediacies, who think incorrigibly in terms of the present.

Teach us, O Lama, the physical levitation of bodies and how we may be earthbound no longer.

For you know well to what lucid liberation of souls, to what freedom of the Mind within the Mind (O true Pope of the soul!) we now refer.

It is with Inward Eye that I perceive you, O Pope, on the heights of inwardness. It is Inwardly that I truly resemble you: I, dust, idea, lips and levitation; dream, cry, renunciation of all fixed ideas, suspended among all forms, and longing for nothing but the wind.

— M. B.

INVOCATION TO THE MUMMY

These nostrils of bone and skin
where shadows begin
of the absolute, and the coloring of those lips
you close like a curtain

And this gold life slips you in dreams
life that robs you of your bones
and the flowers of that false stare
linking you back to the light

Mummy, and these spindly hands twisting
to overthrow your entrails
these hands whose horrible hovering shadows
take the shape of a bird

All this death decorates itself with
as if with some chance irregular rite
this chattering of shadows, and gold
where your blackened entrails float

This is the way I come to meet you
down the road of vitrified veins,
and your gold is the same as my pain
my worst yet most trustworthy testimony

— M. B.

LOVE WITHOUT A TRUCE

These triangulations on thirsty water
this route without a sign
Madame, and the mark of your masts
on this sea I drown myself in

The messages of your hair
the signalflare of your lips
this storm which carries me away
in the wake of your eyes

This shadow finally, on the shore
where life calls truce, and the wind,
and the terrible trampling footsteps
of the crowds as I pass.

Each time I lift my eyes to you
it is as if the earth trembled
while the fires of love resembled
the caresses of your husband.

— M. B.

NOCTURNAL FESTIVAL

This festival links these lakes
To the flashing chariots of the stars
With their harvest cornucopias
Heavy with our brilliant thoughts.

Somewhere between earth and sky
It flings out the waste of souls
Which anyone might, in the flaming night
Take for flying swans

And we, complacent observers
At these transfusions of our marrow
Can also see the stars sinking
From our exhilarating dream.

— M. B.

296

RENÉ DAUMAL

1908-1944

D AUMAL WAS ONE OF THE FEW WRITERS to have the distinction of
being invited by Breton himself to join the Surrealist movement,
and of resisting. Breton's enthusiasm (expressed in the Second
Manifesto of Surrealism) was evidently inspired by Daumal's
poem, "Fires at Will," about which Breton remarked: "He who
speaks in this manner, having had the courage to say that he is
no longer in control of himself, has no reason to prefer being
separated from us, as he will soon find out." This explicit invita-
tion to join official Surrealism was never accepted, despite the
increasingly obvious reasons furnished by Daumal's poetry for
accepting it (as the Surrealist leader predicted).

Before this as well, Daumal's background had been extremely
various and independent. A student of Sanscrit, he became a
translator of Suzuki's classic texts on Zen Buddism, and wrote
many essays on the history of philosophy, both Western and
Eastern. In 1928 he co-founded the magazine *Le Grand Jeu*.
Under Daumal's direction the magazine emphasized the mystical
and occult, but with an inflection which caused Breton (despite
the Surrealist interest in a no less secular Beyond) to charac-
terize Daumal's circle as "mere God-seekers."

Collected posthumously in *Poésie noire, poésie blanche* (*Black
Poetry, White Poetry*, 1954),[1] Daumal's poems reiterate Sur-
realist denials of existing external reality, adding a further doubt:
the questioning of Man's right to exist at all. Since Buddhism
taught that reincarnation is likely, Daumal concluded that there-
fore earthly existence itself is an act perpetrated against the
individual will, and even the threat or promise of its termination

is only a ruse, an illusory escape from the inevitable cycle: the ultimate "deception," as the poet called it. The poems are haunted by a scarcely negative consciousness of impending death, seen as the poet's long-lost "double"; and also by a personification of death as a sort of sinister mother, an exacting being, avaricious in her search for beings to extinguish — but only so as to place upon them perversely the burden of further metamorphoses.

Daumal's view of "the Absurd as the purest and most basic form of metaphysical existence," framed in the series of essays published posthumously, *Chaque fois que l'aube paraît* (*Each Time Dawn Appears*, 1953),[2] has been seen as foreshadowing the work of the postwar Existentialists. Daumal himself identified the impulse behind his work as identical with that of " 'Pataphysics," since, he said, "I recognize the same attitude in Alfred Jarry's book, *Gestes et opinions du docteur Faustroll, 'Pataphysicien* [Exploits and Opinions of Dr. Faustroll, 'Pataphysicist]."[3] Like Jarry, he is a patron saint of the College of 'Pataphysics, a large, international, yet still underground literary organization whose other Surrealist-associated members have included the visual artists Marcel Duchamp and Joan Miró, the film-maker René Clair and the poets Raymond Queneau and Jacques Prévert.

Daumal's view of existence as contradiction was perhaps expressed in the manner of his death, which reportedly occurred as the result of inhaling certain potentially toxic materials during an experiment aimed at determining the threshold between consciousness and death.

OTHER PRINCIPAL WORKS

Works by Daumal include: *Le Contre-Ciel* (poems: Jacques Doucet, 1936); *La Grande Beuverie* (semiautobiographical novel: N.R.F., 1938); *Le Mont Analogue* (novel: N.R.F., 1952; tr. by Roger Shattuck as *Mount Analogue*, Pantheon, 1959); *Lettres à ses amis*, Vol. 1 (correspondence: N.R.F., 1958); *Petit Théâtre* (short plays: Collège de 'Pataphysique, ca. 1960; one, *En Ggggarrrde!* [1924], tr. by Michael Benedikt in *Modern French Theatre: The Avant Garde, Dada, and Surrealism*, E. P. Dutton 1964); *Les Pouvoirs de la parole* (essays: N.R.F., 1972).

THE PHANTOM SKIN

I drag my hope along with my bag of nails,
I drag my strangled hope to your feet,
you who are not yet,
and I who am no more.

I drag my bag of nails across the beach of fire
singing all the names I'll give to you
and those I have no more.
Here in the hut, on the beach, it rots, that rag
in which my life fluttered around;
it was perfectly shipshape, the deck planks were all nailed down,
so he died there in his own little bunk-bed
with his eyes unable to see you,
his ears deaf to your voice,
his skin too thick to feel you
when you grazed him
when you passed in a wind of sickness.

And now I have peeled back that putrefaction,
and pale, and in whiteness I come unto and into you,
my new phantom skin
already trembling in your air.

— M. B.

These translations are based on the original Daumal manuscripts, which differ slightly from the posthumously published versions. We are grateful to Mr. Claudio Rugafiori, the poet's literary executor, for his care and generosity in transmitting these definitive texts to us. — M. B.

THE SKIN OF LIGHT

The skin of light enveloping this world lacks depth and I can actually see the black night of all these similar bodies beneath the trembling veil and light of myself it is this night that even the mask of the sun cannot hide from me I am the seer of night the auditor of silence for silence too is dressed in sonorous skin and each sense has its own night even as I do I am my own night I am the conceiver of non-being and of all its splendor I am the father of death she is its mother she whom I evoke from the perfect mirror of night I am the great inside-out man my words are a tunnel punched through silence I understand all disillusionment I destroy what I become I kill what I love

— M. B.

"IT COMES FROM DEEP CAVERNS . . ."

It comes from deep caverns
It comes from the caves of myself
a step stamped in the snow
a suggestion of emptiness against whiteness
a white-tongued silence
a solid void in the midst of motionless air
it comes from deep caverns
a whiff of the cave, yet with a head.

The forehead of a breath batters at my door
beats at the whiteness of my open door
a sad head
against all the sadness of the snow

A breath with a forehead convulses
blindly then leaps toward me
— it is this cry from the caves of myself
this bubble filled with silence
in the frozen block of my voice.

Blinded, this face forced against my door
which is open wide yet filled with an impenetrable void,
it tears itself forth from the most invisible darkness
then tears itself to bits across the swords before my door.

— **M. B.**

REVOLUTION IN SUMMERTIME

The light is excessive. Men run off to buy handkerchiefs; and not to blow their noses in.

Last resort: Eclipse, that celestial acrobat.

In the midst of this cosmic carnival, this man who takes his role of planetary body seriously. Everybody else is busy burning the sun in effigy, irony of fate, pleasantry of slaves.

Impossible to laugh enough. Now the slaves revolve around the millstone that grinds up life. Their sweat intoxicates the stars, the fattened sun drags itself along through the dust of the highways, a broken eye opens in the sky and the slaves all laugh, shoulders aglow.

— M. B.

ARTIFICE AFIRE

The merry-go-rounds go round
with their painted plaster coaches,
and their golden-haired sirens exhale
from their hollow heavy chests,
unhappiness enters the city,
among palaces built by jesters and jokers,
unhappiness enters the houses of cards,
enters the plaster carcasses of houses,
enters the gilded carousels.

Let's set fire to the city,
so the carousel mermaids burn,
the colors of their cheeks become still brighter
misery with its steel grip triumphs
amid the laughter of burnt embers,
and the odor of varnished pasteboard
burnt bright red.

The steel grip reigns
Every moment more confident and bright,
lovely misery shining in the ashes,
last certainty, what are you hiding there in your palm?
open your fingers, hard but firm hand,
so I may place my burning forehead
in your vital, living, dependable flesh,
bleeding from the assassination of the sun.

— M. B.

THE MONSTER-MENDER

The monster-mender has just passed by in a hail of broken
   windows.
For an instant, I saw his twisted lip penetrate and part the veils
   of shattered glass;
His single, grayish lip
the great snarl of that lip,
his clotted saliva and the crapulous beach of his teeth.
The monster-mender just made a second jump and here he is
   watching over us now from his watchtowers.
His eye, that rotten old tangerine, has only one story to tell, the
   tale of a little Berber shepherd who, one day, was devoured by
   an army of white worms,
his eye, Babel built of dead flesh,
his eye, which it would be nice to see bleed.
The monster-mender suspended all activities for a moment,
then came tottering over in my direction.
But I knew that he would, I'd known it from the beginning of
   time,
you can't scare me, I shouted at him
— I was shrieking like a locomotive so close it grazes your ear,
   at daybreak in a misty city, a city of slag-heaps and tall
   chimneys.
All the monster-mender was able to get for his stockpile was a
   little fragment of metal fear-frozen into numbness by a
   death-spasm

— M. B.

ONE WORD WILL DO

Name, if you can, your shadow, your fear
and measure the circumference of its head,
circumference of your world and if you can
speak it out, the catastrophe-causing word,
if you dare break this silence
woven of silent laughter — if you dare
without help to break the ball,
to shatter the texture,
all alone, all alone, and plant your eyes there
and come forth blind to the night,
come toward your own death who hardly even notices you,
alone if you dare break apart the night,
paved with dead eyeballs,
with no assistance whatsoever if you dare to
come along naked alone to the mother of the dead —

in the heart of her heart your eye remains shining —

listen to her calling you: my child
listen to her calling you by your name.

— M. B.

CONSOLATRICE

Silence worsened the loss of a friend,
candle flames froze in white flowers,
and I laughed at my finger in the mirror,

The drawers were opening of themselves in the morning breezes,
a flattened sun slid in my hand,
I made stupid calculations slobbering.

A woman came in with white eyes of ivory,
holding out arms to me and smiling: she had
in place of teeth bits of red flesh.

— M. B.

FLESH OF TERROR

Somewhere in the night a mollusc is growing
— but where does he get his flesh from?
he grows with the little pale balls
in the pits of childish stomachs
these knots that inflate in the belly and beneath the ribcage
and that people call "fear-of-death."
It's fear of the death of the whole world,
this mollusc with his fat snout,
his unseeing eyes wrinkling up space.

— M. B.

SORCERY

A child with a stupid expression watches a crack in a window.
The man behind the window is spinning a little copper wheel. The
window wavers, the crack trembles and the child has a split skull.

The man makes the child enter a large empty shop. A bull
reduced by one hardly knows what procedure to the size of a
mouse gallops furiously through the dust on the floor. In a
corner, an old cock gulps down nuts.

"This child is mine!" cries a lady striding down the sidewalk.
She has the red, damp muzzle of a young lamb.

The man gives a second spin, this time backwards, to the
copper wheel, tapping with his fingers upon his brass forehead,
and then returns the child to the woman.

The child takes his mother upon his back and tramps across
the town, shouting: "Glazier!"

— M. B.

RETURN TO AN EVIL DOMAIN

The long long journey down the open road
and all the otters awakened
at dawn beside babbling brooks!

The tall beggar staggers
pouring from one haunch to another
his old bear's torso.

Apocalyptic children
come at us with their cheeks all red
to announce: "You will find your house afire,
your sons all fled."

This whole country is finished: time to return to beginnings:
O wolves with your attracting embraces,
we return now to your magnetic eyes.

— M. B.

307

THE LAND OF METAMORPHOSES

Here I am, still standing at the crossroads, with this shining terror which still and always awaits me. My accomplishments drip out of my fingertips, my lovely conquests, so learnèd, so mad, red, green, all turning like outmoded, useless lighthouses. And this bright white fear shines against the cliffside, a white trembling jelly lying on earth. The sparks of ancient disasters burn out on my carbon hands. Oh no! this time it won't happen without my crying out, without my breaking something; and here, here are my most precious baubles of all which I smash up beneath my feet and it's all for your eyes, eyes of lucid insanity, chalk-white moon which denies me all access to the seas. To get it over as fast as possible here before your eye which nothing can blind, and to begin all over again then — Oh! that's your eternal deception! Look, you even dictate my anger! — yet already it's beginning to subside. . . . The floes float down the yellowish river and the lightning flashes reveal only the drifting dead.

I return to considering my own particular human situation, but just what can I say? Ah, so — it's only a question of myself alone then? These accidental interruptions break up my voice into bits, do we have to knock down all the walls to be heard just a tiny bit better? No, even so, it still wouldn't be enough.

A merciless master with a smile of the brightest ice suggests I try out another body; and here I am, having accepted the disgraceful exchange, still as always standing before the same trembling jelly on the white cliffside; this time before this formless body which I have no idea how to bring to life. It's the scandalous passion they've designated for me — I mean the one I've chosen, alas! I've become as dumb and stupid as an adolescent before his first woman, with these eyes that certainly must be bulging further and further out of my head, as inwardly I calculate the number of seconds contained in a single year, in an effort to get myself to refuse to believe it can really be. Back here I must tailor for myself a set of eyes, ears, a mouth, nostrils, limbs and an entire body to suit my desire; but life continues to be a traitor; she refused to leave me but kept clinging to my bones; but look, now she's just letting me go — but no, I'd lack the necessary strength to enter this sea, since I engender only additional corpses. The lights atop the dunes go on revolving, only now they've all turned gray. Oh! — it's true then: no, it's not worth the trouble to keep on hiding oneself in the swamps, these corpses and more corpses, corpses forever, faster and faster; at every revolution of blood and fear beneath the light-house of the dunes, yet another body falls. And on and on it goes. All my despair is incapable of shaking even a single grass-blade, and I speak with the bright white voice of the dead — no, that's not right, since I have neither voice nor breath, no, I really don't know — but in any case, who cares? It's a shadow speaking here, one whom the living can't recognize; but some day will they recognize its reflection echoing in the cruel smiles of dead men who have died absolutely alone?

— M. B.

FIRES AT WILL

The human being consists of a superimposition of various vicious circles. The big secret is that the revolutions of these circles are entirely self-propelled. But the centers of these circles are themselves set upon a circle; Man slips out of the latter only to enter into the former. This revolution does not pass through the eyes of the wise unnoticed, they alone escape the whirling, and as they depart from it, they can contemplate it: — The harmony of the spheres, cosmology of hearts, all astral gods of thought, passionately glowing systems forged from flesh meeting flesh, whether they be red with blood, orange-tinted from dreaming or yellow with meditation; astrolabes like arrows heated white-hot, far from the hair-triggered traps, beneath the staircases of the underlying devil and the general public air of ebullience which is already beginning to thicken into mud. The genuine trajectory of celestial steel flung across the abyss while the men living below strain themselves in an attempt to sneeze — since one sees everything from an aerial perspective and with no relief, and everything is true in at least a thousand ways, but all these ways of knowing are only significant when taken together, in one big block, black and white together, a divine zebra of extraordinary alacrity. . . . Oh! tell me, haven't primitive people at least managed to erect in their virgin forest the monstrous statue of the zebra-god? God of all contradictions resolved among four lips: but — and this is saddest of all — their energy is all spent and so the world crumbles apart, the light has no further need of prisms to break it up into rainbows, and everything which is real is finally transformed — shock of words, inevitable madness of human communication, a fit spasming out its cries, its false aspirations — the swindle of Prometheus, bringer of fire and truth, Oh how handsome he is, how fine! Prometheus, desperately gasping victory himself given over to the tongues of fire, the whirlwind-crowns of the suns, those minor allies of man . . . BUT THE GREAT BLACK ANTI-SUNS, WELLSPRINGS OF TRUTH IN THE ESTABLISHED SURFACE OF THINGS, IN THE GRAY VEIL OF THE SKIN, COME AND GO AND BREATHE ONE ANOTHER IN, AND MEN NAME THESE ABSENCES. Who will teach them what it is

to be, and what makes them think nonbeing a better thing to be?
You, fed to the tongues of fire, turn your faces toward the flames,
towards the divine kiss which will yank out all your teeth with
a single pull.

— M. B.

DISILLUSIONMENT

White and black and black and white,
pay attention now, I'm about to instruct you in how to die,
close your eyes now, touch your teeth together,
click! see, it's not so hard,
nothing to get so upset about.

And I'm speaking to you without excitement, myself,
black and white and white and black
click! look how soon you've become used to it,
I'm not speaking to you with any excess of sympathy either
still I'm certain that nonetheless you really must realize . . .
— it's so obvious it's ridiculous —

White and black and black and white and white and black,
if our souls exchanged places with our bodies
nothing would be altered at all,
so you can stop speaking now about bodies and souls.

White, black, click! it's the only thing
all mankind understands
(but isn't there something a bit tragic about that?)

I'm speaking to you without excitement, myself,
white, black, white black, click,
it's my perpetual dying cry,
white cry, black hole . . .
Oh! you haven't heard a word,
you don't even exist,
and I'm the only one left here really dying.

— M. B.

ICILY

Attention, there he goes now with his pen,
look out, he's going to explain himself,
he's going to cry out, he's completely alone now.

Shut up and be quiet, is what I have to tell them all;
— *Tell who?* The skins of words fall off,
they're naked and cold in my hand.

Oh, my shiniest, iciest knife,
my best feigner of murder,
is this phrase: *tell who?*

I'm not speaking to anyone anymore,
I stumble around beneath the streetlamps,
I tear myself to bits beside the riverside.

I wish I could say: you . . .
and add almost anything at all;
but an eye, a shining white eye, a pitiless eye,
— a lifeless eye too, no doubt about that — has nailed me down
here.

So then, why bother to go on investigating the coming seasons,
the animals in the fables, calamities, wrecks, deaths, and
disasters,
the usual embodiments of illness and misery,
the slack complacency of tempered steel,
and everything else in the world?

Really now, yes — completely alone; so enough, that's all there
is to tell, that's it!

— M. B.

DECEPTIONS

"Here are flowers soluble in the eyes
of marvelous birds,"
I'll tell you, and I'll open my hands:
they'll be empty, and you'll smile

and I will tell you: "Here is truth,
the secret of secrets."
Before you I'll unfold a leaf:
it will be pure white, and you'll laugh, won't you, you'll laugh,

and I'll tell you: "Come to my palace
of winged diamond,
there you'll see me at last. Look."
You won't see anything and you'll laugh, won't you, you'll laugh,
and that's fine, since I'll end up that way
taking myself seriously.

— M. B.

JACQUES PRÉVERT

1900-

In view of the poet's worldwide reputation as a kind of contemporary folk poet in a somewhat Marxist vein, and his later work as a quasinaturalistic scenarist for the film maker Michel Carné in the late 1930's (*Quai des brumes, Le Jour se lève,* and *Les Enfants du Paradis* [*Quay of Mists, Daybreak,* and *Children of Paradise*]),[1] it may come as a surprise that Prévert's initial writings, such as one of his very first works to be published, "Tentative de description d'un dîner de têtes à Paris-France" ("Attempt at a Description of a Dinner of Various Heads in Paris, France," 1931),[2] are classics of Surrealist satire — and a far cry from the gentle, somewhat sentimental writing for which he became better known in later years.

Actually, Prévert wrote no poetry at all before he joined the Surrealists — this event the direct result of a suggestion in 1924 by a good friend, the painter Yves Tanguy, whom he had met in the army during a mobilization tour in 1920 and with whom he shared a small private home. Soon meetings of the movement were held regularly *chez* Prévert-Tanguy; but it was as an occasional painter and collagist that Prévert participated. His collages appear as illustrations in many of his later books.

At one of these meetings the favorite Surrealist game of *cadavre exquis* ("exquisite corpse")[3] was invented. Prévert's first poetry reflects its violently juxtaposing approach to imagistic creation. Such plastic/verbal violence prophesies a further anger as well: like Aragon's poem, "The Brothers Lacôte," which Tanguy is said to have copied out on one wall, Prévert's early poetry is relentlessly concerned with the castigation of such prime Surrealist targets as the constricting family, the authoritarian father, the simple-mindedly patriotic ideal of country, the military mentality, moralistic sexual hypocrisy, and so forth. Prévert sees these not so much as conventional political antagonists (though this view is involved) but rather as the leading perpetrators of moral blackmail with respect to individual desires. A particular disdain is reserved for a species of secular self-righteousness.

Prévert's dictional style is clearly the result of a feeling that these opponents betray themselves in their speech, which is all too perfectly in tune with their thinking. As the poem "Glory" suggests, its tone is formal, inflexible, inert, and in general, plain dull. The poet's own diction is an implicit rebuke to this: casual, colloquial, and fluid, alive with sudden shifts of mood, it moves with ease from sentiment to irony, anger to tenderness, flatness to a kind of ecstasy of delicacy, transmitting the poet's ideal, which is that of a kind of transformed earth: perhaps an Eden. As he says in "In Vain," "for those who loved it, the garden stays open." With its flexibility and grace, the poetry is often evocative of folk song or nursery rhyme, analogies which Prévert would probably approve.

During the 1930's the poet published literally scores of poems in extraliterary and "ephemeral" media. His first collected volume, *Paroles (Words)*,[4] was gathered by a friend from a wide variety of sources, and was issued in 1945. Several new printings appeared almost at once. Although Prévert broke with the Surrealists in the early 1930's, his poetry continued to attack its primary social targets and to reflect its sense that the human imagination is far too infrequently reflected in human "reality."

During the postwar years, musical settings of Prévert's poetry by both "pop" and classical composers became popular and were learned by heart by schoolchildren throughout France — appropriately enough, in view of Prévert's long-standing conception of childhood as a period of unique, since unself-righteous, goodness.

Poems: *Spectacles* (N.R.F., 1951); *Fatras* (N.R.F., 1955); *La Pluie et le beau temps* (N.R.F., 1955); *Histoires* (N.R.F., 1963). Tales: *Contes pour enfants sages* (Ed. du Pré aux clercs, 1947).

GLORY

Coiffed in a crown of thorns
With spurs on her heels
Stark naked beneath her robes of ermine
The bearded woman entered the room
I represent magnificence of spirit incarnate
As a sideline I give lessons in diction
Also lessons in pontification in affliction in prediction in
    malediction in persecution in subtraction in multiplication in
    benediction in crucifixion in moralizing in mobilizing in
    distinction in mutilation in self-destruction and in the
    imitation of Christ Our Lord with a detailed program of the
    entire evening's activities with photographs of all the great
    men who are participating in this play and as an extra added
    attraction I give you the authoritative handbook and official
    guide to the great apes published under the august sponsorship
    of some celebrated acknowledged national official cannibal
    congressional or state publishing house
And also a handbook of perfect deportment
The fully expurgated Kama Sutra
And the latest official list
Of unclaimed state lottery prizes
And also a catechism of stick-to-it-ism
And a dozen bottles of mineral water too
For foreign parts
With a tricky handy little key
For screwing them all open.

— M. B.

317

THE ECLIPSE

Louis XIV also called the Sun King
used to sit quite frequently on a chamberpot-chair
towards the end of his reign
one night when it was very dark
the Sun King rose from his bed
went out to sit upon his chamberpot-chair
and disappeared.

— M. B.

THE LAST SUPPER

They sit at table
They eat not
Nor do they touch their plates
Yet their plates stand straight up
Behind their heads.

— M. B.

ATTEMPT AT A DESCRIPTION
OF A SUPPER OF VARIOUS HEADS
IN PARIS, FRANCE

Those who piously . . .
Those who copiously . . .
Those who wave the flag
Those who inaugurate
Those who believe
Those who believe they believe
Those who when they speak might as well go caw caw caw
Those who dress in fancy feathers without a flaw
Those who spare neither tooth nor claw
Those who orate
Those who gunboatate
Those who punctuate
Those who keep perfect time
Those who polish until whatever it is sparkles and shines
Those who throw out their bellies in their pride
Those who avoid your eyes
Those who are not afraid to take the bull by the balls when he's
    dead
Those who've grown bald on the inside of their heads
Those who give their blessings to all the churning masses
Those who distribute the kicks in the asses
Those who prop up and stuff up the dead with their great regret
Those who bayonet
Those who let their children play with guns
Those who let guns play with their children
Those who float who refuse ever to sink
Those who believe the best of all mankind though here and there
    some few may stink
Those whose gigantic wings alone prevent them from
    superhuman flight
Those whose only dream is sticking pieces of broken bottle on
    the top of the Great Wall of China at midnight
Those who cover up their faces in wolves'-heads when chewing
    on a lambchop

Those who make off with the eggs but refuse to take the
responsibility for whipping up the omelette
Those who own four thousand eight hundred and ten yards of
Mount Blanc, three hundred of the Eiffel Tower, twenty-five
centimeters of chest expansion and what's more those who are
proud of it
Those who suckle at the bosom of the nation
Those who do the running, the raiding, and the revenging on our
behalf, the whole mob of them, and a lot more besides, who
proudly enter the President's Residence, crunching along the
gravel road, all pushing and shoving, all hurrying each other
along, because there is to be a great banquet of heads right
now and everyone can choose the head that best fits his taste.
One head the head of a clay pipe, the other the head of an English
Admiral; as a side dish there are heads made out of bombs,
the heads of Galliffet, the heads of gentle beasts with bad
headaches, Auguste Comte-heads, Rouget de Lisle-heads,
Saint Theresa-heads, heads made out of heads of headcheese
even, heads of feet, heads of men of the cloth, milkmen-heads.
Some of them, just for a laugh, carried on their shoulders
delightful little calf-faces, and these faces were so lovely and so
sad — with little sprigs of parsley sticking out of their ears like
seaweed sprouting from reefs deep beneath the seas — that
nobody even noticed them.
A mother wearing a dead skull's head smilingly presented her
daughter wearing an orphan's head to a venerable old diplomat
friend of the family who had on the head of Soleilland.
It was truly deliciously charming and all in such perfect taste
that when the President arrived wearing an overstuffed Colum-
bus'-egg head everybody went absolutely crazy.
"Actually, the idea was quite simple; the whole trick was in
being the first to think of it," announced the President unfolding
his napkin; and before the spectacle of so much simplicity and
malice the guests could no longer overcome their emotions:
through cardboard crocodile-eyes a fat factory-owner let flow
a few tears of uncontrollable joy, a slightly smaller industrialist
nibbled on the table legs, all the pretty ladies jiggled their tits
a bit and the Admiral, carried away by his own enthusiasm,
tipped his champagne glass in the wrong direction, broke off the
stem in doing so, and died of a ruptured appendix just standing

there, feet locked on the arms of his chair, shrieking: "Save the children first!"

By strange coincidence, the seafarer's widow — on the advice of her maid — had that very morning concocted a striking war-widow's head, with two long lines of pain running down from either side of the mouth part, and two neat little pockets of grief, touches of gray beneath blue eyes.

Standing on the seat of her chair, she addresses the President, howling at the top of her lungs to demand increases in war-widows' pensions and the right to wear as a brooch, crosswise on the bosom of her evening gown, the deceased's favorite sextant.

Finally, slightly calmer now, she lets her lonely widow's gaze wander over the table, and, spying among the hors d'oeuvres a plate of filets of herring, sobbing, she gobbles down several, one after another, like a machine; then she swallows up the rest, in memory of the Admiral who "seldom indulged himself during his long lifetime," but who "nevertheless did love them so very much." Interruption: The Minister of Protocol is requesting that everyone stop eating, since the President is about to speak.

The President has arisen, you can see that he's just broken the top of his cranial egg with his knife because he prefers it a bit less warm, only just a modicum less warm. . . .

Now he is speaking and the silence is suddenly such that you can hear the flies in flight and suddenly such that you can hear them flying so distinctly that you can't even hear the President speaking anymore which is really quite regrettable because it's specifically about flies he's speaking, about flies and their incontestable usefulness in every area of life and in the realm of colonial activities in particular.

". . . For, without flies, we would be without fly-swatters, without fly-swatters there would be no Governor-General of Algiers, no French consulate . . . no insults to revenge, no olive-trees, in fact no more Algeria, which means no more hot spells, Gentlemen, and those bracing heat waves in the desert, Gentlemen, aren't they the very health of the weary traveler, and besides . . ."

But when flies become bored they die, and all the stories of past glories, all these statistics of ours fill them with the full weight of sadness, so that first they lower one foot from the ceiling, then the next and then they fall, as flies will do, in our dinnerplates . . . all over our clean white shirt-fronts, dead as the songs say.

"The most noble conquest of man is the horse," the President was announcing, "and were there but one horse left in the entire world, I would want to be him."

The speech is over; and like an overripe orange flung against a wall with all his might by a badly brought-up child, the Marseillaise explodes and the entire audience, dazzled by the gradual general growth of moss and spiderwebs over everything, and the stunning brilliance bouncing off the copper band instruments, rises as one to its feet, choked up, drunken, just at the thought of the History of France and that of the illustrious Pontet-Canet.

Everyone is standing, except for the man with the head of Rouget de Lisle* who takes all this in his stride and who is of the opinion that the performance was well executed indeed and then, gradually, the music dies down and then the next thing you know the mother with the corpse-head has taken advantage of this peaceful moment to push her little orphan-headed daughter toward the President's table.

Flowers in her hand, the child begins her memorized speech: "Monsieur President, Sir . . ." But her emotion, plus the heat, plus the flies are such that she keels over and falls with her face flat in the flowers, teeth snapped tight as the jaws on a pair of nail-clippers.

The man with the head made out of a truss and the man with the head completely formed from an abscess fling themselves forth, and the little thing is borne up, subjected to an autopsy, and disowned by her mother who — discovering on the child's card listing dancing-partners certain doodles of an unspeakable obscenity — wouldn't even dream for a single moment that the one who had amused himself that way was the family's dear old diplomat friend upon whom the father's job depends.

Concealing the paper in her dress, she stabs at her bosom with a stub of white chalk while giving out a loud shriek and her grief is painful to behold for all those who think that this is the genuine article, the actual grief of a mother just deprived of her child.

*Author of "The Marseillaise" [Editor's note].

Delighted to be the center of attention, she lets herself go, she really lets them have it, she moans and she groans, singing out:

"Where oh where is my dear little daughter, oh where oh where can Barbara be/who threw grass to the rabbits, and rabbits to the cobras . . ."

But the President, whose first experience with a lost child this is certainly not, makes a certain practiced gesture with his hand, and the banquet goes on.

And those who had come to peddle coal and wheat peddle coal and wheat and also certain large green islands entirely surrounded by water; lush lands with pneumatic trees and metal pianos exquisitely crafted so that your ears need not be assaulted by the outcries of the natives around the plantations when the good-natured fun-loving colonialists go for target-practice after dinner.

With one bird on his shoulder, another inside his pants so he can prepare roast fowl while he waits, sits that oddest duck of all, at whose house later on the poets would go, talking of Michelangelo.

"This is really," one was saying to another, "I mean *really* quite a success." But then, in the glare of a spotlight, the Minister of Protocol is caught *in flagrante delicto*, eating a plate of chocolate ice-cream with a coffee-spoon.

"That there should be no special spoon for chocolate ice-cream is insane when you stop to think about it," the Governor was saying, "it's unimaginable in fact — after all, the dentist has his drills, the paper its proper scissors, and even red radishes, as opposed to white, have their appropriate radish-dish."

But suddenly everyone starts to tremble with fear, because a man wearing a man's head just entered, a man nobody there seems to have invited and who sets down atop the table, in a basket, the head of Louis the Sixteenth.

It's really the horror of horrors: its teeth, the old men and the doors all chatter with fear.

"We're done for, they've done in a locksmith,"* screamed the burghers of Calais in their shirts all gray as Cap Gris-Nez, as they slid away down the banisters.

The overwhelming terror, the tumult, the feeling of despair, the straw that broke the camel's back, the state of siege and

* This king's hobby was fiddling with locks [Editor's note].

outside, in a full-dress uniform, with blackened hands beneath white gloves, the sentry who sees blood gushing forth from the gutters and a bug on his tunic realizes events have taken a turn for the worse and that now it's time to go, while the going's still good.

"I had intended," announces a smiling man, "to bring you the ashes of the royal family, who are rumored to be buried in the 'Caucasian Vault' somewhere beneath the rue Pigalle, but those crazy Cossacks who keep weeping and sighing over there, dancing the Kazatsky and buying each other drinks, keep quite a close watch over all the dead men they protect.

"Still, you can't have everything, I'm no Ruy Blas, nor am I Cagliostro, I'm no crystal ball, I'm no mess of coffee grounds. No, I'm not one to keep a collection of prophets' beards in cotton wadding. Certainly, I love an occasional laugh with a few friends, but I'm speaking here for the shut-ins, I monologue for the longshoremen, I broadcast for the magnificent idiots in the suburbs and it's only by accident that I'm paying this visit to your little world.

"First to say, 'Oh cut the crap!' is as good as dead. But you're all silent — too bad, I was kidding all along.

"Yes, you have to have a little laughter in your life so if you want, I'll take you on a guided tour into the heart of town but of course I realize that you're a little afraid of traveling, you know what you know, which is to say that the Tower of Pisa is crooked and that vertigo overcomes a man when he leans over for a look yes that applies to you too over there on the terraces of those cafés.

"Still, you'd have a good time for yourself, just like the President when he goes down to inspect a mine, just like Rudolph down at the tavern when he sits around with the local cut-throat, just like it was when you were but a child and they took you to the Municipal Zoo for a look at the Great Anteater.

"You'd have been able to see beggars with no Skid Row, lepers without begging bowls and shirtless men stretched out along the benches, stretched out abbreviatedly, however, in view of the fact that it's illegal.

"You'd have seen men in flophouses making the sign of the cross in exchange for a bed and families with eight children in a 'one-room dwelling' and — if you'd really behaved yourself, you'd have had the opportunity and privilege of seeing this: the Father who arises with a case of the shakes, the Mother expiring with worry over the last of her babies, the surviving members of the family escaping on the run and taking a blood-covered road to escape the pain.

"You just must see — believe me, it's a sight for sore eyes — you just *must* behold the moment when the Good Shepherd leads his sheep to the slaughterhouse, the moment when the eldest son with a resigned sigh throws in his lot with the junkies, the moment when children bored to tears switch beds in their room, you just absolutely must see the man lying in his bed surrounded by its bars just as the alarm-clock is preparing itself to go off in his ear.

"Look at him now, listen to that snoring, he's dreaming, he's dreaming he's going on a long journey, dreaming that everything is going smoothly, that he has a reserved seat in a private compartment . . . but the hand on the clock collides with the light on the train and the awakened man soaks his head in a sinkful of cold water if it's winter — or hot water, if it's summer.

"Look at him hurrying along, gulping down his morning coffee, entering the shop for work, except that he's still not awake, the alarm didn't ring loudly enough or the coffee wasn't strong enough, he's still dreaming, dreaming he's going on a long, long journey, dreaming that a comfy place on the train is waiting for him, except that he leans out a little too far and falls headfirst into a garden, then tumbles straight into a cemetery, awakes and screams like a bloody animal, two fingers are missing, the machine tried to eat him alive, but he wasn't hired to dream away the day was he and just the way you're thinking now — he got what he deserved.

"You're thinking also that after all a thing like that doesn't happen too often and that one swallow doesn't make a spring or anything, you're logicking it out that an earthquake in New Guinea can't stop the grapes from growing in Provence, much less cheeses from aging or the earth itself from turning.

"But I wasn't asking you to logic; I was asking you to look, to listen, to accustom yourself, so as not to be surprised to hear your cue-ball brains breaking open when the elephants come around, looking to take back their ivory.

"Because this half-dead head of yours, the one you keep

mostly buried under dead cardboard, these bleached brains behind their amusing pasteboard mask, this head with all its lines and wrinkles, with all its practiced grimaces — some day with all your detachment you'll shake this head clean off its little connecting link, and as it goes tumbling off, rolling away in the sawdust, you won't even cry out, won't even cry out yes it's O.K.!; much less no.

"And if it isn't actually your very own, it will be one of your friends' heads, because you know the old tales well enough, with their shepherds and their dogs; no, as far as having a really good, solid head on your shoulders, you needn't be ones to worry. . . .

"I'm still only kidding, of course, but after all, as people say, a flyspeck is enough to change the course of human history. A little guncotton instead of surgical cotton in the ear of an ailing King and couldn't the King himself just explode . . . the Queen rushes to his bedside, but there is no more bedside anymore: there is no more palace anymore. All there is, is in ruins, and draped in mourning. The Queen feels her mind going. To relax her a bit, a stranger with a nice smile gives her a cup of strong coffee. The Queen drinks it, the Queen dies from it, and the servants begin pasting labels on the children's luggage. The man with the nice smile returns, opens the largest trunk, shoves all the little princes inside, snaps the padlock on the trunk, checks the trunk at the baggage-room at the station and walks off rubbing his hands.

"And when I speak, Monsieur le President, Mesdames, Messieurs, of 'the King, the Queen, and the little Princes,' you understand of course that it's only to disguise things a little, since you can't logically blame regicides who haven't a king around if they make use of their talents with respect to those in the immediate environs, can you?

"Particularly that is with respect to people who think that a handful of rice is more than enough to keep a family of oriental peons going for eons.

"Or with respect to people who snicker at International World's Fairs because a black woman is carrying a black child on her back just the way they've been carrying in their white insides a pale-as-death white child for six or seven months.

"Or with respect to 30,000 reasonable people actually supposed to consist of both a body and a soul who marched to the

326

rally on the Sixth of March in Brussels, military music leading them on, parading before the statue erected to the memory of the self-sacrificing Carrier-Pigeon Soldier and with respect to those who will march tomorrow in places with names like Brive-the-Dauntless, Rose-the-Rosy-Cheeked or Carpa-the-Jewess before the monument 'to the innocent young sailor-teenager who died in the war as a representative symbol of. . . .' "

But a coffeepot thrown from some distance by an indignant our-strength-is-in-might advocate lands on the head of the man who was telling a group of people how useful a sense of humor can sometimes be. He falls flat. The Soldier-Pigeon is revenged. The official cardboard-heads trample the head of the smiling man with a rain of kicks, and the young woman, I mean the one over there dipping the tip of her umbrella into the blood for a souvenir, bursts into a tiny tinkle of laughter. The music begins again.

The head of the man is all red now, like an overripe tomato, one eye dangles at the end of a single vein, but all over the demolished face, the remaining living eye — the left one — goes on beaming like a flashlight in the ruins.

"Transport him hence," says the President; and the man, who is outstretched on a stretcher with his face covered by a police-captain's raincoat, marches off horizontally out of the President's Residence, one man in front of him, another close behind.

"You have to have a good laugh now and then, don't you?" he mumbles to the sentry on duty at the door and the sentry watches him being carried away with the same stunned expression you sometimes see a good man adopt when faced with the presence of pure malignancy.

But now, penetrating the shutters before the plate-glass windows of the pharmacies, shines a bright star of hope and, like wise men who fail to recognize Child Jesus when they see him, all the butcher-boys, itinerant bed-linen salesmen and other men of good will observe the star which tells them that the man they saw is inside, that the man isn't quite dead yet, that perhaps they are about to nurse him back to health back in there; and so everyone awaits his re-emergence, in the hope of doing him in once and for all.

They wait; and soon, on all fours because of the narrowness of the opening below the shutters, the chief magistrate creeps into the little shop, the druggist helps him to his feet and shows him the supposed dead man, head propped up on a baby-scale.

And the judge demands to know, and the druggist looks at the judge in return, wondering whether this isn't actually the very same joker who threw confetti on that General's coffin a little while ago and who, even earlier than that, planted the time bomb in Napoleon's path.

And then they chit-chat about this and that, about their children, and their various coughs and colds; day breaks, and the curtains are drawn back at the President's Residence.

Outside, it's spring, with animals, with flowers, and in the nearby park one can hear the sound of children's laughter; yes, it's spring all right, the needle goes crazy in the compass, the metal flange scampers about beneath the drill-press and the magnificent dolichocephalic once more falls on her ass on the chaise longue and plays the fool.

It's getting a little warmer now. It's Spring, with lovers like safety matches rubbing each other a little along their striking surfaces, with adolescent acne cases on the increase; and here we have the sultan's daughter and the mandrake-root reader, here we have pelicans, flowers out on every balcony; everywhere flourish tin watering-cans, the most beautiful season of the year is upon us.

The sun shines for all mankind, except of course for prisoners and miners, and also for

those who scale the fish

those who eat the spoiled meat

those who turn out hairpin after hairpin

those who blow the glass bottles that others will drink from

those who slice their bread with pocketknives

those who vacation at their workbenches or their desks

those who never quite know what to say

those who milk your cows yet who never drink their milk

those you won't find anesthetized at the dentist's

those who cough out their lungs in the subway

those who down in various holes turn out the pens with which
    others in the open air will write something to the effect that
    everything turns out for the best

those who have too much to even begin to put into words

those whose labors are never over

those who haven't labors
those who look for labors
those who water your horses
those who watch their own dogs dying
those whose daily bread is available on a more or less weekly
   schedule
those who go to church to keep warm in their winter
those whom Swiss Guards send outdoors to keep warm
those who simply rot
those who enjoy the luxury of eating
those who travel beneath your wheels
those who stare at the Seine flowing by
those whom you hire, to whom you express your deepest thanks,
   whom you are charitable toward, whom you deprive, whom
   you manipulate, whom you step on, whom you crush
those from whom even fingerprints are taken
those whom you order to break ranks at random and shoot down
   quite methodically
those who go on forced marches beneath the Arch of Triumph
those who don't know how to fall in with the custom of the
   country any place on earth
those who never ever see the sea
those who always smell of fresh linen because they weave the
   sheets you lie on
those without running water
those whose goal is eternally the blue horizon
those who scatter salt on the snow in all directions in order to
   collect a ridiculous salary
those whose life expectancy is a lot shorter than yours is
those who've never yet knelt down to pick up a dropped hairpin
those who die of boredom on a Sunday afternoon
        because they see Monday morning coming
        and also Tuesday and Wednesday and Thursday and Friday
        and Saturday too
        and the next Sunday afternoon as well.

                                              — M. B.

PALL-BEARERS

An old man with a gold armband and a black watch
a Queen of means with a man of the May
and some toilers of the peace with some justices of the sea
a boa-grinder with a coffee-constrictor
a dead joke with the butt of a soldier
a belly-hunter with a head-dancer
a music-bit with a gallows-composer
a funeral pipe with a briar pyre
a flat bicycle with a tandem tire
a girl in a black cassock with a priest in a bikini
a porcelain professor with a philosophy mender
a little Bengal sister with a tiger of the poor
a conscientious director with a company objector
a winged duck with a lame victory
a tugmaker with a matchboat
a duck with measles with a boy cooked with orange
a director of the round table with the Knights of the British
    Broadcasting Corporation
the pilot of a large family with the father of a ship on the high
    seas
the Society of oysters with Jesus on the half-shell
a member of the prostate with a hypertrophy of the French
    Academy
a dental son with a prodigal surgeon
a fat horse of the diocese with a seven-hand bishop of the circus
*radioactive disarmament with world fall-out.

— TEO SAVORY

* With the poet's permission, this last line has been added by the translator
[Editor's note].

330

FAMILIAL

The mother knits
the son makes war
She finds this perfectly natural the mother does
And the father what does he do the father?
He goes to work
His wife knits
His son's at war
He's at work
He finds this perfectly natural the father
And the son and the son
What does he find the son?
He finds absolutely nothing the son
The son his mother knits his father goes to work he's at war
When he finishes the war
He'll go to work with his father
The war continues the mother continues she knits
The father continues he goes to work
The son is shot he doesn't continue
The father and mother go to the graveyard
They find this natural the father and mother
Life continues life with the knitting the war the work
The work the war the knitting the war
The work the work and the work
Life with the graveyard.

— MARK STRAND and JEAN BALLARD

I SAW SEVERAL OF THEM

of them who sat on the hat of another
pale
trembling
as waiting for something . . . it doesn't matter what . . .
the war . . . the end of the world . . .
it was absolutely impossible for him to make a gesture or speak
and the other
the other who was looking for "his" hat was even paler
and he was trembling too
and he kept repeating to himself endlessly:
my hat . . . my hat . . .
and he wanted to cry.
I saw one of them who was reading the papers
I saw one of them who saluted the flag
I saw one of them who was dressed in black
he had a watch
the chain of a watch
a wallet
the legion of honor
and a pince-nez.
I saw one of them who pulled his child by the hand
and who cried . . .
I saw one of them with a dog
I saw one of them with a sword-cane
I saw one of them who was crying
I saw one of them who was going to church
I saw another of them who was coming out . . .

— MARK STRAND and JEAN BALLARD

WRESTLING WITH THE ANGEL
For J.-B. Brunius

Don't bother
The fight's fixed
The match is rigged
and when he or she or it appears aloft above the ring
surrounded by spotlights
they'll all start singing the Te Deum
and even before you have the chance to get up from your little
    chair in the corner
their gong will sound
they'll throw their sacred sponge in your eyes
And you won't even get in a quick jab to the feathers
before they all grab you
and he or she or it will hit you below the belt
and you'll fall flat
arms stuck out stiff in an idiotic cross
outstretched in the sawdust
and you may never again be able to make love.

— M. B.

BIRD-CATCHER'S SONG

The bird that flies so sweetly
The bird red and warm as blood
The bird so tender the bird mocking
The bird that suddenly is afraid
The bird that suddenly hurts itself
The bird that would like to flee
The bird alone and enraged
The bird that would like to live
The bird that would like to sing
The bird that would like to cry
The bird red and warm as blood
The bird that flies so sweetly
It's your heart pretty child
Your heart that beats for the wings so sadly
Against your breast so hard so white

— MARK STRAND and JEAN BALLARD

TO PAINT THE PORTRAIT OF A BIRD

For Elsa Henriquez

First of all paint a cage
its door standing open
then paint
something appealing
something shining
something beautiful
something tasty
for the bird
then lean the canvas up against a tree
in a garden
in a forest
or in the woods
find another tree and hide yourself behind it
silently
without moving a muscle . . .
Sometimes the bird will come right away
but it could also take many long years
before it decides to
Don't become discouraged
but wait
wait if you have to year after year after year
the earliness or lateness of its arrival
has no relation
to the success of the work
When the bird appears
if he appears
maintain the most total silence
while you wait for the bird to enter the cage
and once he's in
softly shut the door with a quick stroke of your paintbrush
then
one by one blot out all the bars of the cage
taking care not to touch the bird's feathers
Then paint the tree's portrait

choosing the most beautiful of all its branches
for the bird
also paint the green foliage and the freshness of the breeze
the dust afloat in the sunlight
and the noises of the insects in the grass in the intense heat of
    summer
and then wait for the bird to sing
If the bird does not sing
it's a bad sign
a sign that the picture is bad
but if it does sing that's a good sign
that is to say a sign that you can sign
Then you reach out and gently pluck
one of the feathers of the bird
and you write your name over in one corner of the picture.

— M. B.

FREE QUARTERS

I slipped my cap into the cage
and went out with the bird on my head
So
you've given up saluting
asked the commanding officer
That's right
you don't have to salute anymore
answered the bird
Ah so
excuse me please I thought everybody still saluted
said the commanding officer
You are fully excused everybody makes mistakes
said the bird.

— M. B.

THE HUNTING OF WHALES

A whale-hunting we will go, a whale-hunting we will go,
Said the father in an angry roar
To his son Prosper, as he lay stretched out flat, hiding beneath
the chest of drawers,
A whale-hunting we will go, a whale-hunting we will go,
But you don't want to go,
So how come?
What I'd like you to tell me is how come I have to go and kill a
creature
Who never did me any harm, Papa,
Go catch whales yourself, Papa, by yourself a-hunting go
Since you're dying to,
I'd rather stay here at home with our dear old Mom,
And Cousin Gaston.
So then that father sailed off alone in his little boat
Upon the bounding main. . . .
So here we see the father all at sea
And here we see an angry thrashing whale's tail
And here we see Cousin Gaston who just overturned the soup-
tureen,
The soup-tureen full of fish broth.
It was a mean and a nasty sea,
But the soup was quite good.
And here we see Prosper in his corner chair, accusing himself:
A whale-hunting we will go, except that I didn't go,
And just why didn't I anyway?
Perhaps she could have been caught,
And perhaps I could even have been able to eat some afterwards
But here we see the door bursting open, and shedding oceans
The father appears, all out of breath,
The whale upon his back.
He throws the beast down on the table, a gorgeous lovely whale
with blue eyes,
A beast such as is seldom seen,
And he says in a horrid harried voice
Hurry up and carve it up,

I'm hungry, I'm thirsty, I'd like to have my supper.
But now we see Prosper stumbling to his feet,
Staring his father in the very whites of his eyes,
In the whites of his papa's sweet blue eyes,
Eyes just as blue as those of the blue-eyed beast
And asking: So how come I have to carve up a poor creature who
    never did a thing to me?
To hell with it, I won't do it, I'm finished with this farce,
Then he flings the knife to the floor
But the whale gets angry too, and throws herself on the father,
And slices him up into little slivers.
Oh, oh, cries Cousin Gaston,
It reminds me of when I used to go a-hunting, a-hunting for
    butterflies as a boy
And see
See Prosper, writing out the death-notice for the newspaper,
The mother mourning over her poor old husband
And the whale, with tears in her eyes too, contemplating the sad
    shattered family
And suddenly crying out:
Why oh why did I have to go and kill that poor idiot,
Now others will come chasing after me in their big powerboats
And they'll end up exterminating my dear little family finally,
But then, breaking into uneasy laughter,
She made her way to the door but pleadingly
Shouted through the window as she shot past:
    Madame, if someone should come looking for me,
    Be a nice person and tell them:
    The whale had to leave,
    Sit down,
    Stay calm, don't worry, rest easy
    In another fifty years she's almost certain to come back this
    way again.

          — M. B.

THE BROKEN MIRROR

That jolly little fellow who sang without stopping
that jolly little fellow who once danced in my head
The jolly little fellow of my youth
broke his shoelace
and all the attractions at the fair
collapsed at once
and in the empty silence of this carnival
I heard your joyous voice
your broken fragile voice
childlike yet desolate
coming from far off and calling me
and I placed my hand on my heart
where
were vibrating
covered with blood
the seven glass slivers of your starlit laughter

— M. B.

THE GARDEN

Millions and millions of years
Would still not give me half enough time
To describe
That tiny instant of all eternity
When you put your arms around me
And I put my arms around you
One morning in the cold winter light
In the Parc Montsouris in Paris
In Paris
On this earth of ours
This earth which is a star.

— M. B.

IN VAIN

An old man howling at death
rolls his hoop across the square
He cries that it's winter and all is done
that the match is rigged the dice are thrown
the bets are made the mass is sung
the piece is played and the curtain down
In vain
in vain
They call me, those friends who can't stand me
they're running to fat and they stand watch in hand
asking me questions they don't understand
In vain
in vain
Others more dead than alive walking blind
trailing their childhood dreams behind
And those well-tailored clubmen
bore you to tears with political fears
that the country's in danger the course is run
the statue's of clay the time has come . . .
Already I hear at the foot of the square
the roll of the muffled drum
the bugle is blowing
the garden is closing
In vain
in vain

For those who loved it the garden stays open

— TEO SAVORY

AIMÉ CÉSAIRE

1912-

ONE OF THE FIRST BLACK POETS to gain wide recognition in France, coiner of the term "Négritude" (which might be translated as "Black consciousness"), Césaire is also an historically significant figure in the political development of the Antillean and Caribbean region, where he has been a leading reform figure since the mid-1940's.

Born in Martinique, Césaire left that island in 1931 to study in Paris; shortly thereafter he was instrumental in founding two magazines expressing Antillean and Black interests, *L'Etudiant Noir* (*The Black Student*) and *Légitime Défense* (*Legitimate Defense* — named after an essay by André Breton). A small, active Antillean Surrealist group was formed in 1932; it was in the late 1930's that Césaire was discovered by the Surrealists, after Breton (in one of those chance encounters which are so frequent in Surrealist history) came upon a mimeographed copy of some of the poet's early verse on a counter in a clothing store. Breton's recommendations facilitated the publication of Césaire's early work in Surrealist-associated reviews. Later, during the war, Breton included his work in the review *Hémisphères* and also published the younger poet's work in *VVV*, a magazine which he edited.

Even before the war Césaire had written the long verse narrative, *Cahier d'un retour au pays natal* (*Notebook of the Return to My Native Land*).[1] Issued in part in France in 1939, and finally in book form in 1947 with an introduction by Breton entitled "Un Grand Poète Noir" ("A Great Black Poet"), it is, in addition to being one of the finest long poems to come from Surrealism, considered an essential text with regard to the "Blackness" movement in France as well as elsewhere. Specifically Black concerns, seen according to Surrealism's emphasis on the need of each man to reach psychic fulfillment and maturity, also prevail in *Tropiques*, the review the poet founded upon his return to the islands in 1940 and which he edited until 1945, and in the volumes of non-narrative poetry written for the most part before the war but published, respectively, in 1946, 1948, and 1949. These shorter poems especially echo the Surrealist concept of criticism through "black bile" or "black humor," terms first entered in the movement's lexicon to denote a certain darkly bitter humor.

Another side of Césaire expresses his version of the movement's desire that the world become more "in tune with thought," the poet speaking in tones of Apollinairean prophecy in picturing a state opposite to struggle: a condition of earthly, perhaps visionary, bliss. Although these evocations often involve vivid Antillean imagery, local landscapes are viewed without recourse to either conventional naturalism or "Socialist Realism." Often the beneficence of natural surroundings is associated with an enfolding feminine presence and erotic love, the poet indicating both the desirability and the possibility of relating inner and outer goals. Césaire's technical and philosophical sophistication, and his relationship to the Surrealist heritage generally, is acknowledged by the title of his second collection, *Soleil cou coupé*,[2] the final line of one of Apollinaire's most adventurous poems, "Zone."

In 1946, Césaire, who had been deeply involved in politics since his student days in Paris, ran for and won the posts of both mayor of the capital city of Martinique, Fort-de-France, and Communist deputy. However, in 1956 the poet separated from the Communist party in protest against its wish to exert explicit local control, founding the Progressive party of Martinique, which he still heads. Césaire's rejection, the *Lettre à Maurice Thorez* (*Letter to Maurice Thorez*, 1957),[3] is a complaint about psychic as well as political dictatorship on several levels, the poet pointing out to Thorez that "if the aim of all progressive politics is one day to restore their freedom to colonialized peoples, then the day-by-day actions of progressive parties must at least not contradict the projected objective and not regularly wreck the

very foundations of this future freedom, foundations both organizational and psychological. . . ."

The later writings include a series of historical dramas, and a collection of poems, *Ferrements* (*Gratings*, 1960),[4] including a long memorial poem to Paul Eluard, reflecting an undiminished Surrealist outlook.

OTHER PRINCIPAL WORKS

Collections of poems: *Les Armes miraculeuses* (N.R.F., 1946; reissued 1970 — includes the drama *Et les chiens se taisaient*); *Cadastre* (Ed. du Seuil, 1961 — contains both *Soleil cou coupé* of 1948 and *Corps perdu* of 1949). Other plays include: *La Tragédie du roi Christophe* (Présence Africaine, 1963); *Une Saison au Congo* (Ed. du Seuil, 1967); *Une Tempête* (Ed. du Seuil, 1960 — adaptation of Shakespeare's *Tempest*). Other political works: *Discours sur le colonialisme* (Présence Africaine, 1951); *Toussaint Louverture* (Présence Africaine, 1963).

RAINS

Rain which in your most regrettable overflowings never forgets
the way the girls of Chiriqui suddenly pull out from between
   their darkened breasts lamps made out of flickering
   glow-worms
Rain capable of absolutely anything except washing away the
   bloodstains on the fingertips of assassins of entire peoples
   startled beneath the tall treetops of innocence

— M. B.

SINCE AKKAD   SINCE ELAM   SINCE SUMER

Sleep-shatterer, uprooter,
Breath-breaker, breath-quickener,
Master of the three highways, you see before you now a man
    who has walked a long, long time.
Since Elam. Since Akkad. Since Sumer.
Master of the three highways, you see before you now a man
    who has borne a great, great deal.
Since Elam. Since Akkad. Since Sumer.
I have borne the body of the commandant. I have borne the
    commandant's railroad. I have borne the commandant's
    locomotive, the commandant's cotton. I have borne on my
    woolly head — which is so serviceable it needs no other
    cushion — God, the machine, the highway (that is to say, the
    God of the commandant).
Master of the three highways, I have been a bearer beneath the
    sun, I have been a bearer through the mist I have borne across
    potsherds across hot coals among man-eating army ants. I
    have borne the parasol I have borne explosives I have borne
    neck shackles.
Since Akkad. Since Elam. Since Sumer.
Master of the three highways, master of the three viaducts, allow
    me for once — the first time since Akkad since Elam since
    Sumer — with my face apparently still more weathered and
    tanned than the calluses on my feet but in reality more delicate
    than the crow's impeccable beak and as if draped funereally by
    the bitter folds that my borrowed gray skins form for me (this
    costume Man imposes upon me every winter) — allow me
    now to move forth across the dead leaves taking my patient
    little sorcerer's steps

toward the place where triumphantly menace the inexhaustible
    injunctions of mankind flung forth in the face of the snarling
    snickerings of the winter hurricane.
Since Elam. Since Akkad. Since Sumer.

— M. B.

DEMONS

I struck out at its legs and arms. They turned into paws made of
steel terminating in powerful claws covered by supple little
greenish feathers composing a subtle yet highly calculated
exterior. From one fearful conception within my brain its beak
was born, snout of a ferociously armored fish. And so the
animal before me became a bird. Regular as clockwork its stride
tyrannically paced out the red sand like some measurer of a
sacred field descended from the disgraceful tears of a
river. And as for its head? In a flash I noticed it was constructed
out of translucent glass inside of which its eye ran a
complicated system of pulleys and connecting rods which from
time to time with an exceedingly impressive display of pistons
polluted the atmosphere of the time with a mixture of mercury
and chrome
Already the monster was all over me, invulnerable.
Beneath its breasts and enveloping its entire abdomen located
just beneath its neck and also over the entire back were what
at first sight one took for feathers were scales of rustproofed
painted iron which when the creature opened and closed its
wings to shake off the rain and the blood made a vista which
nothing could conceal with its stale odors and sounds of
serving spoons being clashed together by the white seismic
hands of an earth seizure there among the sordid basket-
weavings of a far too unhealthy summer

— M. B.

346

SWAMP NOCTURNE

The swamp unrolling its lasso which had previously been kept
coiled around its navel

and here I am settled thanks to the insistent assistance of
quicksand activity beneath the swamp and puffing away on the
finest tobacco any lark on earth has yet had to smoke.

Miasma they called it what could only suggest the reign of some
kind of twilight. I hereby declare that they have led me down
the path of error. From the other side of this life, from death,
bubbles arise. They burst to the surface with the sound of
lightbulbs exploding. They are the deep-sea divers of
withdrawal returning to the surface in order to remove their
glass-and-lead heads, returning their tenderness.
Every creature is some watch-bird of the guard to me way down
here.
Every plant the silphium laciniatum, blind witness of both
North and South.
Still alert here however.
There are snakes around.
One of them hisses along the length of my spinal column, then
coils itself around the lower section of my rib cage, then darts
his head forward as far as my spasmodically choked throat.
After a while constriction becomes a pleasant sensation and here
beneath the sand I celebrate

THE HYMN TO THE LUMBAR SERPENT

— M. B.

OFFERING TO THE STORM

Hele helele the King is a great king
long may his majesty deign to look within my asshole to see if it
    contains any diamonds
long may his majesty deign to explore my mouth to see how
    many carats it might contain
tom-tom laugh
tom-tom laugh
I carry the king's litter
I unroll the king's carpeting
I *am* the king's carpeting
I carry the king's diseases
I *am* the king's parasol
laugh laugh tom-tom from the kraals
tom-tom from the mines all laughing up their sleeves
holy tom-tom with your rat-teeth and hyena grinning laughing
    in the faces of the missionaries
tom-toms of the forest
tom-toms of the desert
tom-tom cry
tom-tom cry
burn down to the hot-blooded silence of our limitless shoreless
    river of tears
and roll
roll softly, with a ball-bearing motion
the pure carbon motion of our endless death-throes come of age
thunder thunder mighty speechless deliriums
lions bright scarlet yet maneless
tom-toms protecting my three souls which are my brain my heart
    and my liver
thunderous tom-toms which from their peaks watch over my
    habitation in the star-filled wind
whose foundation is the storm-tossed rock of my black head
and you brother tom-tom for whom I've frequently
    secreted in my mouth all day long a word which is alternately
    cool and burning like our seldom-expressed taste for revenge
tom-toms of the Kalahari

tom-toms of the Cape of Good Hope who round the cape with
   your threats
O Zulu tom-tom
tom-tom of Chaka
tom, tom-tom
tom, tom-tom
King our mountains are great mares in heat taken at the peak of
   their convulsiveness
King our fields are rivers provoked by the shipments of
   putrefaction which flow from the sea and your freighters
King our precious stones are the flickering lamps of a widowed
   dream of an eventual dragon
King our trees have the elaborate form of a flame too enormous
   for our hearts yet certainly too tiny for a dungeon
So laugh laugh tom-toms of Kaffirdom
like the beautiful question-mark at the tail end of the scorpion
drawn in pollinated form against the blackboard of the sky the
   blackboard of our brains at midnight
like the thrilling of some sea serpent enchanted by the thought of
   foul weather
like the muffled inverted laughter of the sea gurgling through the
   gorgeous portholes of the wreck

— M. B.

THE TORNADO

That time when
    the senator noticed that the tornado had been napping
    on his fluttering
    napkin
and the tornado flew high rampaging through the air above
    Kansas City
That time when
    the preacherman noticed the tornado reflected in the deep
      blue eyes
    of the sheriff's wife
and the tornado was everywhere at once suddenly sticking out its
    big face in front of everybody
stinking like ten thousand blacks packed together for shipment
    in one train
that meant the time had come for the tornado to burst out into
    laughter
and the tornado made over everything a most handsome
    laying-on of hands with its beautiful white ecclesiastical hands
and that meant the time had come for God to notice that he had
    had too much to drink of late for example two hundred glasses
    of blood delivered by the lynch-hangman
and to notice that the city now consisted of a true fraternity of
    black and white stains
shed by the corpseful against the background of the skin of a
    horse slaughtered as it was streaking away to escape
And the tornado by now having had some experience of the
    suburbs of a richly wreckage-filled memory
spat down from a sky gorged on hysterical oaths
so that for a second time steel "twisted like pretzels" was
    "twisted like pretzels"
And the tornado which had gulped down like a pondful of
    bullfrog's tongues its flock of rooftops and chimneys loudly
    exhaled a unifying conception the prophets themselves had
    never thought to predict

                            — M. B.

MILLIBARS OF STORM

Refuse to silence the light of this day and let us depart now with
    faces exposed
to face those unknown countries where the very whistlings of
    birds are interrupted
our ambush opens fire with sounds like those of planetary
    circumferences spinning by
pay no attention to those caterpillars slithering past
instead look only to the millibars which take their stand at the
    storm's central eye
in order to create the space where the heart of all things and the
    coming of man may be erected

O Dream let us refuse to silence
among the hoofbeats of these frothing horses
the sound of tears groping their passageway toward the great
    wingtips of eyelids

— M. B.

TO SCREAM

I salute you birds who break into and disperse the formations of
    herons and the genuflections of their deferentially dipping
    heads
in sheaths of white down

I salute you birds who with blows of your beaks pierce through
    to the center of the swamp
and the heart of the sunset commandant

I salute you wild cry
    resin-fed torch
    entangled with streaks
    of fleas of the flying rain and white mice

Raving mad on the verge of screaming I salute you with my
    shouting which is whiter even than death itself

My time will come the time the one I welcome here and now
enormous generous
simple
so that every word every gesture will shed some new light of
    understanding
on your blonde she-goat's face
browsing there in the infatuating hollow of my hand

And there right there
O sweet leech
there we have the origin of all time
there we have the end of everything existing in time

and the upright majesty of the original eye

— M. B.

MOMENT OF CALM

Time will surely not be in the least evil anymore then
doors will collapse before the assaults of the waters
orchids will hold out their delicate heads crazed like those of the
    tortured
through the latticework gateway where words are sent forth two
    by two
the tendrils of vines will send out from the depths of their
    restlessness a lucid army of leeches whose embracing will
    evoke the irresistible power of perfumes
from every grain of sand a bird will be born
from every innocent bloom a scorpion will come (everything on
    earth having been recreated)
the trumpets of venus-flytraps will flourish to announce the hour
    of abdication of my thick lips pierced with needles in favor of
    the more flexible armor of the bitter herbs of the future
and the gradual formation of naïve flesh around the heart of
    misery will be general
and far beyond any connection with the bivalvular incrustations
    of tapeworms
while the swallows which fly out of my saliva pile up
together with seaweed carried along in the tidal waves produced
    by you
the bleeding seething myth of an unannounced moment arriving
so that from every level of the towers of silence vultures will take
    off
with in their beaks scraps of our former flesh much too uncalm
    for our skeletons

— M. B.

THE WHEEL

The wheel is not only the most beautiful discovery of mankind
    but the only one as well
there is the sun which turns
there is the earth which turns
there is your face which rolls back and forth around the axis of
    your neck when you weep
so how about you minutes of all time won't you coil yourself
    around this take-up reel of life
like lapped-up blood
the art of suffering sharpened like the stumps of trees against the
    knives of winter
the deer drunken with thirst
which balances on the unforeseen wellstones of your face like a
    storm-struck schooner
your face
like an entire village asleep at the bottom of a lake
but which is reborn again during the days of rising grass and the
    season for flowering

— M. B.

INCLINATION

O mountain O dolomites like a bird's heart beneath my childlike
    hands
O icebergs O ghosts old gods sealed up in all their glory
and nonetheless in a ring around a fire among three stones
    crowned with a vibrating halo of flies
a pond for the drowned is filling once more
O region of the dead you collide in vain against the revolutions
    of the twisting roads
zone where the processional progresses from the level
    of green flames up to the ditches of witchcraft
inclination of all things come fight it out with me it is I who
    wear the solar tiara
gong multiply this pit where the death-struggles of beasts
    evoke the exclamations of men preserved in the
    petrifications of thousand-year-old forests

O beloved let us lean down here together over the geological
    layers

                                         — M. B.

SAMBA

Everything which projects which curves into space has compacted
    to create your breasts all the bells of the blossoming
    hibiscus all the pearls of the oysters all the entanglements
    that form a mangrove all there is of sun stored in reserve
    inside the lizards of the sierras all it takes of iodine to make
    a day beside the seaside all the mother-of-pearl required to
    concoct the echoes of conch shells undersea
If you wanted it to happen
    blowfish would float by holding hands
If you wanted it to happen
    all day long peronia-vines would make trails out of their
    tails and bishop-birds would be so unusual that nobody will
    be surprised to hear they have been swallowed up by the
    cross-shaped petals of the trichoma-blossom
If you wanted it to happen
    psychical power
    would inspire confidence all night long thanks to its lifebuoy
    relay system of bird's-beak-flowers
If you wanted it to happen
    in even the poorest worker's quarters chain-belts would
    arise with their cups filled with perfumed fragrances of the
    freshest sounds in the world thanks to which the earth and
    its infernal wrinkles would all become totally stoned
If you wanted it to happen
    all wild animals would drink from fountain-spray
    and in our minds
    the violent nations
    would already be pointing out to the birds the impression of
    motionlessness transmitted by the tallest tamarack trees

—— M. B.

THE THUNDER'S SON

And without her having stooped to seduce her jailers
a bouquet of hummingbirds has fallen sprinkling from between
her breasts
the first few flowers arising from dead reefs have sprouted out of
her ears
she speaks to me in a language so gentle and subtle that at first I
can't quite understand it but after a while I understand that
she confirms for me
that Springtime has arrived after swimming upstream
that every thirst is satisfied that Fall and ourselves have been
reconciled
that the stars in the street have been blossoming in broad
daylight and hold out their fruits to us now low and easily
within reach

— M. B.

JUDGMENT OF THE LIGHT

Transfixing muscles and blood
devouring all eyes this intense bright mass of foliage
crowning with truth our usual lights
a ray a spray from the triumphant sun
by means of which
justice will be done
and every arrogance washed away

Household vessels and human flesh slip away into the thick
    neck of the waves
silences by way of contrast have begun to exert the most
    substantial pressures

Around the circumference of the circle
among public activities along the riverbanks
the flame
stands solitary and splendid in its upright judgment

— M. B.

NOTES AND SOURCE DATA

Notes

GUILLAUME APOLLINAIRE

1. Ed. *Sic.* 2. Tous les Arts; reissued 1922, 1950. Tr. by Lionel Abel (Wittenborn, Schultz, 1949). 3. Kahnweiler; reissued Gallimard/N.R.F., 1921. (Note: Here and in all bibliographies, we refer to this firm as N.R.F. for the sake of brevity.) 4. Ed. de la Sirène; tr. by Louis Simpson in George Wellwarth's and this editor's anthology, *Modern French Theatre: The Avant-Garde, Dada, and Surrealism* (Dutton, 1964; Faber, 1966). 5. *L'Oeuvre de Marquis de Sade* (Bibliothèque des Curieux, 1909). 6. *Cinquantenaire de Charles Baudelaire* (Maison du Livre, 1917). 7. Barcelonnette; anonymous translations of two of these works, *Les Mémoires d'un jeune Don Juan* and *Les Amours d'un hospodar*, appear in *Two Pornographic Novels* (Olympia Press, 1961). 8. Mercure de France. 9. Messein. 10. Mercure de France. 11. Ed. du Bélier, 1949.

PIERRE REVERDY

1. N.R.F. 2. Mercure de France. 3. Mercure de France. 4. Ed. du Rocher. 5. N.R.F. 6. N.R.F. 7. N.R.F. 8. Collection Peintres Français Nouveaux.

TRISTAN TZARA

1. *Les Premiers poèmes*, tr. by Claude Sernet, Seghers, 1965. 2. Ed. Jean Budry. 3. Collected with other Dada manifestos in *Sept Manifestes Dada/ Lampisteries*, Pauvert, 1963; tr. by Ralph Manheim in *The Dada Painters and Poets* (Wittenborn, Schultz, 1951). 4. G.L.M., 1946; tr. as "The Gas Heart" by Michael Benedikt in *Modern French Theatre: The Avant-Garde, Dada, and Surrealism* (Dutton, 1964). 5. Fourcade, 1931; reissued by N.R.F., 1969. 6. Nagel.

PHILIPPE SOUPAULT

1. Au Sans Pareil. 2. *Littérature* #16, 1920; tr. by George Wellwarth in his and this editor's *Modern French Theatre: The Avant-Garde, Dada and Surrealism* (Dutton, 1964). 3. Le Sagittaire. 4. Plon. 5. University of Washington Bookstore (Seattle). 6. These essays include: *Guillaume Apollinaire* (Cahiers du Sud, 1927); *Henri Rousseau* (Quatre-Chemins, 1927); *Lautréamont* (Ed. des Cahiers Libres, 1927); *William Blake* (Rieder, 1928); *Paolo Uccello* (Rieder, 1928); *Baudelaire* (Rieder, 1931); *Souvenirs de James Joyce* (Charlot, 1943); *Lautréamont* (Seghers, "Poètes d'aujourd'hui" No. 6, 1946); *Essai sur la poésie* (Eynard, 1950); *Profils perdus* (Mercure de France, 1963).

ANDRÉ BRETON

1. Kra; in *The Manifestoes of Surrealism* (tr. by Richard Seaver and Helen R. Lane, University of Michigan Press, 1969, together with texts referred to in Notes 10 and 20; also several others). 2. N.R.F. 3. Au Sans Pareil. 4. *Entretiens* (N.R.F., 1952). 5. N.R.F. 6. N.R.F. 7. Kra. 8. N.R.F.; reissued 1963. 10. Kra. 11. Ed. des Cahiers Libres. 12. Ed. Surréalistes. 13. Ed. Surréalistes. 14. Sagittaire. (This text, and also those referred to in Notes 6 and 12, tr. by Richard Howard in *The History of Surrealism*, by Maurice Nadeau [Macmillan, 1965].) 15. Reprinted in *Documents Surréalistes*, ed. Maurice Nadeau (latest ed., 1964). 16. Beaux-Arts. 17. Sagittaire. 18. Brentano's; reissued by Sagittaire, 1947, and Pauvert, 1965. 19. N.R.F. 20. Ed. Fontaine. 21. Sagittaire, in *Les Manifestes du surréalisme*; enlarged edition reissued by Pauvert, 1962: this is the definitive edition of the Breton manifestoes to date, including the two manifestoes issued by Kra in 1924 and 1930 and the entire Sagittaire volume of 1946. 22. Ibid.

LOUIS ARAGON

1. In *Le Mouvement perpétuel/Feu de joie* (N.R.F., 1970); originally issued in separate volumes by N.R.F. and Au Sans Pareil in 1926 and 1920, respectively. One of the rediscovered texts is a draft of part of the novel *Anicet ou la panorama* (*Anicet or the Panorama*, N.R.F., 1921), suggesting that this work also owes much to automatism. 2. In *Littérature*, No. 13. 3. N.R.F. 4. N.R.F. 5. N.R.F. 6. N.R.F.; reissued by Livre de Poche, 1966; tr. by Frederick Brown as *Nightwalker* (Prentice-Hall ,1970). 7. *La Peinture au défi* (Galerie Pierre, 1930). 8. Text in *Histoire du Surréalisme* by Maurice Nadeau; tr. by Richard Howard in *The History of Surrealism* (Macmillan, 1965). 9. Ibid. 10. Denoël & Steele, 1935. 11. Tr. by Haakon Chevalier (G. P. Putnam's Sons, 1961).

PAUL ELUARD

1. G.L.M., 1935. 2. A. J. Gonon. 3. Privately printed. 4. Au Sans Pareil. 5. Au Sans Pareil. 6. Au Sans Pareil. 7. N.R.F. 8. G.L.M. 9. N.R.F. Contains selections from Eluard's earlier poetry in addition to middle-period writings. 10. N.R.F.

JEAN (HANS) ARP

1. *Vingt-cinq Poèmes* (Collection Dada, 1918); *Cinéma calendrier du coeur abstrait* (Collection Dada/Au Sans Pareil, 1920); *De nos oiseaux* (Ed. Kra, 1923); *Vingt-cinq-et-un Poèmes* (Ed. Fontaine, 1946; new edition of previously named work with new drawings). 2. *Le Passager du transatlantique* (Collection Dada/Au Sans Pareil, 1921). 3. A long list. A complete bibliography in English appears in Arp's *On My Way: Poetry and Essays, 1912–1947* (tr. by Ralph Manheim, Wittenborn, Schultz, 1948). 4. Ed. de la Librairie de l'Art Indépendent, 1914. 5. Verlag Paul Steegemann. Arp wrote poems in German throughout his life; those collected in *Wortträume und schwarze Sterne: 1911–1952* (Limes Verlag, 1953) include two cycles from his Surrealist-associated period, "Der gestiefelte Stern" (1924–1927) and "Vier Knopfe zwei Locher vier Besen" (1924–1930). 6. Tr. by Eugene Jolas, from *Transition*, 1932. 7. Quoted from Ralph Manheim's translation in *On My Way*.

BENJAMIN PÉRET

1. Collection Littérature. 2. Ed. Surréalistes. 3. Ed. Surréalistes. 4. Ed. Surréalistes. 5. Poésie et Révolution, reissued Pauvert, 1965. 6. Albin Michel. 7. Albin Michel. 8. Galleria Arturo Schwarz.

ROBERT DESNOS

1. Kra, 1927, confiscated that same year; reissued by N.R.F. in 1962 with the short novel *Deuil pour deuil*, originally issued by Kra, 1924. 2. Collected, with Desnos' film criticism, in *Cinéma* (N.R.F., 1966). 3. Collection "Humour," 1945; tr. by Michael Benedikt in *Modern French Theatre: The Avant-Garde, Dada, and Surrealism*. 4. Reprinted in *Documents Surréalistes*, ed. by Maurice Nadeau (Ed. du Seuil, latest ed., 1964). 5. Reprinted in *Domaine public* (N.R.F., 1953). 6. Ibid.

ANTONIN ARTAUD

1. Included in *Correspondance avec Jacques Rivière*, in the *Oeuvres complètes*, Vol. I (N.R.F., 1956). 2. In *Oeuvres complètes*, Vol. I. 3. Ibid.; tr.

by George Wellwarth as *Jet of Blood* in *Modern French Theatre: The Avant-Garde, Dada, and Surrealism* (Dutton, 1964). 4. In *Oeuvres complètes*, Vol. II (N.R.F., 1961). 5. Ibid. 6. Ibid. 7. *Oeuvres complètes*, Vol. IV (N.R.F., 1964); tr. by Mary C. Richards in *The Theatre and Its Double* (Grove Press, 1958). 8. *Oeuvres complètes*, Vol. VII (N.R.F., 1967).

RENÉ DAUMAL

1. N.R.F. 2. N.R.F. 3. 1911; latest ed. issued by Fasquelle, 1955.

JACQUES PRÉVERT

1. Translations of the two last-named scenarios by various hands appear in Simon and Schuster's Classic Film Script series (1968). 2. Reprinted, together with the major part of the earlier poetry, in *Paroles*. 3. Described in the introduction to this volume. 4. Collection La Calligraphe, 1945; initial standard edition, N.R.F., 1947. Selections tr. by Lawrence Ferlinghetti in *Paroles* (City Lights Books, 1958).

AIMÉ CÉSAIRE

1. Bordas, 1947; tr. by John Berger and Anna Bostock (Penguin Books, 1969). 2. Editions K, 1948. 3. Présence Africaine. 4. Ed. du Seuil.

364

Source Data

GUILLAUME APOLLINAIRE

(All poems have been collected in *Oeuvres poétiques*/N.R.F./1956.)

Hôtel/*Banalités*/*Oeuvres poétiques*/1956; written 1913
1909/*Alcools*/Mercure de France/1913; written 1913
Automne/*Alcools*/Mercure de France/1913; written 1905
Les Colchiques/*Alcools*/Mercure de France/1913; written 1907
Zone/*Alcools*/Mercure de France/1913; written 1912
Saltimbanques/*Alcools*/Mercure de France/1913; written 1908
Un Fantôme de nuées/*Calligrammes*/Mercure de France/1918; written 1913
Le Musicien de Saint-Merry/*Calligrammes*/Mercure de France/1918; written 1913
Rosemonde/*Alcools*/Mercure de France/1913; written 1912
Lundi rue Christine/*Calligrammes*/Mercure de France/1918; written 1913
Océan de terre/*Calligrammes*/Mercure de France/1918; written 1918
La Petite Auto/*Calligrammes*/Mercure de France/1918; written 1914
L'Oeillet/*Calligrammes*/Mercure de France/1918; written 1914
Il pleut/*Calligrammes*/Mercure de France/1918; written 1914
Liens/*Calligrammes*/Mercure de France/1918; written 1913
Coeur/*Calligrammes*/Mercure de France/1918; written 1914
Il y a/*Calligrammes*/Mercure de France/1918; written 1915
En allant chercher des obus/*Poèmes à Lou*/Cailler/1955; written 1915
La Jolie Rousse/*Calligrammes*/Mercure de France/1918; written 1918
Toujours/*Calligrammes*/Mercure de France/1918; written 1917

PIERRE REVERDY

(All poems have been collected in *Main d'oeuvre*/Mercure de France/1949, and *Plupart du temps*/N.R.F./1945.)

Son de cloche/*Les Ardoises du toit*/Ed. du Nord-Sud/1918

Départ/*Les Ardoises du toit*/Ed. du Nord-Sud/1918
Saltimbanques/*Poèmes en prose*/N.R.F./1915
Spectacle des yeux/*Sources du vent*/Mercure de France/1929
Quai aux fleurs/*Sources du vent*/Mercure de France/1929
La Lutte des mots/*La Balle au bond*/N.R.F./1928
Chauffage central/*Sources du vent*/Mercure de France/1929
Crève-Coeur/*Cale sèche*/Mercure de France/ca. 1914
Temps de mer/*La Balle au bond*/N.R.F./1928
Là ou là/*La Balle au bond*/N.R.F./1928
Au bout de la rue des astres/*La Balle au bond*/N.R.F./1928
Toujours là/*La Lucarne ovale*/N.R.F./1916
L'Invasion/*Pierres blanches*/Mercure de France/1930
Clair Hiver/*Grande Nature*/Mercure de France/1925
Encore l'amour/*Sources du vent*/Mercure de France/1929
Voyages sans fin/*Sources du vent*/Mercure de France/1929
Une Autre Explication du mystère/*La Balle au bond*/N.R.F./1928
L'Esprit sort/*Poèmes en prose*/N.R.F./1915
Ce souvenir/*Grande Nature*/Mercure de France/1925
Couleur des fenêtres/*Grande Nature*/Mercure de France/1925

TRISTAN TZARA

La Mort de Guillaume Apollinaire/*De nos oiseaux*/Kra/1923
Epiderme de la nuit croissance/*De nos oiseaux*/Kra/1923
Les Saltimbanques/*De nos oiseaux*/Kra/1923
Pélamide/*Vingt-Cinq Poèmes*/Collection Dada/1918 (reissued by Ed. de la
    Fontaine/1945
Droguerie-conscience/*Vingt-Cinq Poèmes*/Collection Dada/1918 (reissued
    by Ed. de la Fontaine/1945)
Soir/*De nos oiseaux*/Kra/1923
Une Route seul soleil/*Terre sur terre*/Ed. Trois Collines/1946
L'Homme approximatif, I/*L'Homme approximatif*/Fourcade/1931 (reissued
    by N.R.F./1968); written 1925–1930
Tonique/*Indicateur des chemins de coeur*/Jeanne Bucher/1928
Accès/*Indicateur des chemins de coeur*/Jeanne Bucher/1928
Fluide/*Le Signe de vie*/Bordas/1946
Les Portes se sont ouvertes/*Où boivent les loups*/Ed. des Cahiers Libres/
    1932
V/"40 Chansons et déchansons" in *De la coupe aux lèvres*/Edizioni Rap-
    porti Europei/1961
Maturité/*Entre-temps*/Point du jour/1946
L'Eau creusait de longues filles . . ./*L'Antitête*/Ed. des Cahiers Libres/
    1933
Voie/*Indicateur des chemins de coeur*/Jeanne Bucher/1928

PHILIPPE SOUPAULT

(Many of the earlier poems have been collected in *Poésies complètes*/
    G.L.M./1936.)

Route/*Rose des vents*/Au Sans Pareil/1920
Dimanche/*Rose des vents*/Au Sans Pareil/1920
Servitudes/"Bulles billes boules: 1920–1930" in *Poésies complètes*/G.L.M./ 1936
Articles de sport/"Bulles billes boules: 1920–1930" in *Poésies complètes*/ G.L.M./1936
Médaille d'or/*Georgia*/Ed. des Cahiers Libres/1926
Georgia/*Georgia*/Ed. des Cahiers Libres/1926
Horizon/*Rose des vents*/Au Sans Pareil/1920
Le Nageur/*Georgia*/Ed. des Cahiers Libres/1926
Médaille de sauvetage/"Bulles billes boules: 1920–1930" in *Poésies complètes*/G.L.M./1936
Les Mains jointes/*Georgia*/Ed. des Cahiers Libres/1926
Conseils au poète/*Sans phrases*/Girard/1953
Fleuve/*Georgia*/Ed. des Cahiers Libres/1926

ANDRÉ BRETON

(Many of these poems have been collected in *Poèmes*/Gallimard/1948.)

L'Aigrette/*Clair de terre*/Collection Littéraire/1923
Toujours pour la première fois/*L'Air de l'eau*/Ed. Cahiers d'Art/1934
Le Marquis de Sade . . ./*L'Air de l'eau*/Ed. Cahiers d'Art/1934
Vigilance/*Le Revolver à cheveux blancs*/Ed. des Cahiers Libres/1932
Les Ecrits s'en vont/*Le Revolver à cheveux blancs*/Ed. des Cahiers Libres/ 1932
Une Branche d'ortie entre par la fenêtre/*Le Revolver à cheveux blancs*/Ed. des Cahiers Libres/1932
Au beau demi-jour/*L'Air de l'eau*/Ed. Cahiers d'Art/1934
Un Homme et une femme absolument blancs/*Le Revolver à cheveux blancs*/Ed. des Cahiers Libres/1932
L'Union libre/*L'Union libre*/Ed. Surréalistes/1931
Monde/1935–1940 in *Poèmes*/N.R.F./1948
Aux yeux des divinités/*Clair de terre*/Collection Littérature/1923
On me dit que là-bas . . ./*L'Air de l'eau*/Cahiers d'Art/1934
Rideau rideau/*L'Air de l'eau*/Ed. Cahiers d'Art/1934
Cours-les-toutes/1935–1940 in *Poèmes*/N.R.F./1948
Poème-Objet: Ces terrains vagues et la lune . . ./Collection of the Museum of Modern Art, New York City/constructed 1941
Poème-Objet: J'ai salué à six pas . . ./*Breton*, "Poètes d'aujourd'hui," No. 18/Seghers/drawn 1943
Sur la route de San Romano/"Oubliés" in *Poèmes*/N.R.F./1948.

LOUIS ARAGON

Serrure de sûreté/*Le Mouvement perpétuel*/N.R.F./1926
Déclaration définitive/*La Grande Gaîté*/N.R.F./1929
Les Frères Lacôte/*Le Mouvement perpétuel*/N.R.F./1926

Chanson à boire/*La Grande Gaîté*/N.R.F./1929
Tercets/*La Grande Gaîté*/N.R.F./1929
Air du temps/*Le Mouvement perpétuel*/N.R.F./1926
Les Débuts du fugitif/*Le Mouvement perpétuel*/N.R.F./1925
Sans famille/*Le Mouvement perpétuel*/N.R.F./1925
Partie fine/*La Grande Gaîté*/N.R.F./1929
Tant pis pour moi/*Persécuté persécuteur*/Ed. Surréalistes/1931
Une Fois et pour toutes/*Le Mouvement perpétuel*/N.R.F./1926
J'inventerai pour toi la rose . . ./*Elsa*/Gallimard/1959
L'Aurore/*Le Fou d'Elsa*/N.R.F./1963

PAUL ELUARD

(All poems have been collected in *Oeuvres complètes*, Vols. 1 and 2/N.R.F./
1968.)

Poule/*Les Animaux et leurs hommes, les hommes et leurs animaux*/Au
Sans Pareil/1920
Porc/*Les Animaux et leurs hommes, les hommes et leurs animaux*/Au
Sans Pareil/1920
Patte/*Les Animaux et leurs hommes, les hommes et leurs animaux*/Au
Sans Pareil/1920
Mouillé/*Les Animaux et leurs hommes, les hommes et leurs animaux*/Au
Sans Pareil/1920
Plumes/*Les Animaux et leurs hommes, les hommes et leurs animaux*/Au
Sans Pareil/1920
L'Amoureuse/*Mourir de ne pas mourir*/N.R.F./1924
L'Extase/*Le Temps déborde*/Ed. Cahiers d'Art/1947
Pour vivre ici/*Choix de poèmes*/N.R.F./1951; written 1917
A Pablo Picasso/*Les Yeux fertiles*/G.L.M./1936
Nous sommes/*Chanson complète*/N.R.F./1939
Tu te lèves . . ./*Facile*/G.L.M./1935
Notre mouvement/*Le Dur Désir de durer*/Bordas/1946
Sans âge/*Cours naturel*/Sagittaire/1938
Paroles peintes/*Cours naturel*/Sagittaire/1938
Max Ernst/*Répétitions*/Au Sans Pareil/1922
Yves Tanguy/*La Jarre peut-elle être plus belle que l'eau*/N.R.F./1951;
written 1930's
Finir/*Le Livre ouvert(I)*/Ed. Cahiers d'Art/1940
Du dehors/*Poésie et vérité*/Ed. de la Main à Plume/1942
Liberté/*Poésie et vérité*/Ed. de la Main à Plume/1942 (enlarged edition,
Baconnière/1943)
Médieuses/*Médieuses*/N.R.F./1939
"La Poésie doit avoir pour but la vérité pratique"/*Poèmes politiques*/
N.R.F./1948
Quelques-uns des mots qui jusqu'ici m'étaient mystérieusement interdits/
Cours naturel/Sagittaire/1938
La Terre est bleue comme une orange . . ./*L'Amour la poésie*/N.R.F./1929
Le Miroir d'un moment/*Capitale de la douleur*/N.R.F./1926

JEAN (HANS) ARP

Je suis un cheval/*Le Siège de l'air*/Vrille/1946; written 1934
Une Goutte d'homme/*Sciure de gammes*/Parisot/1938
Ce que chantent les violons dans leur lit de lard/"Poems 1939–1942" in *Le Siège de l'air*/Vrille/1946; written 1939
Sciure de gammes/*Sciure de gammes*/Parisot/1938
Manifeste millimetre infini/*Jours effeuillés*/N.R.F./1946; written 1938
Les Pierres domestiques/"Poems 1917–1935" in *Le Siège de l'air*/Vrille/1946
Blocs blancs/"Poems 1939–1942" in *Le Siège de l'air*/Vrille/1948
Les Pieds du matin/*Le Siège de l'air*/Vrille/1946; written 1938
L'Eléphant tyrolien/*Le Blanc aux pieds de nègre*/Fontaine/1945
L'Etc. blanc/*Le Blanc aux pieds de nègre*/Fontaine/1945
Les Saisons leurs astérisques et leurs pions/*Des Taches dans le vide*/Sagesse/1937
Veines noires"Poems 1945" in *Le Siège de l'air*/Vrille/1946
Joie noire/*Le Siège de l'air*/Vrille/1946; written ca. 1943

BENJAMIN PÉRET

(All poems have been collected in *Oeuvres complètes*, Vols. 1 and 2/ Losfeld/1969, 1971.)

Allo/*Je sublime*/Ed. Surréalistes/1936
Où es-tu/*Un Point c'est tout*/Editions K./1947; written 1942, reissued in *Feu central*
Qui est-ce/*De derrière les fagots*/Ed. Surréalistes/1934
Ça continue/*De derrière les fagots*/Ed. Surréalistes/1934
Mille Fois/*De derrière les fagots*/Ed. Surréalistes/1934
Clin d'oeil/*Je sublime*/Ed. Surréalistes/1936
Tout à l'heure/*Un Point c'est tout*/Editions K./1947
Le Premier Jour/*A tatons*/Editions K./1947; written 1942, reissued in *Feu central*
Chanson de la sécheresse/*Le Grand Jeu*/N.R.F./1929
Pour passer le temps/*De derrière les fagots*/Ed. Surréalistes/1934
A suivre/*Un Point c'est tout*/Editions K./1947; written 1942, reissued in *Feu central*
Quatre à quatre/*De derrière les fagots*/Ed. Surréalistes/1934
Faire le pied de grue/*De derrière les fagots*/Ed. Surréalistes/1934
Nébuleuse/*Je sublime*/Ed. Surréalistes/1936
On sonne/*Un Point c'est tout*/Editions K./1947
Louis XVI s'en va à la guillotine/*Je ne mange pas de ce pain-là*/Ed. Surréalistes/1936
Mes derniers agonies/*Le Grand Jeu*/N.R.F./1928
Vent du nord/*A tatons*/Editions K./1947; written 1942, reissued in *Feu central*
Atout trèfle/*De derrière les fagots*/Ed. Surréalistes/1934
Nuits blanches/*De derrière les fagots*/Ed. Surréalistes/1934

(All poems have been collected in Domaine public/N.R.F./1953.)

Destinée arbitraire/*C'est les bottes de 7 lieues cette phrase "Je me vois"*/
Galerie Simon/1926
Il fait nuit/*Corps et biens*/N.R.F./1930; written 1926
Les Espaces du sommeil/*Corps et biens*/N.R.F./1930; written 1927
Identité des images/*Corps et biens*/N.R.F./1930; written 1927
La Voix de Robert Desnos/*Corps et biens*/N.R.F./1930; written 1927
L'Idée fixe/*Corps et biens*/N.R.F./1930; written 1927
Paroles des rochers/*Corps et biens*/N.R.F./1930
Le Suicidé de nuit/*Corps et biens*/N.R.F./1930; written 1927
Coucou/*Les Sans Cou*/privately printed/1934
Si tu savais/*Corps et biens*/N.R.F./1930; written 1926
Pour un rêve de jour/*Corps et biens*/N.R.F./1930; written 1927
J'ai tant rêvé de toi/*Corps et biens*/N.R.F./1930; written 1926
De la rose de marbre à la rose de fer/*Corps et biens*/N.R.F./1930; written
1927
Un Jour qu'il faisait nuit/*Corps et biens*/N.R.F./1930; written 1923
Mî-Route/*Les Sans Cou*/privately printed/1934
Vie d'ébène/*Corps et biens*/N.R.F./1930; written 1927
Désespoir du soleil/*Corps et biens*/N.R.F./1930; written 1927
Au bout du monde/*Fortunes*/N.R.F./1942; written 1936
Les Grands Jours du poète/*C'est les bottes de 7 lieues cette phrase "Je me
vois"*/Galerie Simon/1926

(All poems have been collected in *Oeuvres complètes*, Vol. 1/N.R.F./1956.)

Poète noir/*L'Ombilic des limbes*/N.R.F./1925
L'Arbre/"Bilboquet" in *Oeuvres complètes*, Vol. 1/N.R.F./1956; written
1925
L'Orgue et le vitriol/*Tric-trac du ciel*/Galerie Simon/1923
Orgue allemand/*Tric-trac du ciel*/Galerie Simon/1923
Romance/*Tric-trac du ciel*/Galerie Simon/1923
Neige/*Tric-trac du ciel*/Galerie Simon/1923
Prière/*Tric-trac du ciel*/Galerie Simon/1923
La Trappe/*Tric-trac du ciel*/Galerie Simon/1923
Lune/*Tric-trac du ciel*/Galerie Simon/1923
Le Mauvais Rêveur/"Bilboquet" in *Oeuvres complètes*, Vol. 1/N.R.F./1956;
written 1925
La Nuit Opère/"Bilboquet" in *Oeuvres complètes*, Vol. 1/N.R.F./1956;
written 1925
Vitres de son/"Bilboquet" in *Oeuvres complètes*, Vol. 1/N.R.F./1956;
written 1925
Adresse au Dalaï-Lama/"Bilboquet" in *Oeuvres complètes*, Vol. 1/N.R.F./
1956; written late 1920's

Invocation à la momie/"Bilboquet" in *Oeuvres complètes*, Vol. 1/N.R.F./ 1956; written late 1920's
L'Amour sans trêve/"Bilboquet" in *Oeuvres complètes*, Vol. 1/N.R.F./1956; written late 1920's
Fête nocturne/"Bilboquet" in *Oeuvres complètes*, Vol. 1/N.R.F./1956; written late 1920's

RENÉ DAUMAL

(All poems have been collected in *Poésie noire, poésie blanche*/N.R.F./ 1954.)

La Peau du fantôme/*Le Contre-Ciel*/Cahiers Jacques Doucet/1936
La Peau de lumière . . ./"Poems 1924–1931" in *Poésie noire, poésie blanche*/N.R.F./1954
Il vient des profondes cavernes . . ./"Poems 1924–1931" in *Poésie noire, poésie blanche*/N.R.F./1954
La Révolution en été/"Poems 1924–1931" in *Poésie noire, poésie blanche*/ N.R.F./1954
Feu aux artifices/"Poems 1924–1931" in *Poésie noire, poésie blanche*/ N.R.F./1954
Le Raccommodeur de monstres/"Poems 1924–1931" in *Poésie noire, poésie blanche*/N.R.F./1954
Il suffit d'un mot/*Le Contre-Ciel*/Cahiers Jacques Doucet/1936
La Consolatrice/"Poems 1924–1931" in *Poésie noire, poésie blanche*/N.R.F./ 1954
La Chair de terreur/"Poems 1924–1931" in *Poésie noire, poésie blanche*/ N.R.F./1954
Sorcellerie/"Poems 1924–1931" in *Poésie noire, poésie blanche*/N.R.F./1954
Retour au pays mauvais/"Poems 1924–1931" in *Poésie noire, poésie blanche*/N.R.F./1954
Le Pays des métamorphoses/"Poems 1924–1931" in *Poésie noire, poésie blanche*/N.R.F./1954
Feux à volonté/*Le Contre-Ciel*/Cahiers Jacques Doucet/1936
La Désillusion/*Le Contre-Ciel*/Cahiers Jacques Doucet/1936
Froidement/*Le Contre-Ciel*/Cahiers Jacques Doucet/1936
Les Déceptions/"Poems 1924–1931" in *Poésie noire, poésie blanche*/N.R.F./ 1954

JACQUES PRÉVERT

(All poems except "In Vain" were selected from *Paroles*/N.R.F./1947.)

La Gloire
L'Eclipse
Le Dernier Souper
Tentative de description d'un dîner de têtes à Paris-France/written ca. 1930
Cortège

371

Familiale
J'en ai vu plusieurs . . .
Le Combat avec l'ange
Chanson de l'oiseleur
Pour faire le portrait d'un oiseau
Quartier libre
La Pêche à la baleine
Le Miroir brisé
Le Jardin
En vain

AIMÉ CÉSAIRE

(All poems were selected from *Soleil cou coupé,* originally published by
Editions K. in 1948; reissued in *Cadastre*/Ed. du Seuil/1961.)

Pluies
Depuis Akkad depuis Elam depuis Sumer
Démons
Marais nocturne
Ex-Voto pour un naufrage
La Tornade
Millibars de l'orage
A hurler
Calme
La Roue
Allure
Samba
Fils de la foudre
Jugement de la lumière

Acknowledgments

The author is grateful to the following for permission to reprint translations of poems in this book:

Librairie Gallimard, Paris, for the poems of:

Guillaume Apollinaire — from *Oeuvres poétiques* (1956): "1909," "Automne," "Rosemonde," taken from *Alcools* (1920). "En allant chercher des obus," taken from *Poemes à Lou* (1957). "Un Fantôme de nuées," "Lundi rue Christine," "Océan de temps," La Petite "Patte," "Pour vivre ici," taken from *Poésies* (1913–1926). "Mouillé," "Médieuses," taken *poétiques* copyright © 1956 by Editions Gallimard.

André Breton — "Toujours pour la première fois," "Le Marquis de Sade a regagné," "On me dit que là-bas," "Vigilance," "Les Ecrits s'en vont," "Une Branche d'ortie entre par la fenêtre," "Un Homme et une femme absolument blancs," "Rideau rideau," "Au beau demi-jour," taken from *Clair de Terre*, preceded by *Mont de Piété*, followed by *Le Revolver à cheveux blancs* and by *L'Air de l'eau* (1966). "L'Union libre" from *L'Union libre*. "Monde," "Cours-les toutes," "Sur la route de San Romano," "L'Aigrette," taken from *Poèmes* (1949). Copyright 1949, © 1966 by Editions Gallimard.

Paul Eluard — "Plumes," taken from *Les Animaux et leurs hommes, les hommes et* from *Choix de poèmes* (1951–1954). *Oeuvres complètes* copyright © 1968 by Editions taken from *Le Temps déborde*. "A Pablo Picasso" taken from *Les Yeux fertiles* (1936). "Nous sommes," taken from *Chanson Complète* (1939). "Tu te lèves," taken from *Facile*. "Notre mouvement," taken from *Le Dur Désir de durer*. "Sans âge," "Paroles peintes," "Quelques-uns des mots qui jusqu'ici m'étaient mystérieusement interdits," taken from *Le Cours naturel* (1938). "Max Ernst," taken from *Répétitions* (1926). "Yves Tanguy," taken from *La Jarre peut-elle être plus belle que l'eau* (1930–1938). "Finir," taken from *Le Livre ouvert* (1938–1944). "Du Dehors," "Liberté," taken from *Poésie et vérité*. "La Poésie doit avoir pour but la vérité pratique," taken from *Poèmes politiques* (1948). "La Terre est bleue comne une orange . . . ," taken from *L'Amour la poésie* (1964). "Le Miroir d'un moment," taken from *Capitale de la douleur* (1964). "Porc," "Poule," "Patte," "Pour vivre ici," taken from *Poésies* (1913–1926). "Mouillé," "Médieuses," taken from *Choix de poèmes* (1951–1954). *Oeuvres complètes* copyright © 1968 by Editions Gallimard.

Robert Desnos — from *Domaine public* (1953): "Destinée arbitraire," taken from *C'est les bottes de 7 lieues cette phrase "Je me vois."* "Il fait nuit," "Les Espaces du sommeil," "Identité des images," "Paroles des rochers," "L'Idée fixe," "Le Suicidé de nuit," "Coucou," "Si tu savais," "Pour un rêve de jour," "J'ai tant rêvé de toi," "De la rose de marbre à la rose de fer," "Un Jour qui'il faisait nuit," "Mî-route," "Vie d'ébène," "Désespoir du soleil," "Au bout du monde," "Les Grands Jours du poète," "La Voix de Robert Desnos," taken from *Domaine public*. *Domaine public* copyright 1953 by Editions Gallimard.

Antonin Artaud — "Poète noir," "L'Arbre," "Orgue allemand," "Neige," "Vitres de son," "L'Orgue et le vitriol," "Prière," "Adresse au Dalaï," "Le Mauvais Rêveur," "Lune," "La Nuit Opère," "L'Amour sans trêve," "Invocation à la momie," "Fête nocturne," "Romance," "La Trappe," taken from volume I of *Oeuvres complètes* (1956).

374

Joachim Neugröschel for his versions of poems by Philippe Soupault and Louis Aragon.
Rosmarie Waldrop for her versions of poems by Philippe Soupault.
Keith Waldrop for his version of "Le Marquis de Sade" by André Breton.
David Antin for his versions of poems by André Breton. The translations of "Une Branche d'ortie entre par la fenêtre," "Un Homme et une femme absolument blancs," and "L'Union libre" originally appeared in *Poems From The Floating World*, Vol. 4. Copyright © 1962 by David Antin. "Cours-les toutes," never published before, was translated by Mr. Antin in 1963.
Lou Lipsitz for his translation (with Jean Gillou) of "L'Aurore" by Louis Aragon.
James Laughlin and New Directions Publishing Corporation for Mr. Laughlin's versions of "Chanson de la sécheresse," "Faire le pied de grue," and "Mes dernières agonies" by Benjamin Péret. Copyright 1940 by New Directions Publishing Corporation.
Teo Savory for her versions of poems by Jacques Prévert. All three poems translated by Miss Savory were originally published by Unicorn Press in *Prévert*. Copyright © 1967 by Teo Savory.
Mark Strand for his versions (with Jean Ballard) of poems by Jacques Prévert.

The following translations by the editor have previously appeared in books and periodicals, to whose editors grateful acknowledgment is made:
"There Is," © 1972. Originally appeared in *Ironwood*, Vol. 1, #2, Fall 1972.
"Saffron," © 1960. Originally appeared in *Fresco*, Vol. 10, #2, Winter–Spring 1960.
"Central Heating," "The Spirit Escapes," © 1971. Originally appeared in *The Dragonfly*, anthology issue, 1971. "Flower-Market Quay," © 1972. Originally appeared in *The Dragonfly*, Vol. 3, #1, Spring 1972.
"Another Explanation for the Mystery," "At the End of the Street of Stars," "Time of the Sea," © 1969. Originally appeared in *Extensions*, Vol. 1, #2.
"Our Movements," © 1972. Originally appeared in *The Dragonfly*, Vol. 3, #3/4.
"Painted Words," © 1972. Originally appeared in *The Milk Quarterly*, #2.
"Some Words Which, up until Now, Have Remained Mysteriously Forbidding for Me," © 1972. Originally appeared in *Kayak*, #30, December 1972.
"Ageless," © 1972. Originally appeared in *The Falcon*, #5, Winter 1972.
"Medusas," © 1973. Originally appeared in *The Falcon*, #6, Spring 1973.
"The Beloved," © 1973. Originally appeared in *UnMuzzled Ox*, #6.
"Hello," "Twinkling of an Eye," © 1972. Originally appeared in *Kayak*, #29, September 1972.
"Where Are You," © 1972. Originally appeared in *Field*.
"And on the Very First Day," "Someone's Knocking," "It Keeps Going On," "Sleepless Nights," © 1973. Originally appeared in *The American Poetry Review*.
"Half-way," © 1969. Originally appeared in *The Bennington Review*, Vol. 3, #4, Winter 1969.
"Arbitrary Destiny," "Nightfall," "The Spaces inside Sleep," "Identity of Imagery," "L'Idée fixe," "Words from the Rocks," "Suicided by Night," "Cuckoo-Clock," "If You Only Knew," "I've Dreamed of You So Much," "The Rose of Marble and the Rose of Iron," "One Day When It Was Night Out," "Half-way," "Ebony Life," "Despair of the Sun," "At the World's Last Outpost," "The Great Days of the Poet," © 1971. Originally appeared in *22 Poems of Robert Desnos*, published by Kayak Press.
"For a Daylight Dream," © 1972. Originally appeared in *The Falcon*, #5, Winter 1972.
"Consolatrice," "Sorcery," "Deceptions," © 1962. Originally appeared in *Quagga*, Vol. II, #2.
"Flesh of Terror," "The Monster-Mender," © 1969. Originally appeared in *Stony Brook*, #3/4, 1969.
"Return to an Evil Domain," © 1972. Originally appeared in *Hearse*, #17.
"Rains," "The Wheel," © 1971. Originally appeared in *Tri-Quarterly*, #20, Winter 1971.
"The Tornado," © 1973. Originally appeared in *Chelsea*, #32, August 1973.